Semi-Conducting

Figure 0.1 The author and his mother, Tanahuilín, Chile, 1960. Photo by Hilde Vorwerk Crasemann.

Semi-Conducting

Rambles Through the Post-Cagean Thicket

Nicolas Collins

BLOOMSBURY ACADEMIC
NEW YORK • LONDON • OXFORD • NEW DELHI • SYDNEY

BLOOMSBURY ACADEMIC
Bloomsbury Publishing Inc
1385 Broadway, New York, NY 10018, USA
50 Bedford Square, London, WC1B 3DP, UK
29 Earlsfort Terrace, Dublin 2, Ireland

BLOOMSBURY, BLOOMSBURY ACADEMIC and the Diana logo are trademarks of
.Bloomsbury Publishing Plc

First published in the United States of America 2025

Cover design by Louise Dugdale
Cover image: Drawing by Samuel Lucas, 1863 © The Trustees of the British Museum

Bloomsbury Publishing Inc does not have any control over, or responsibility for, any
third-party websites referred to or in this book. All internet addresses given in this
book were correct at the time of going to press. The author and publisher regret
any inconvenience caused if addresses have changed or sites have ceased to exist,
but can accept no responsibility for any such changes.

Library of Congress Cataloging-in-Publication Data
Names: Collins, Nicolas, author.
Title: Semi-conducting : rambles through the post-Cagean thicket / by Nicolas Collins.
Description: [1.] | New York : Bloomsbury Academic, 2025. | Includes
bibliographical references.
Identifiers: LCCN 2024026855 (print) | LCCN 2024026856 (ebook) |
ISBN 9798765127568 (paperback) | ISBN 9798765127551 (hardback) |
ISBN 9798765127575 (ebook) | ISBN 9798765127582 (pdf)
Subjects: LCSH: Avant-garde (Music)–History–20th century. | Music–20th
century–History and criticism. | Avant-garde (Music)–History–21st
century. | Music–21st century–History and criticism. | Computer music–
History and criticism. | Electronic music–History and criticism. | Collins, Nicolas.
Classification: LCC ML197 C743 2025 (print) | LCC ML197 (ebook) |
DDC 780.9/04--dc23/eng/20240723
LC record available at https://lccn.loc.gov/2024026855
LC ebook record available at https://lccn.loc.gov/2024026856

ISBN: HB: 979-8-7651-2755-1
PB: 979-8-7651-2756-8
ePDF: 979-8-7651-2758-2
eBook: 979-8-7651-2757-5

Typeset by Deanta Global Publishing Services, Chennai, India
Printed and bound in Great Britain

To find out more about our authors and books visit www.bloomsbury.com and
sign up for our newsletters.

Contents

Preface

The impact of John Cage on the culture of post-war America and Europe is well documented. For avant-garde music, there has been no equivalent paradigm shift since, yet the world we live in—the music and art we make and enjoy, and our relationship to the technologies that enable that making and enjoying—are profoundly different from anything Cage would have imagined (or in all probability liked). His most durable legacy, the thing that stretches beyond any individual personal aesthetic, has been the ethos usually termed "experimentalism."

Semi-Conducting is a subjective survey of the post-Cagean musical world and its evolution. Beginning with the generation of composers whose youthful trajectories were upended in the 1950s and 1960s by the discovery that *anything* might be listened to as music, it follows the succeeding generations who reached out into popular culture, consumer technology, and social practices to investigate new varieties of aural experiences and to engage new kinds of audiences. The invented gerund "semi-conducting" is meant to invoke an approach to creation that is both directed and open to accident, and a period in which the familiar borders between performers and audiences, producers and consumers, playable instruments and machines have been redefined.

This book is also a memoir. Using personal experience to make connections between aesthetic experience and experimentation tangible, the text moves between accounts of hands-on making—the technical challenges and impetuses—and observation of the surrounding cultural scenes. It considers questions such as the relative claims of improvisation and of scores as ways of structuring performances, and compares the implications of analog versus digital resources in the production of music.

On the first day of 2016, I made a New Year's resolution to write a story a day from memory. The exercise was entertaining, rewarding (like weight-training for writing muscles), and surprising. The anecdotes jotted down covered a lot of ground. I wrote about raising children and paying the rent, but mostly I wrote about the musical ideas, scenes, and artists I had engaged with over four decades—many of them poorly documented in their heydays.

People who became aware of this project asked to read it, but while an anecdote archive is fun to write, it is not a fun read. Its short tales were too abbreviated and quixotic for anyone living outside my own head—like being trapped at a dinner party with someone who can tell a great story but never shuts up. So, in the stasis of the Covid lockdown, I set about transforming those 350,000 words into a more cogent tour of unusual music.

This is not a musicological text. There is no omniscient narrator. The book's trajectory is my own, as a composer, curator, and audience member in locations from Northern Norway to Southern Chile, and from CBGB to the Concertgebouw.

A child of the New York art world, I moved from teenage adventures with electronics to studying minimalist experimental music with Alvin Lucier, and then to the maximalist semi-conducted mayhem of New York's Downtown improvisers scene in the 1980s. In Europe for a decade, I curated festivals, led a music research foundation, and composed for chamber ensembles and soloists, with circuits and computers, traditional instruments, and homemade ones. At the cusp of the millennium, I joined the Department of Sound at the School of the Art Institute of Chicago, where students cajoled me into teaching them to build simple circuits and hack commonplace gizmos, a class that bloomed into a book and a global network of workshops.

The book discusses not only the experiences and ideas in the art of others, but I also take time to explain a number of my own works, in part because I think some readers might be interested in the pieces themselves, and also because I see these now as responses to what was going on around me, lenses through which to view the activities of others. (A companion website featuring audio and video files of these pieces, as well as additional figures and documentation, can be found here: https://www.nicolascollins.com/semi-conducting/. Most of my works referenced in the text can be accessed more efficiently through this site, with its chapter breakdowns, than the individual urls in the end notes).

Most of what I have learned as an artist came through oral transmission. There were no textbooks on experimental music in 1972: Alvin Lucier told stories. When I studied Indian music, my tabla teacher didn't hand out notation, he recited solfège. I learned circuitry and programming by interrogating smarter peers. John Zorn talked me through the cues for *Cobra*. These lessons were often elliptical: Alvin might start out explaining composer Gordon Mumma's homemade analog computer, but end on a story about Mumma's eccentric attempt to circumvent jet lag. I have tried to preserve this pedagogical character.

I am immensely grateful to the mentors and peers who guided me along the path to where I am today—their names, familiar and not-so-familiar, appear throughout the book. But I am also beholden to my friends and colleagues who took the time to answer questions and to read and comment on the text as I distilled all those stories into a narrative of sorts: Frank Baldé, Ed Baxter, David Behrman, Nico Bes, Vicky Bijur, John Bischoff, Prudence Crowther, Tom Demeyer, Andrew Raffo Dewar, James Fei, Kyle Gann, Jay Hogard, Jonathan Impett, Stuart Jones, hans koch, Ron Kuivila, Marina LaPalma, George Lewis, You Nakai, Ben Neill, Bob Ostertag, Matthias Osterwold, Robert Poss, Simon Reynolds, Veniero Rizzardi, Jon Rose, Viola Rusche, Richard Scott, James Staley, Peter Todd, Ed Tomney, and David Toop. I am beholden to Susan Tallman, who has shared with love and patience the last forty-five, often peripatetic, years of my life—attending, critiquing, and often performing in my music. Those who have read her books or articles know that she is a brilliant writer, but she is also the world's second-best editor. (Like me, she owes a debt to Prudence Crowther.) Susan devoted far too many hours to the final draft of this book, and if *Semi-Conducting* rises from workmanlike prose to the height of a pleasurable read, it is the result of her collaboration.

A Hidden Switch

I was not a musical kid.

The cover of the New York Philharmonic Hall 1964–5 program shows a dozen little boys sitting in jackets and ties at one of Leonard Bernstein's Young People's Concerts. I'm in the front at the right, looking vaguely perplexed. The event was my first experience of a live orchestra (see Figure 1.1).

My home life was culturally rich in many ways. My father was a professor at Columbia University, and my mother worked at the Museum of Modern Art. The walls of our "classic six" on Morningside Drive were lined with paintings and prints, some by friends, some by artists with names known to the world at large. The furniture was identified by the names of its mostly Scandinavian designers. The bookshelves sported spines in English, German, Spanish, and Catalan. (My mother, the product of a Hamburg merchant banking family, had grown up in Chile; my father was the preeminent American scholar of Antoni Gaudí.)

The children were regularly trundled around New York galleries and museums, and—given that both parents were architectural historians—we were taught to look analytically at all the spaces around us. Early in his career, during a service at St. Paul's Chapel on the Columbia campus, my father looked up and noticed that the vaults used the same herringbone tile pattern employed by Gaudí in Barcelona; research showed they were the engineering trademark of a Spanish builder, Rafael Guastavino, and indeed derived from Catalan vaulting. (The Oyster Bar in Grand Central Station is another iconic example of his work.)[1] Locating Guastavino vaults became something of an obsession (he was an obsessive man), and the children were useful scouts. "Look up!" was the family mantra.

But music . . .?

My father had a component HiFi system on which he played records of the jazz he came to love as a student in the 1930s. We had a radio, and my mother would sometimes listen to classical broadcasts. But it never occurred to either of them to head out to a club or a concert hall. Both had been told as children that piano lessons were a waste of time and money since no family members had ever shown any musical aptitude, so their three boys were spared that particular rite of passage.

I would like to say that I came home from the Philharmonic that day and demanded a piano or a violin, but I didn't. It was only years later, at the ragged end of the 1960s, when my hair was longer and my attitude more contentious, that music began to sing

Figure 1.1 Philharmonic Hall program book cover, 1964–5 season. The author, lower right, at his first orchestral concert (a Leonard Bernstein "Young People's" concert), 1964. Photo by E Fred Sher/Saturday Review, Inc., courtesy of the NY Phil Shelby White & Leon Levy Digital Archive.

its siren song. And by then it had less to do with Bernstein than with *Rolling Stone* and Rube Goldberg.

A book of Goldberg's drawings—with their physical logic and sublime absurdity, their parkour-runs from parrots to pulleys—entranced me from early childhood. And while modernist paintings at MoMA bored me, the kinetic sculptures of Jean Tinguely were catnip. At home, I constructed long marble runs from cardboard tubes and invented stupidly complicated machines to do simple things like smashing a peanut. The disproportion between the elaborate mechanism and the modest end result was the locus of delight—it transferred attention from the goal to the process. It was another version of "look up!" Even my often-dour dad seemed to enjoy them.

Like many of his generation, my father did not do joyful affection. He had his reasons. The product of emphatically cheerless Yankee stock (the one joke he recalled from childhood was about deprivation, and it was not particularly funny), he had helped liberate Bergen-Belsen in 1945 and three years later found himself suddenly widowed with a young son.[i] Other patriarchs might have bonded with their sons over sports, but games—outdoors or in—were not really in his wheelhouse. Yet he loved to tinker.

Those grim Maine forbears had been craftsmen (the Smithsonian, he told us, owned a Collins-built one-horse shay, a photo of which I found in a storage box alongside piles of po-faced tintypes). A living embodiment of the Emerson dictum that "a man is no worse metaphysician for knowing how to drive a nail home without splitting the board," the esteemed professor delighted in building bookshelves, replacing tap washers, rewiring lamps, rotating tires, and teaching his three boys various craft skills already on the cusp of displacement. My older brother, a math prodigy, ignored these lessons; my younger brother resented them. I loved them.

My father taught me how to change a fuse, tighten a loose woodscrew with a matchstick, saw wood, and use the right kind of glue.[ii] In only one particular did his mastery of mechanical arts falter: Once a year while I was in middle school, we would sit together at the workbench in our summer cottage, plug in a soldering iron the size of a small baseball bat, and try to solder together discarded license plates from a junk pile in the garage. How it was that my father—a chemistry major at Princeton—did not realize that solder won't stick to painted surfaces, I cannot say, though it would not have been out of character for him simply to relish the frustration.

The cottage was on Cape Cod, and I spent hours face down in the waters of Buzzard's Bay, monitoring the profusion of dull brown fish whose names I learned at

---

[i] The joke, as I heard it from my grandfather's lips: "If we had some ham we'd have some ham and eggs . . . if we had some eggs."

[ii] He had a particular fondness for glues and brought home a fresh tube every time a new technology came onto the market. Our first epoxy arrived shortly after the shattering of the crystal decanter from which my parents served their cheap red wine at dinner. Twenty-four hours later, the jug was back on the table. It performed admirably for several years until one night it dissolved in mid-pour. Epoxy had been advertised with the claim that it was used to hold together sections of the B-52 bombers then raining terror on Hanoi. As we mopped up, my father observed that the North Vietnamese should consider spraying US planes with wine.

the Children's School of Science in Woods Hole, or cheering on mosquito-devouring bats from my perch on the back porch. (A small twist of fate's dial would have seen me happily employed at the Marine Biological Laboratory or Woods Hole Oceanographic Institute.)

Rounding out the family's atlas were periodic visits to my mother's home in Chile, where we would wander in the foothills of the Andes, ride rotund horses on the family's sprawling sheep ranch in the north, feed rose petals to the tiny Pudu deer on their tree farm in the south, or follow the twilight swoops of what my grandmother—a resident of the country since 1920—still referred to as *Fledermäuse*. With endless patience, my grandparents' gardener let me pad around after him on his daily rounds of placing and removing the little water gates (*tacos*) in the canals that served their orchard outside Santiago. The socio-economic and political implications of all this would come home to me later, but to a New York City child in the 1960s it was simply magical.

Though we had no musical instruments, my brothers and I did share a kiddie record player with a built-in speaker on which we worked our way through a small stack of child-appropriate discs. When I was seven, in what may have been my first act of audio hacking, I stuck a pin in the base of a paper drinking cup and used it as a stylus, listening to "Big Rock Candy Mountain" spill over the cup's rim as if it were the acoustic horn of an old gramophone. With less success, my little brother and I shouted into the cup in an attempt to record over Burl Ives, on the not-completely mad assumption that the needle would scribe new grooves in the vinyl.

My grade school years dovetailed with the age of the transistor radio, whose allure as an object was as powerful as that of the pop music that came out of it. When I finally persuaded my parents to buy me one, I chose the smallest affordable model—nine square inches of black plastic and white metal. In third grade, I fell in love with the bands of the British Invasion—the Beatles, the Rolling Stones, the Animals—and pop's evolution became mine. As I grew older, friendships developed or fell to the wayside around the axes of musical taste. Social life moved from the Beatles to Jimi Hendrix and San Francisco psychedelia, and on to Miles Davis and Rahsaan Roland Kirk.

Radio, record stores, and *Rolling Stone* magazine kept teenagers apprised, and in a New York prep school full of nerdy, well-connected, well-heeled boys, there was always someone who had found something newer, hipper, and more challenging to catch the beauty of. I was mesmerized by Ravi Shankar and the tabla player Alla Rakha in D. A. Pennebaker's 1968 film of the Monterey Pop Festival. I spent my weekends and babysitting money at the Fillmore East, where I heard Buddy Guy, B. B. King, Jefferson Airplane, and the Grateful Dead.

The Collegiate School for Boys, which I attended for thirteen years, was then on West 77th Street. So was Miles Davis's townhouse, which I would walk by going to and from the bus stop. One spring, shortly after the release of his *Bitches Brew* album, whenever I passed the house on my way home I would hear an amplified trumpet repeating a single bebop riff, over and over and over. Davis had been working with guitarist John McLaughlin and must have borrowed his wah-wah pedal; with each iteration, he would articulate the wah-wah differently, honing this new technique.

It never struck me as remarkable to be privy to these curbside concerts, nor did it occur to me to record them, though I could have dragged the family's Norelco cassette recorder with me to school. I have, however, never forgotten those eavesdropped recitals.[2]

In the spring of 1968, the Columbia campus erupted with protests. The university's plan to build its new gymnasium on the public land of Morningside Park sparked fulsome opposition from neighborhood residents and many members of the university, including my parents. (My mother was photographed sitting with fellow protesters and our family dog in the maw of a bulldozer.)[3] Students occupied several university buildings and shut down classes. I was fourteen and had been dabbling in photography, so whenever I wasn't in school or sleeping, I roamed the campus with a borrowed Nikon, snapping away—students conferring from behind the chained doors of Low Library, cops patting their billy clubs as they leaned on barricades, a waiting paddy wagon. I was young enough (and, I later realized, white enough) to disappear from adult view, and no SDS member, cop, or Black Panther ever questioned my presence. (Half a century later some of these photos would appear in Paul Cronin's documentary, *A Time to Stir*).[4]

Columbia '68 was a sonic experience as well as a visual one. Megaphones sprouted like spring flowers, the earnest words interlaced with feedback and obscured by distortion. Amplifying one's voice to address a handful of friendly comrades under a tree was more of a conceptual statement than an acoustic necessity. The inflection of politics by art seemed natural: Music had long been a conspicuous vehicle of political expression—my kiddie records included the subtly subversive Burl Ives (blacklisted in 1950), while Pete Seeger (indicted for contempt of Congress in 1957) provided an occasional musical backdrop in the adult living room. But by 1968, the folksy sincerity of banjo and acoustic guitar had been displaced by electronic whine and chatter. In Jimi Hendrix's *Are You Experienced*, which I bought in that same momentous year, the artifacts of feedback and distortion seemed as much an anti-authoritarian statement when applied to the guitar as they were when they rang out at a sit-in. This was the sound of subversion, not ideology. While Seeger overlaid timeless, politically neutral chords and melodies with pointed lyric statements, Hendrix reshaped the underlying musical material; his message lay inside the sound itself (see Figure 1.2).

In high school, my listening became more eclectic and more electric. Several of my friends played in bands, one or two of them quite seriously. My classmate Doane Perry worshiped Clive Bunker, the drummer for Jethro Tull, and dreamed of assuming his mantle (twelve years after graduating high school he did, and played with Tull until he retired in 2012). I dabbled with guitar, flute, and percussion, trying to find some way to *make* music, not just play it back. However, self-conscious about the lack of childhood piano lessons or even minimal musical literacy, I felt I was always playing catch-up to the kids who had been at it for years.

Counterintuitively, becoming a composer seemed somehow more realistic because I associated it with planning and thinking rather than playing. And while there were plenty of guitar-hero wannabes in my school, there was no one who claimed to be a

Figure 1.2 Megaphone being used to speak to a gathering of six students during the protests at Columbia University in May 1968. Photo by Nicolas Collins.

composer. So, fueled by the adolescent urge to distinguish myself from the pack, I began writing aspirationally avant-garde notes on paper for small ensembles. Unsurprisingly, I had little success enticing the instrumentalists I knew to execute them. They all had better things to do with their time.

To hear those notes, I would have to play them myself, but I could only handle one instrument at a time. After a few experiments with the family cassette recorder, I realized that with a proper reel-to-reel tape recorder, it would be possible to overdub myself playing all the parts. This was common practice in professional multitrack music production, and with some difficulty it could be emulated using a consumer-quality machine. With babysitting money and Christmas gift checks, I bought a used Tandberg Model 64 the size of a small suitcase, and adopted a complicated system for turning myself into a band: I would record a guitar passage in the left channel, then rewind the tape, and play it back while performing on flute. Adjusting the volume controls, I could mix the playback of the guitar from the left channel with the new flute part, recording them both on the right channel. I'd then play back the right channel (guitar + flute) and mix it with a new part played on percussion, now recording in the left channel, replacing the first track of guitar alone. By repeating this "bouncing" (as the technique was known) I could layer multiple parts (see Figure 1.3).

The tape recorder I bought turned out to have two unexpected features. As the tape spooled from one reel to another, it passed over three tape heads: the left one erased any audio already on the tape, the middle one recorded new material, and the right one played sound back. The playback head was engaged by default when

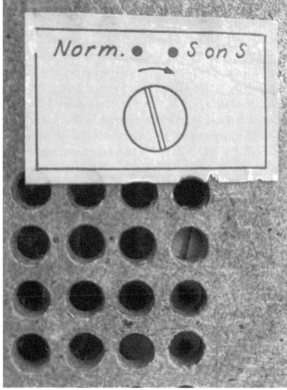

Figure 1.3 Above: the author's first electronic music machine: a Tandberg Model 64 tape recorder, 1971. Photo by Simon Lonergan. Below: detail of the back panel. Hidden switch recessed behind hole, second row, far right. Photo by Nicolas Collins.

you played a previously recorded tape. But if you listened to the playback head while *recording*, you heard the sound you were recording back at a slight delay. This delay was a function of the tape speed and the one-inch distance between the playback head and the record head: on the Tandberg's slowest speed (1 7/8 inches per second [IPS]), an echo came back about 1½ seconds after playing; at higher speeds, the slap-back was faster. Playing back while recording an instrument in tempo with the delay provided a rhythmic underpinning that I recognized from rockabilly music, which used similar "head-delay" for its characteristic slap-echo on vocals. At 1 7/8 IPS, the delay provided a driving pulse of around 37 beats per minute (BPM); increasing the tape speed to 3¾ IPS doubled the tempo to 75 BPM; 7½ IPS yielded a feisty 150 BPM.

If I played on beat, the delay superimposed each new note over the one that had been played a moment earlier, creating a two-note vertical harmony from a horizontal melodic sequence. I began to incorporate the delay tempos and overlap of notes into the musical structure of improvised playing, rather than using the machine as a passive recording device for pre-composed music. These effects are familiar to anyone who has ever used one of the myriad digital-delay pedals now available to guitarists, but my modest experiments, a decade before the advent of such devices (and not yet aware of the similar use of tape effects in other music), felt like a revelation.

The Tandberg's other hidden talent was far stranger. On the back of the machine, I found a hole next to a paper label marked "NORM • → • S ON S." Behind the opening was a two-position switch that could be rotated with a screwdriver: in the NORM position, the tape recorder functioned as expected; S ON S not only enabled the "Sound on Sound" overdubbing function but also induced unexpected feedback inside the machine (see Figure 1.3). It was as if turning up your radio caused some hidden microphone to feed back with the speaker. The buttons and knobs on the front, which normally adjusted the sounds being recorded or their playback volume, now manipulated internally generated electronic sound.[iii]

This mystery switch was documented nowhere in the manual, and I never learned whether its behavior was an intended feature of the original design or a fault in my machine. Either way, it did something astonishing: in combination with the tape-head echo, the switch transformed a familiar recording device into a unique performance instrument—not as potent as Hendrix's guitar, but my very own playable feedback machine. I spent many hours mucking about with it, hunting for music lurking inside.[iv]

These two hidden attributes of the Tandberg revealed a music that sounded fresher and more seductive than anything I could imagine scribbling down on manuscript paper, and with much less effort than my bouncing process entailed to record the notes.

[iii] This kind of internal electronic feedback, I learned later, was central to David Tudor's electronic pieces of the 1960s and 1970s, and, in the 1990s, to the style of music known as "no-input mixing."

[iv] During the Covid lockdown, I unearthed the old machine in the attic of the Cape Cod house, though not the user's manual. An online search, however, turned up a scan of it, still lacking any reference to the "NORM • → • S ON S" switch.

Exhilarated by my discoveries, I now wanted to build some kind of noise-making circuit of my own. Synthesizers held obvious appeal, and Robert Moog's eponymous machines had been on the market since 1967, but at $3,000 to $8,000 (over $60K today), they were beyond the budget of all but the richest pop stars and institutions. (In 1970, only twenty-eight were in the hands of individual musicians.) To build something myself, I figured I would need to come up to speed on how electricity worked. Happily, like many private schools at that moment, mine had begun to augment its hoary college prep curriculum with a menu of wacky electives intended as a sop to student fractiousness. One was a class on basic electronics. It was taught by Bob Sakayama, a recent graduate of Brown University who had arrived at the school in 1968 to teach math and physics, and brought a much-needed whiff of diversity to a largely older and almost uniformly white faculty. Taking advantage of the school's loosened requirements, I had bypassed physics—an omission I would later regret—so this was my first exposure to electrical theory. At the end of the trimester, I still had more questions than answers, but Bob asked if I would be willing to teach the class the following year in his stead. Remarkably, neither administrators nor parents seemed to object to their children (exclusively my close friends) being taught by a poorly prepared high-school student.

The experience gave me enough confidence that I invested in my first integrated circuit or "chip." This one had been designed and marketed as the bleating heart of the Touch-Tone telephone. Aided by an article in a hobbyist magazine, I managed on my third attempt to build a working oscillator—a circuit whose electrical waves make pitched sound. This is the core "synthesis" of synthesizers. Different waveforms produce different timbres: sine waves would be heard as mellifluous flute-like tones, square waves as raucous or brassy rasps, with other curves in between.

Professional synthesizers added a host of bells and whistles for tweaking and controlling those sounds, as well as keyboards for hitting particular pitches with time-honored muscle memory. My little circuit wasn't as versatile as one from Robert Moog's brilliant mind, but one Moog oscillator cost $395, while mine cost $5.

The Touch-Tone chip sat regally in the center of an oversized prototyping circuit board, encased in a phenomenally ugly (yet, to my eyes, very professional-looking) metal box with a crinkly matte-black finish that I festooned with orange Dymo labels officiously designating the mismatched knobs, switches, and jacks as "pitch," "output," and "on." (Years later, when I showed my oscillator to my future wife, Susan Tallman, she observed, "it looks like something made by Fred Flintstone.") Ugly or not, it made electronic music the moment I turned it on (see Figure 1.4).

Though I had no way of knowing it at the time, this chip—the Signetics SE/NE566—was also being used by real grown-up composers on both coasts: it animated the electronic *shruti* box that was the first circuit of composer and early hacker Paul DeMarinis in California, as well as an extraordinary homemade synthesizer built by Sonic Arts Union member David Behrman. The 566 may have been to the development of experimental electronic music what the Stratocaster was to the rise of rock and roll.

The most influential arbiter of my musical acquisitions was *Rolling Stone*, and I read it cover to cover. The February 7, 1970, issue included four bemused paragraphs on Terry

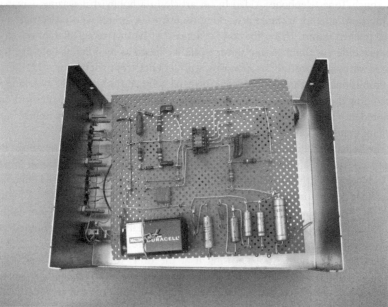

Figure 1.4 The author's first home-built circuit, an oscillator, 1972. Photos by Nicolas Collins.

Riley's experimental *Rainbow in Curved Air* alongside a pair of reviews of the Grateful Dead's landmark *Live/Dead* album. (One of the Dead reviews employed *Rolling Stone*'s default journalistic style; the other was a probably fictional account of sexual activity synchronized to the album's track sequence.)[5] I bought both records within weeks of each other—a snapshot of the tangled state of my musical interests. The Riley record *should* have alerted me to the precedent of the tape recorder as a performance instrument, since his keyboard improvisations were driven by the same head-echo rhythmic pulse I found so inspiring in the Tandberg, but there was so much else going on in the music I didn't make the connection. Riley's dreamy liner notes—"the concept of work was forgotten"—were in any case useless as a technical guide.

Rainbow was released on the Columbia Records Music of Our Time series produced by David Behrman (he of the homemade synthesizer), which aimed to introduce composers of experimental music to a more pop-oriented public. Had I bought other records in the series, I would have heard the electronic experiments by Pauline Oliveros and others active at the San Francisco Tape Music Center. Instead, I bought more Dead. (I was sixteen, after all.)

My awareness of "electronic music" did not extend far beyond Karlheinz Stockhausen and Tonto's Expanding Head Band. And I knew I did not want to follow in the steps of either: Stockhausen was rooted in a high modernism that felt alien to me, while Tonto was pop-ish but lacked the depth of proper rock and roll. Where I felt comfortable was fiddling about in the consumer-unfriendly ends of household objects (a family tradition) and inventing impractical electronic structures that were not so different from my childhood Rube Goldberg variations.

I understood, however, there was more to music than the devices that played it. To self-educate, I assembled a listening list going back a few centuries, filling the gaps in my education with records, scores, and books from the Lincoln Center branch of the New York Public Library. I took a music history course taught by the organist and choir director of West End Collegiate Church, Allen Jay Sever. (My school was still nominally associated with the Dutch Reform Church that had founded it in 1628.) An open-minded sort, he asked the students—all three of us—to bring in LPs of what we were listening to at home. I brought in Grateful Dead's "Dark Star," track one on *Live/Dead*. Mr. Sever listened carefully and pronounced: "Improvisations in the Dorian mode."[v] I resolved to find out more about this Dorian and enrolled in a theory class at Manhattan School of Music.

I learned the difference between modal music, which uses seven distinctive arrangements of whole and half steps, each of which is fixed, and tonal music, which relies on just two common configurations of steps (major and minor), but can shift from one key to another in the course of a single composition. In European musical history, modal had preceded tonal, with Bach as the tipping point. Tonal is the sound of Beethoven's *Moonlight Sonata*; modal is sixteenth-century music like that of Claudio

---

[v] I have fond memories of Mr. Sever, who, in addition to serving at West End Collegiate Church for more than fifty years, also played for the flamboyantly left-wing Stephen Wise Free Synagogue for more than forty years, and taught throughout the city.

Monteverdi. Or the Grateful Dead on *Live/Dead.* (Coincidentally, the Terry Riley record I paired with the Dead was also in a modal scale.)

Meanwhile, the Group for Contemporary Music at Columbia offered performances of works by Mario Davidovsky, Charles Wuorinen, and other brainy twentieth-century composers working in styles commonly referred to as "12-Tone," "Serial," or simply "Atonal." Contravening the favoritism of both modal and tonal systems, these schemes refused to emphasize any one note or perceived key, making sure that each pitch of the chromatic scale was heard as often as the others.

Under the illusion that the road to composing always begins with the piano, I persuaded my reluctant parents to rent an upright, on which I plinked out whatever ideas I had that did not involve squeals of feedback. I had one mentor—a graduate student in electronic music at Hunter College named Danny Feldman, who worked with my mother in the Museum of Modern Art library. Danny listened uncomplainingly to my pieces and my ideas, took me seriously and, when I aired my insecurities, gave me a crucial piece of advice: "There is no 'correct' musical background; listen to the music you love, not the music you think you should love." He assured me that a composition didn't have to be "about" the legacy of European musical masters, though it remained unclear to me what might take its pedagogic place.

As I approached the prospect of college, my dreams turned away from the city to small liberal arts schools in bucolic, white-steeple, New England settings. The flakier and more hedonistic, the better. Studying lute-making in a leaky geodesic dome 200 miles from a major city seemed a perfect way to spend four years and my parents' money. I was enjoying a flirtation with Marlboro College in Vermont when I happened to thumb through a copy of John Cage's *Silence* (1965) in my parents' library (an indication of his pervasive influence in art world circles). Cage, I learned, had drifted in and out of Wesleyan University, so I paid a visit to the school. Middletown, Connecticut, proved to be a bleak, post-industrial hamlet bereft of both white steeples and hippy hemispheres, but the course catalog was a candy shop: there were classes in electronic music and marine biology and Latin American literature and all the other domains I could see myself adulting in. There was a famous program in what was then termed "World Music," where I could learn to play the *tabla* that had so impressed me in *Monterey Pop.* How could I say no to a school that offered the two-semester philosophy sequence "Language as Cosmos" and "Cosmos as Language"?

My last months in New York were spent studying synthesizer technique at Manhattan School of Music and producing rudimentary tape compositions as a high-school capstone project. My first review came from the headmaster: "If I didn't know it was you, Collins, I'd assume it was a bunch of drunks at a party."[6]

I Am Sitting in a Classroom

On my second day at Wesleyan, I met with the faculty advisor who had been assigned to me. Jon Barlow was a brilliant pianist, a Charles Ives scholar, and a polymath of extraordinary range. He listened patiently as I rattled off a list of alluring classes from a dozen different disciplines, then zeroed in on my mention of electronic music.

"Do you know the composer Alvin Lucier?"

I admitted I did not.

"Well, you should call him up. He makes music with bats."

I didn't know if he meant flying mammals or Louisville Sluggers, but either way, it caught my interest.

I called Professor Lucier and was invited over to his house on the edge of campus. This casual access was a surprise: no Columbia undergraduate had ever set foot in the apartment of Professor Collins. I was received in a living room that suggested I had missed one hell of a party the night before, and I noted the absence of what I thought of as the obligatory composer's piano. We made our introductions. He stuttered, which I assumed was hangover-related. After a few minutes, I proposed that I opt out of his introductory lecture course on the basis of the synthesizer class I'd taken that summer. He was damningly diplomatic: "I'm sure you know much more about synthesizers than I do, but I like my students to be familiar with the music that's already out there. I hate having to say the words, 'that's very nice, but it's been done before.'"

Chastened, I signed up for "Introduction to Experimental Music," which was held in a surprisingly large hall otherwise used for introductory lectures in the sciences. What drew so many students wasn't their fascination with avant-garde sounds; the class had a reputation as a "gut," an easy credit for pre-meds and athletes and others with pressing claims on their time. In his opening lecture, Lucier spoke about hearing the music of John Cage for the first time.

It was the summer of 1960 and Lucier was in Venice, en route to Rome on a Fulbright Fellowship. He had been writing what he described as "neo-classical music in a vaguely Stravinsky style" and had just bought some beautiful handmade manuscript paper on which to notate it. A friend called him up and said, "come with us tonight, we're going to hear this crazy composer John Cage at La Fenice, it should be a laugh." They went. The lights dimmed, and pianist David Tudor—a highly respected interpreter of contemporary music—ran down the aisle, jumped onto the stage, slid under the piano, and started banging on the underside of the soundboard. Later, Cage rose up on a hydraulic lift, playing another piano and then turning on a radio. "The audience was furious," Lucier told us, before inserting a dramatic pause. "For the next year I couldn't write a note of music. My mind was a blank. I did nothing but eat pasta and drink red wine." The beautiful handmade manuscript paper sat untouched.[1] I have since heard similar tales from other composers of that generation about their own year of silent shock that followed their first encounter with Cage.

By the time Cage turned fifty, Lucier explained, he had challenged fundamental assumptions about music and the roles of composer and performers. He embraced sounds many would have dismissed as noise. He invented methods of removing personal taste—the putative locus of artistic genius—from compositional decisions. He elevated impersonal sounds, like those of the natural world, to the same aesthetic level as the violin or piano. He pioneered the use of electronics in live performance. The list went on and on.

Twice a week for the next nine months, I listened as Lucier played records and tapes, passed around scores, and talked. We were soon on a first-name basis (something else that never happened with my father's students). The first semester covered a period from around 1939 to the mid-1960s, focusing on the "New York School" that consisted of Cage, Morton Feldman, Earl Brown, and Christian Wolff. Every lecture on Cage was a revelation, from the earliest works for junkyard percussion to the unexpectedly romantic pieces for prepared piano and the uncompromisingly radical *4'33"*. (This last, John Cage's landmark "silent" composition, had been premiered by Tudor in 1952 in a small chapel near Woodstock, New York—an event Alvin asserted "was the *real* Woodstock, not all those hippies naked in the mud.") Feldman had put a spin on the paradox of octaves in twelve-tone music (the idea that a C is a C is a C within the serial rule set, regardless of octave) in pieces that transposed intervals so widely the listener could never tell if they were consonant or dissonant, with the result that his music—unlike Cage's—always sounded sublimely beautiful. I have to admit I didn't fully appreciate Brown at the time, a pioneer in graphically notated scores, despite his openness to aspects of improvisation that overlapped with my other musical interests.

It was Cage's *Cartridge Music* (1960) that resonated most profoundly with me. Earlier electronic music, like that of Pierre Schaeffer or Herbert Eimert, had usually been made by recording various sounds, slicing up the tape and stitching it back together in a studio; performances, such as they were, consisted of playing the tape back from speakers on a stage. Everything, with the possible exception of the machine breaking down or an audience member having a coughing fit, was determined in advance. On stage there was no drama, no risk, no visceral evidence of thinking on one's feet.

Cartridge Music was the opposite. In place of sophisticated studios or synthesizers, Cage adapted the stylus cartridges from record players—something almost every American home had—to act as contact microphones, instructing players to replace the needle with anything that would fit in the opening: pipe cleaners, straws, guitar strings, and Slinkies (this last was later adopted by Ben Burtt to create the iconic lightsaber sound for the first *Star Wars* movie).

The score was similarly built on the principle of adaptability, consisting of twenty sheets of paper covered in amoeba-like blobs, along with an array of transparencies bearing forms like a clock face, polka dots, little circles, and dotted lines that might have been lifted from a pirate's treasure map. By superimposing the various sheets, the performers created graphics that told them when to insert and pluck at the pipe cleaners, springs, or whatever; how to adjust the loudness and tone of each cartridge, and when to use another microphone as a secondary sound source. The volume could sometimes ratchet up loud enough to generate feedback, but Cage's instructions dictate: "All events, ordinarily thought to be undesirable, such as feed-back, humming, howling, etc., are to be accepted." [2]

Instead of papers or exams, Alvin required every student in the class to prepare a fifteen-minute realization of the score of *Cartridge Music* and perform it live, which we did together in the Wesleyan Faculty Club shortly before Thanksgiving. This was my electronic music concert debut, and it was chaos. I loved the sounds; I loved Cage's acceptance of the player as a partner in the preparation of the performance score; I loved the opening of the stage to "non-musicians" by exchanging conventional instruments for consumer technology. I now understood that electronic music could be a *performed* music rather than the recorded output of a studio process.

Of the four members of the New York School, Wolff intrigued me as much as Cage. I was smitten with his "coordination scores" such as *For 1, 2 or 3 People* (1964), in which he "reduced the tempo to zero" (his words), replacing tempo-based notation— the familiar array of whole notes, half notes, quarter notes, and so on—with graphic symbols that specified when a musician might start and stop in relation to others: for example, "play after a previous sound has begun, hold till it stops."

Home for Thanksgiving that fall, I rattled on to my parents about this exciting new music and mentioned that Wolff had, as a high-school student in New York, approached Cage for composition lessons. (Cage later told me that they gave up after three lessons because Wolff "didn't want to follow my assignments.")

My mother glanced up from the turkey. "Not *little* Christian Wolff?" she asked.

A brief genealogical tour ensued: Christian's parents were the eminent publishers and editors Kurt and Helen Wolff. My great-aunt Ena in Santiago was Helen Wolff's sister, making Christian my cousin, at least by Chilean standards. When my mother had come to New York to study at Columbia in the late 1940s, she had seen a lot of the Wolffs and their teenaged son.

This connection was charming (like both Aunt Ena and Helen Wolff), but it did not endow me with any special insight. Child of the 1960s that I was, I had interpreted the conductor-less democracy of Christian's ensemble interaction as an early step toward the overtly anti-authoritarian political works he began composing soon after. And later, when I began to study computer programming, these same pieces struck me as a kind of proto-computer music, given the similarity of his instructions to logical operations. Eventually, Christian kindly disabused me of both ideas: he had developed his notational system when a time-strapped student at Harvard, looking for an efficient way to produce a rhythmic complexity that would otherwise take hours of painstaking work to score conventionally. It was just one of my many useful misunderstandings of the music I heard that first year with Alvin. (Christian didn't hold my ignorance against me; I was touched when he composed an extension of *For 1, 2 or 3 People* for a group of four performers that included myself: *Or Four People* [1994].)[i]

The second term of Alvin's class brought us to the present day, examining composers of Alvin's generation who had been affected by Cage: Terry Riley, LaMonte Young, Pauline Oliveros, Steve Reich, Philip Glass, Robert Ashley, Gordon Mumma, David Behrman, and Alvin himself. Post-war European music was better documented and more widely taught, but Alvin chose to focus on the New World and on "Downtown" music (at the time it was largely confined to lofts below 14th Street), in contrast to the "Uptown" fare I had encountered through the Columbia Group for Contemporary Music on 116th Street. Many of the Downtown composers were described as "Minimalist" for their penchant for stretching a small amount of musical material to extreme lengths—a tendency I interpreted as a reaction against the overwrought complexity of late serialism. (The paradigm of durational minimalism was the score of La Monte Young's *Composition 1960 #7*, which consists, in its entirety, of the interval of a perfect fifth and the instruction: "to be held for a long time.") Their instrumentation often deviated from the conventional ensembles of the time: electric organs instead of pianos, homemade circuits in lieu of violins. Most of what we heard in class had been composed within the previous five or ten years. This music was not just new to me, it was new, period.

Alvin was a member of the rather grandly titled Sonic Arts Union, a quartet of young composers that also included Ashley, Behrman, and Mumma. They had joined forces in 1966 as an outgrowth of the ONCE Festivals of New Music that Ashley and Mumma had helped found in Ann Arbor in 1961. The Sonic Arts Union was not an ensemble in the usual sense: they did not perform repertoire as instrumentalists. Instead, each composer presented his own work, sometimes solo, sometimes assisted by the others. They shared some equipment, like amplifiers and speakers, but unlike the Beatles or the Budapest String Quartet, their collective identity was secondary to that of its individual members. Lucier's music revolved around acoustical phenomena such as architectural resonance. Ashley worked extensively with voice, which gave equal weight to literary content and the physicality of the vocal performance. Behrman used circuits (initially rather simple) and feedback networks in group performances that balanced on the border between control and chaos. Mumma built his own, more complex circuits that often interacted with conventional instruments, producing intermittent shrieks in response to his French horn playing, for example. (It was he who taught Behrman and pianist David Tudor how to build circuits, and the other members of the Sonic Arts Union tended to defer to him on technical matters.)

---

[i] The four performers for the premiere concert, in Groningen (NL) in June 1994, were David Tudor, Takehisa Kosugi, Wolff, and me.

What exactly drew me to Cage and the composers who flourished in his wake? It felt like surfing the crest of a paradigm shift in the very idea of music itself. As Behrman explained that moment: "established techniques were thrown away and the nature of sound was dealt with from scratch."[3] The *methods* fascinated me at least as much as the resulting sounds. This music felt like an open call for invention.

In his accounts of young composers whose conservatory-instilled cosmologies were shattered by Cage, Alvin invoked a collective impulse to "return music to the year zero"—to scrutinize music's most fundamental axioms and assumptions. He offered a parable about Philip Glass: after graduating from Juilliard and receiving a Fulbright scholarship, Glass went off to France to study with Nadia Boulanger, a legendarily demanding teacher of formal compositional technique. Despite his rigorous training, Glass found mastering the methods to her satisfaction a challenge. In the midst of his struggles, he was hired to help with a score Ravi Shankar was writing for Conrad Rooks's film *Chappaqua* (1967). His task was to listen to Shankar and Alla Rakha play and notate their performance so it could be recreated by a French orchestra. Like most Westerners at the time, Glass knew nothing about Indian music, and his attempts to pin down the intricate rhythmic structures and pitch nuances using traditional five-line notation were frustrating for everyone until, finally, he removed the bars between measures. For Boulanger, this would be an unthinkable act, but now Glass could see the repeated patterns endemic in Indian music, and he has spoken about the liberating influence this had on his own compositional trajectory.[4]

Alvin's version of this story added (or possibly invented) a detail missing from Glass's own account. The rules of Western counterpoint had been laid down by Johann Joseph Fux's 1725 textbook (followed by Boulanger, and still in use today), and one of the most important of these rules was "no parallel fifths."[5] Noticing the prevalence of parallel fifths in Shankar's preferred orchestrations, Glass pointed out that this wasn't allowed.

"But why not?" Shankar asked. "We've been playing parallel fifths in India for thousands of years, since long before your counterpoint."

Glass then asked himself what would happen if he went back to Fux's directive and did the opposite: instead of *no* parallel fifths, use *only* parallel fifths. He derived a new compositional technique from this contrarian starting point and, in 1973, released an LP with the first results, *Music in Fifths* (1969) and *Music in Similar Motion* (1969).[6] The story may be apocryphal, but for me, it served as a fitting illustration of the reinvention of musical structures in that heady time. Glass rewrote counterpoint from its own year zero and let a new species evolve from one critical mutation.

I had no particular interest in counterpoint (not then, anyway), but the nature of Alvin's own "year zero" had a massive impact on me. He had reconsidered not just what constituted acceptable intervals or instrumentation, but the most basic phenomena of aural experience—the meeting of physical acoustics and biological perception. His 1969 composition *Vespers* bears the poignant and expansive subtitle:

> For any number of players who would like to pay their respects to all living creatures who inhabit dark places and who, over the years, have developed acuity

in the art of echolocation, i.e., sounds used as messengers which, when sent out into the environment, return as echoes carrying information as to the shape, size, and substance of that environment and the objects in it.[7]

In *Vespers*, blindfolded performers use handheld echolocation devices called Sondols to navigate a dark room by sound alone.[ii] (This was the bat allusion that intrigued me in my first advisory meeting; no Louisville Slugger after all.) Lucier had taken sound back to before a composer's year zero, to before its role in music, to its use as a practical tool by pre-hominid flying sonic virtuosi.

The physical structure of any space, indoors or out, is friendlier to some frequencies of sound than others: some are absorbed and die away quickly, while other "resonant" frequencies ricochet longer. When you hold a conch up to your ear, what you hear is the white noise of wind and surf filtered by the shell's cavity to emphasize certain resonant frequencies. In his best-known work, Alvin explained this phenomenon even as he allowed it to subsume his voice.

I am sitting in a room (1969) bounces a recorded text back and forth between two tape machines, playing and re-recording the sound through a speaker and microphone in a room, recycling the words as the resonant frequencies of the architecture reshape the speech into mellifluous gongs and whistles—"musical" sounds for sure, but as much "echoes carrying information" as the minimal clicks of *Vespers*—while at the same time charting the inexplicable journey from prose to song, from explanation to experience, and from presence to absence.

I may have had only a nodding acquaintance with Mozart, but I had observed the behavior of bats on two continents and had spent innumerable family outings identifying ceiling vaults. Alvin's example filled in the essential bit missing from Danny Feldman's advice that "there is no 'correct' musical background." It was possible to make musical—or at least sonic—works about the things that fascinated me. Ideas were common currency in the world I grew up in, but I didn't want to be a musicologist. I wanted to be a composer, and Alvin handed me a toolbox I understood.

He taught me how to listen—not just to music, but to the acoustical phenomena that underlie and precede it. By the end of the year, I noticed that whenever I entered a bathroom, I could hum the resonant frequency of the room, no doubt from recognizing, subconsciously, the filtering of my footfall in a hard-tiled space. My parents had taught me the importance of noticing details: the herringbone tile pattern of a Guastavino vault, the droopy organic lines of the art nouveau chotchkes they collected, the trifoliate horror of poison ivy. Alvin shifted my attention from eyes to ears.

His was a lesson that has enriched my life immeasurably. Even now, despite the declining high-frequency sensitivity of older ears, I find I am ever more sensitive to "roomtone"—that filtering of ambient sound—and how it shifts when I cross a

---

[ii] The size of a large flashlight, the Sondol was developed in the 1960s by Listening Incorporated in suburban Boston as a navigational aid for the blind. It was unsuccessful in its intended market, probably because its slightly threatening appearance and ominous "tick . . . tick . . . tick" sound drew unwanted attention to the user.

threshold. When I lie in bed in the morning, I hear the acoustic changes that accompany my wife closing the door to the bathroom. On the landing outside our apartment, I hear the space expand when the elevator door opens. Clicking the car's key fob in a parking garage, I visualize the wave front of the beep as it spreads away, rebounds off distant walls, superimposes on itself, then slowly decays into the ambient noise, like the ripples in a pond or physics lab wave tank.

Alvin's approach to teaching—drawing largely from his own first-hand experience— dovetailed nicely with the oral pedagogy of Wesleyan's World Music program, a prominent part of the music department's identity. There were a few ethnomusicology programs around the country where you could study the music of India or Japan or Indonesia from books, scores, and recordings in the manner of Western musicology. At Wesleyan, however, you could learn to *play* the sitar, shakuhachi or bonang through one-on-one lessons with a master musician, whose own training had often been primarily or entirely oral. When I began studying tabla, Sharda Sahai taught me by reciting the *bols*, the North Indian rhythm equivalent of solfège.

Alvin taught us about recent music by telling stories illustrated with tape recordings from his own collection, often given to him by fellow composers since there were few records available.[8] He handed out scores, some of them published, others just photocopies of hand-drawn drafts. In the absence of textbooks, Alvin passed around issues of *Source: Music of the Avant Garde*, a journal published irregularly from 1967 to 1973 under the direction of composer Larry Austin, which featured scores and essays submitted by emerging artists.[9] Most importantly, perhaps, Alvin also arranged visits by composers and would deploy his students to meet them at the bus station (an inexpensive ticket from New York City). We would drive them around, tech their concerts, and listen to their stories.[10]

Lacking any unifying theoretical dicta about this music, we were left to our own devices to connect the dots—to consider how (or whether) works such as *Music in Fifths* and *Vespers* linked to each other or to the larger histories of music. We were asked to listen, perceive, and think for ourselves. One of the central issues in my mind had to do with intentionality—the relationship between the composer and the composition. I came to see each piece of music as arising somewhere on a spectrum that runs from aspirational randomness to unfettered personal choice. Cage's use of chance methods (shuffled transparencies, star maps, and, most famously, the *I Ching*) to remove personal preference lives at one end, while at the other lay the kind of "free improvisation" I would come to know through the performances of British guitarist Derek Bailey or the AMM group.[iii] Terry Riley's *In C* (1964)—a single sheet of paper bearing fifty-three short riffs

---

[iii] The *I Ching* is an ancient Chinese divination text. Yarrow sticks or coins are tossed to generate, pseudo-randomly, sixty-four possible hexagrams, each mapped to a text that is interpreted to answer questions or give advice. Helen and Kurt Wolff—composer Christian Wolff's parents—published a translation that Christian presented to Cage in 1951. Cage used the *I Ching* methodology to decide musical parameters—such as pitches, durations, dynamics, and so on—in many of his subsequent compositions.

which can be repeated any number of times by each of the players before proceeding to the next—sat somewhere in the middle, evoking a jazz chart and a skipping record in equal measure. Nearby Riley would lie structures like those Sol LeWitt alluded to when he wrote: "the idea is the machine that makes the art": mechanisms and methods that point to themselves, not just to their output.[11] Fugue, serial form, and twelve-bar blues are familiar examples of machines for making musical art (admittedly with considerable human intervention), but the music Alvin played introduced a panoply of new ones—systems and processes that stepped up to replace the old engines of instinct, taste, and tradition with which I had always felt slightly uncomfortable.

There was music with no discernible melody, harmony, or rhythm (such as Behrman's *Wave Train*, 1965) and music that used impossibly long sounds (La Monte Young) or equally all-consuming rests (*4'33"*). And while music is reflexively celebrated for its manipulation of emotion, this new music allowed for objective and perceptual phenomena—physics, zoology, neurology—to motivate structures, as in Maryanne Amacher's use of psychoacoustic effects to induce music for the inner ear.

There were "task scores," from which music emerged as the byproduct or trace of a seemingly arbitrary process, rather than as the intentional output of inherently musical actions: Kenneth Maue's *Names* (1972), for example, consists of the instruction: "Make a list of all the persons you have ever personally known or met." There were "impossible scores" where sounds emerged from the failure to execute a difficult act properly: Tom Johnson's *Risks for Unrehearsed Performers* (1977) supplied instrumental virtuosi with a series of instructions that escalated in difficulty until skill reached its inevitable limit and the player was forced to give up.

In "circuit-as-score" compositions, musical decisions were shared with electronic circuits (exemplified by the work of David Tudor, who eventually gave up the piano to devote himself entirely to electronic work) or a computer program. New musical forms might arise from capabilities and limitations intrinsic to a piece of technology, and later be separated from it to live on as independent sonic structures—for example, Steve Reich's compositions for tape loops (*Come Out*, 1966), which led to his body of phase music for purely acoustic ensembles (*Piano Phase*, 1967).

Pieces such as Alvin's *Vespers* were composed for the behavior of sounds *after* they left the instruments, attuning audiences to how sound propagated and transformed in space. Pauline Oliveros turned listening itself into a form of performance in her *Sonic Meditations* (1971). Finally, notions about where and when music happened were being challenged by the emerging fields of sound art, installations, and video, led by artists such as Annea Lockwood, Max Neuhaus, and Nam June Paik.

Many of the scores we studied did not tell you how things would *sound*. Reading the score of a Bach prelude, a musically literate person can imagine the moment-to-moment progression of notes in their mind's ear, but the magic of *I am sitting in a room* is that the flow of sounds you will hear cannot be inferred from the instructions, even though they tell you exactly what is happening. Most of these pieces were lumped under the label "Experimental Music," which served not only to differentiate them from the dominant styles of "Contemporary Music," from Stockhausen to Wuorinen, but to acknowledge the emergence of the unexpected, even from a fixed set of instructions. Some composers took exception to the term, coined by Cage, but to me it made sense.[12] Obviously, this music was not "experimental" in the scientific sense of pitting an established hypothesis against a neatly delimited set of variables; it was "experimental" in the woolier sense of "and what if . . .?" For me, it bridged my new musical interests with the dangling threads of my earliest enthusiasms.

Even within experimentalism, axiomatic concepts arose that many people made use of. Big ideas like "take a sound from one place and put it in another," "do one thing for a very long time," "slow something down a lot," "do something backwards," and "make sound with a very long string" were treated as exercises, points of departure, or new forms to replace more familiar ones like the sonata or blues. Just as many different pieces of music might share the same form, instruments, key, or time signature, Amacher, Lockwood, and Bill Fontana all made pieces that transposed acoustic environments with phone lines. Alan Lamb, Ellen Fullman, Paul Panhuysen, Alvin, and I all did music on long thin wires. Occasionally someone might lay claim to one of these big ideas as a personal invention, dismissing other works in that mode as derivative, but most understood that it was always going to be the specific manifestation of an idea—what it sounded like, how it played out—that counted. (As Robert Ashley once told me, "I'd rather see an old idea done well than a new one done badly.")

In these novel musical methods, I recognized a familiar, Rube Goldberg-like indirection, an upending of efficiency in the name of surprise and discovery. Moreover, many of these "machines for making music" had moving parts that could be observed, and there was pleasure in that. I've always been a fairly monophonic person. Musically, I think in terms of horizontal lines, not vertical harmonies. Most of these compositions made a point of revealing their structure and content in a linear manner. I could follow their naked causality more easily than I could the artfully shrouded voices in a fugue. This music put me at ease.

Of course, things were not quite as simple as I thought during that inspirational first year. What I took to be a world of new musical thought was, in fact, the product of a small group of people—almost all of the same sex, nationality, race, social class, and educational background. The fact that Pauline Oliveros was the only woman whose work Alvin played or discussed in his class was something I only noticed in retrospect. Having grown up with two brothers and having attended an all-boys' school for thirteen years, I was accustomed to a profoundly unbalanced world. Politically, I embraced feminism, and personally, I was thrilled to be (finally) on a coeducational campus, but how endemic gender pressures played out in culture at large—even avant-garde culture—was opaque to me. I had little to go on beyond what Alvin told me, what I read in *Rolling Stone* or the *Village Voice*, and what I heard on my weekend jaunts to The Kitchen (then the most visible center for new music in New York), but these all reinforced the same, unremarked, systemic disparity. I recently dug out the roster for that first class with Alvin. It was 90 percent male and entirely white. I'd like to say that I asked questions about why experimental music appeared to be a mostly male scene, but I did not do so until years later. (An explanation, but not an excuse.)

My other, belated, road-to-Damascus moment had to do with my fundamental assumption of experimental music itself. Yes, you can make a piece "about" anything, but if it's going to work as *music,* you cannot ignore musicality—those ineffable characteristics that make one piece live on in memory while another is forgotten. Numberless pop songs from my childhood share similar chord progressions, but only some are still being whistled by me fifty years on.

When Alvin spoke about taking music back to the year zero, he didn't mean it had to stay there: Glass may have thrown out the old rules of counterpoint, but he created new ones, mapping a fresh fork in the musical road and following it. Everyone was looking for a way through the rubble left by the soundless explosion of *4'33"*, but the most successful pathways retained some axiomatic musical material underfoot: the harmonic series, a rhythm that inspires a bodily response, a perceptible structure, a familiar sound—a hook. As conceptual artist Mel Bochner has pointed out, "there is no *art* that does not *bear* some *burden of physicality.*"[13]

Alvin wasn't concerned with the creation of sound inside a circuit or computer; he was focused on the behavior of sound in space after it leaves the speaker or instrument, which is much more difficult to control or predict. In a radio interview with Felix Kubin, he said, "I'm not so interested in sounds themselves, I'm interested in their reflections."[14] The clicks a Sondol emits are boring and lacking in variety, he admitted. The *music* lies in their reflections, and therein lay the soul of this composition: an homage to the pragmatic sonic genius of the bat, for whom the returning echo contains what really matters—all the information humans usually get through our eyes.

Likewise, the sonic and literary qualities of the initial reading of the text in *I am sitting in a room* are unremarkable, but the words' cumulative reflections eventually yield a musical masterpiece. In *Music for Solo Performer* (1965)—Lucier's breakthrough composition after his post-La Fenice stasis—greatly amplified brain waves are channeled through numerous loudspeakers placed on drums. The 12 Hz alpha waves are barely audible themselves, but their bounce off a drumhead plays the instrument like a stick would.

Years later, reading John Lanchester's short story "Reality" about a haunted house in the English countryside, I found this memorable evocation of the power of such audio reflections:

> Ilona's father had been a poker player in his youth (a very good one, according to him), and he had once said that the best way of telling whether someone was telling the truth was to listen not to what they were saying, or even the tone of their voice, but their echoes. The voices would often be lifted, bright, happy, joking. The echoes sounded flat and angular and full of silences; full of holes, contradictions, meanings that weren't supposed to be there.[15]

Worlds of Music

In the 1970s, what the music department at Wesleyan was best known for was not the presence of Alvin or even its connection to Cage; it was the World Music Program, founded by musicologist Robert Brown in 1963. There were other places where one could study the musicology of other cultures, but Wesleyan was the place to go to learn how to play those musics and instruments. Central to the program was a roster of visiting virtuosi from around the world, as well as a full Indonesian gamelan orchestra on which both PhD students and curious undergraduates could play. There was West African drumming, shakuhachi and koto from Japan, and sitar and veena from North and South India. David McAllister taught classes in Native American music. All this, in addition to a full roster of Western musical instruction, theory, and music history.

I signed up for tabla lessons with Sharda Sahai, a visiting artist from Varanasi with whom I would study for four years. Part of the allure of Indian music for me was its melding of venerable classical traditions and improvisation. Or so I thought, watching the joyful faces and responsive head wiggles of Ravi Shankar and Alla Rakha in the *Monterey Pop* film as they traded riffs like dueling jazz horn players—tossing back and forth phrases sixteen beats long, then eight beats, then four, then two, and finally single beats alternating with seemingly impossible precision as they built their set to a climax.

Some months into my studies, I was sitting behind the tablas on the floor of Sharda's studio as he prepared me for my first public performance.

"Now you will learn the gestures," Sharda explained. "When you play *na* at the end of the second pattern you tip your head like this. And on the third *ta* you turn away a little."

I was nonplussed.

"Wait, are you telling me all those facial expressions are scripted?"

"Of course."

"They're not spontaneous signs of your musical interaction?"

"Oh no," Sharda assured me. "Most of the time I don't even like the musicians I play with."

He went on to tell me that the competition between musicians in Varanasi was so fierce that you had to be careful walking around the city in the week preceding a major concert because rivals would jump out of dark alleys and stomp on your hands. Over the course of four years with Sharda, I learned that improvisation was indeed woven into the music but not always in the places a novice might expect. Moreover, as with many styles of music that incorporate improvisation, students of tabla were first taught to execute fixed material. Improvisation would come later, but in the four years of study, I never reached that level.

There was a curious synergy between the unfenced ear training I was undergoing with Alvin and the far more pedagogically precise education Sharda provided. Entering the tabla studio one day, I saw a sarangi standing in the corner. A string instrument a bit larger than a viola, the sarangi has three fat strings running down a wide steel-wrapped fingerboard, played with a bow, and thirty-five or so sympathetic strings running beneath the fingerboard, as on a sitar. I walked up to take a look as we chatted and found that my voice hung in the air uncannily. Sharda had just borrowed the instrument from the music department's collection, and it hadn't been tuned in a long time. The randomly tuned strings reverberated my voice, as though the sarangi opened a doorway into a cathedral. (Four years later, visiting the Rundfunk Museum in Berlin, I came across examples of early loudspeakers with strings that crisscrossed the opening of the cabinet, like an autoharp. The first electrical speakers struck many listeners as drier and harsher than the gramophone horns that preceded them, which were coupled to the grooves of the record through a mechanism that mimicked the bridge and soundboard of a violin, so more expensive models often incorporated sympathy strings to add warmth, as they do on a sarangi or sitar.)[i]

Home in New York for winter break, I visited the Carroll Musical Instruments store across from the Port Authority in the hopes of finding some of the unusual instruments I had encountered at Wesleyan. The company had started in the 1940s, designing and selling slapsticks, slide whistles, and other novelties for vaudeville and radio sound effects, which led them to importing "exotic" musical instruments. In the 1970s, they were one of the few American dealers of non-Western instruments, although their primary business was now renting out rehearsal rooms in their building.

The owner, Carroll Bratman, would often come out of his office to stand behind the cash register when customers entered the shop. We got to chatting, and I mentioned that I knew how to repair tablas—Sharda taught all his students how to replace the heads on their drums, a lengthy and strenuous process considerably more complicated than putting a new head on a snare drum. Eyes gleaming, Bratman led me to a storeroom full of damaged tablas he hoped I might restore to sellable status. For the next five weeks, I came in every day for a few hours, sat on the floor of the boiler room, stripped off my shirt, and pulled rawhide straps through drumheads for something slightly above minimum wage.

One day, I was wandering the building in search of my supervisor when I came upon a huge room filled with a complete set of Indonesian gamelan instruments and dozens of buckets of water. I tracked down Bratman in his office, and he explained that

---

[i] This idea of sound-resonated strings would underlie the "backwards electric guitars" I created in the 1980s, see Chapter 10.

he had bought them after the 1965 New York World's Fair, where they had featured in the Indonesian pavilion. Two full orchestras worth of instruments had been shipped to New York and sold off at the Fair's end, he explained.

"Some university bought the other set and I keep thinking there's another school out there that would buy mine. Until then, we have to refill the buckets every day to keep the wood from cracking."

I had heard rumors that Wesleyan's gamelan had a missing twin, and now it appeared before me like El Dorado gleaming in an unexpected bit of urban jungle. I suggested a few universities that might consider purchasing the instruments and even tried to interest Wesleyan in buying Bratman's gamelan as a spare, but nothing panned out. (It was eventually donated to the Metropolitan Museum of Art, which sent it to Cornell on a long-term loan, where it is still in use by their Music Department.)

The World Music Program was popular with undergraduates (any number of future doctors, lawyers, and research chemists spent happy undergraduate hours banging away in the gamelan or West African drumming ensemble), but it also attracted professional musicians and composers looking to study outside the Western canon. John McLaughlin—the British guitarist whose wah-wah pedal I heard from outside Miles Davis's house—came to Wesleyan to study the lute-like South Indian veena. He was quite a star at the time, both for his work with Davis and as leader of the Mahavishnu Orchestra, a major act in the emerging Jazz-Fusion movement.

Two weeks into my first semester, the Orchestra played a concert in the hockey arena. McLaughlin had become a devotee of Sri Chinmoy, a trending guru. During freshman orientation, I had met two sari-clad white girls from suburban New York, roommates who were also disciples of Chinmoy and went everywhere together, exuding a cloud of spiritual chasteness (in marked contrast to the hedonistic norm of Wesleyan undergraduate life). They somehow persuaded McLaughlin to attend a post-concert party in their cramped dorm room, to which I was invited. Sometime after midnight, soft drinks drained, McLaughlin stood up to leave, mentioning that he really should start the two-hour drive back to New York since he had a recording session the next morning and was pretty tired. "You can sleep on the floor of our room!" enthused his hostesses in unison, sounding not unlike the eight-score young blonds and brunettes caring for a confused Sir Galahad in *Monty Python and the Holy Grail.*

"Oh no," blushed McLaughlin, "it's a women's dormitory. What if I have to use the bathroom?" (Such modesty from a musician in an era defined by all forms of excess was remarkable.) Without thinking, I chimed in, "Well, you can sleep in my room— I'm in the guys' dorm next door." He agreed.

I offered him the bed, but he chose the floor—wisely, perhaps, given the bed's sagging springs. I can't recall much of what we talked about, but between chanting for a minute and passing out on the linoleum, he offered: "I'm praying to my guru for a full night's sleep in four hours." He was gone when I woke. A few years later, McLaughlin broke with Chinmoy, supposedly after finding his spiritual master in bed with his wife.

I don't remember running into either of the Chinmettes on campus after freshman year, but the summer after graduation, driving to Cape Cod from New York, I stopped to visit one of them at her parents' house on Long Island Sound. Holding a gin and tonic as she reclined in a deck chair on the sand, she was reticent to discuss her time as a disciple.

One of the peculiar charms of American liberal arts colleges is their warm embrace of the clueless applicant. Higher education in most of the world asks the applicant to select in advance their course of study—you apply to the science faculty, or to read law, or to an art school. But liberal arts colleges have a fondness for the aspirant who avows passion for physics, poetry, and pottery in equal measure. And while US schools do ask that students choose a major emphasis in their last two years of study, most also require classes distributed across domains (foreign languages, sciences, quantitative reasoning, humanities, arts). Europeans may leave university knowing more about their field than American students of the same age, but if they're lucky, the beneficiaries of an American liberal arts education know how to think and pursue inquiries across disciplines.

That first semester, in addition to tabla and Alvin's class, I enrolled in Introduction to Ethnomusicology and audited Jazz Big Band, taught by composer Sam Rivers, who had both played with Miles Davis and studied with Alan Hovhaness (I had maxed out on music credits for the term). Rivers commuted from New York and took a relaxed approach to pedagogy—one class consisted of the simple sentence, "You boys jam in D Dorian"—but he was touchingly generous: helping me select a pawn shop saxophone (an instrument I was learning to play at the time), and welcomed me to join the improvisation workshops he hosted in his Studio Rivbea on Bond Street in lower Manhattan. As the registration period drew to a close, however, I was at sixes and sevens about whether to round out my schedule with Russian history or "History of Science to 1600." My father, in a rare instance of engagement with my educational choices, encouraged the history of science. I'll never know what I missed in the way of tsar gazing, but Stuart Gilmore's class was the perfect complement to Alvin's expansion of my musical world. This was my introduction to Greek cosmology, Pythagorean acoustical experiments, theories of universal harmonic proportion, and music of the spheres. It connected so many things.

Having evaded calculus in high school, I chose not to continue to the second semester of post-Newtonian science history, but the physics of sound interested me enough that the following year I enrolled in introductory physics for non-majors. To encourage students to be intellectually adventurous, Wesleyan allowed us the option of taking some classes pass/fail, so you didn't need to worry about dinging your grade point average (GPA). I made an appointment with the professor, Richard Lindquist, an expert in General Relativity, to explain that I was choosing pass/fail not because I was a slacker but because I doubted my math skills. I also mentioned that my understanding of the subject was limited to what I had learned in the history of science class, with its curfew of 1600. (The other students had all studied physics in high school and were pre-meds satisfying a science requirement.) I doubt he took this all in, because when

I raised my hand during an early lecture on momentum (as I recall, a stone was being dropped from the crow's nest of a moving sailboat) and asked, "Where does *vis viva* [an archaic term for kinetic energy] come into this equation?" he was nonplussed. After class, he took me aside and asked if I was pulling his leg.

"No, why?"

"It's just that I've never had a medievalist in a class before. This is going to be very interesting."

And it was, at least for me. I passed the class, but on the obligatory end-of-term evaluation for pass/fail registration, Lindquist wrote: "Collins did the work of a C student."

Similarly, dipping into traditional music, I took classes in Modal Counterpoint (Gabrielli et al.) but opted out of the follow-up Tonal Counterpoint (Beethoven), taking instead a seminar in medieval scale theory. My musical material to this day oscillates between the most contemporary of resources and the artifacts of music written before 1600. (When I started working with brass players, I discovered that many share my preferences, dividing their attention between early music and the avant-garde, and complaining of a dearth of interesting repertoire in the classical period. My hypothesis is that certain musical instruments—of which the trumpet and trombone are good examples—put the player in closer contact with the fundamentals of physical acoustics, which are more present in the underpinnings of modal music than classical forms.)

Acoustics emerged at the intersection of my old world of architectural-historian parents and the new one opened up by Alvin. I read everything I could find on the subject, including a Dover collection of the papers of Wallace Clement Sabine (1868–1919), the American physicist often credited as the first architectural acoustician since Vitruvius. In one paper, he speculated that the structure of Gothic cathedrals may have contributed to the development of polyphonic music—both counterpoint and functional harmony— because the buildings' long reverberation time sustained and superimposed sequential notes.[1] Thus the monophonic "horizontal" melodies of something like Gregorian chant would be heard "vertically" as chords—automatic harmony, an effect not dissimilar to that of Terry Riley's tape delays or my own high-school head-echo experiments.[ii] Sabine contrasts this with how music developed in regions where lighter building materials were used, finding them more likely to emphasize melody and rhythm. Extended reverberation obfuscated rhythmic detail, which he saw as contributing to the relative simplicity of rhythmic structure in classical Western music.

Smitten with this clever notion of causality, I mentioned it to Jon Barlow. He thought for a moment, then suggested that the inverse argument might prove equally valid:

[ii] Riley's tape delays were constructed by threading the tape between two machines. A signal is recorded on one machine, then travels to a take-up reel on the second, where it plays back at a delay proportional to the distance between the two. For example, if the tape is recording at 7½ inches per second (19 cm) and the machines are two feet apart, the sounds play back about 3 seconds after recording (thus were produced the atmospheric canons in Pauline Oliveros' *I of IV* and Terry Riley's *Rainbow in Curved Air*).

that cathedral architecture evolved to support polyphonic music that had emerged independently of any existing architecture.

This ongoing exposure to the interaction of acoustics and music so intrigued me that I began to toy with the idea of studying architecture and becoming an acoustic engineer. I mentioned this idea to my parents. To my surprise, instead of supporting my ambition to enter a field closer to their own than avant-garde music (and undoubtedly more remunerative), my mother reacted in horror: "Oh no, Nicky! You'll spend years executing someone else's ideas before you have the opportunity to create something of your own. Make music instead."

So much for practical parental advice.

In my senior year, I realized that I was running out of time to try something as challenging as calculus, so I signed up for the class with Robert Rosenbaum, a senior member of the mathematics department with a reputation for making complicated things understandable. (He was also famous for his throwing arm: in the midst of writing an equation on the blackboard he could swivel and, seemingly without looking, hurl an eraser directly at the head of a sleeping student anywhere in the large lecture hall, like a pitcher picking off a runner leading off base for a steal.)

Through physics, I had become more comfortable with mathematical concepts but knew that my poor arithmetic skills remained a liability. Calculators were not yet common, but my roommate, fellow Alvin acolyte Ron Kuivila, had a simple four-function model his mother had been awarded for achieving the highest annual sales in her real estate company in suburban Albany. Ron, a skilled mathematician, had no use for it, and loaned it to me at the start of the term.

The day came to complete my first homework assignment. Sitting in the Science Library, I methodically worked my way through the first problem, entering numbers on the calculator keypad as I went. I pressed = and wrote down the result, but the figure surprised me and, thinking I must have mis-transcribed it, I glanced back at the display. It did indeed show a different number, but that also didn't seem right. Then, as I watched, each digit on the calculator gradually evolved into the number 8. The batteries were running down, and the engineers hadn't thought to shut off the calculator when the voltage dropped too low for the chips to function correctly. I struggled through the assignment with traditional paper-and-pencil calculation. When I got back to our apartment, I demonstrated the defect to Ron and asked if I could put in a fresh set of batteries. Fascinated by the display's fatalistic animation, he refused. Once again, at the end of a calculatorless semester, I received a pass/fail evaluation reading, "Collins did the work of a C student."

I have subsequently had many opportunities to think about and make use of what I learned in physics and calculus (and in archaeology, linguistics, geology . . .). I remain profoundly grateful for the opportunity to have been, on certain occasions, a C student.

4

Four Ridiculously Large Speakers

The Wesleyan brochure for prospective students that seduced me in high school had featured beautiful renderings by the architects Roche-Dinkeloo of a multi-building mini-campus for music, art, theater, and dance. When I arrived, the complex was still under construction, and the programs it would eventually host were scattered along the streets that trickled down into the town from College Row. So while the social sciences and humanities were housed in imposing nineteenth-century Portland stone buildings and hard sciences in the mandatory Brutalist concrete tower, the university's resplendent gamelan was laid out in a former A&P supermarket. My tabla lessons took place in a second-floor bedroom of the drafty wooden house that had been allotted to the Indian subcontinent, my shaky rhythms passing through thin walls to blend with the sounds of sitar, mrdangam, vina, and bansuri.

The Electronic Music Studio filled forty square feet at one end of Alvin's office in the Science Center, and consisted of one Arp 2600 synthesizer, a pair of Revox stereo tape recorders, a few microphones, a Dynaco amplifier, and one pair of speakers. This equipment was typical for a small college—Columbia University had more, many places had less—but that's all it was: pieces of equipment. Nothing was fixed in place or wired with the optimizing certainty of a proper studio.

With the new Center for the Arts approaching completion, Alvin was tasked with designing a new facility for making experimental music. It would include a *recording studio*, which was a pretty straightforward proposition: a room with decent acoustics where you fixed ephemeral sounds on tape. The complexity and cost increased as you added tools to the signal chain between performer and tape—microphones, mixers, multitrack tape recorders, and so on—but you could usually count on the musicians to bring their own instruments, supplemented on-site, perhaps, by a piano, a drum kit, and some guitar amplifiers. An *electronic music studio*, on the other hand, needed the core technology of a recording studio along with a host of novel instruments; its goal was to facilitate the creation of new sounds, not just the transcription of familiar ones.

A good recording studio is genre-fluid: a Jimi Hendrix session at the Record Plant in New York might be followed by one with Miles Davis or an advertising jingle. But the design of an electronic music studio—the choice of equipment and its configuration— inevitably imposes a style on the resulting music. The output of the Westdeutscher Rundfunk (WDR) studio in Köln sounds distinctly different from that emerging from the Groupe de Recherches Musicales facilities in Paris, for instance. The Germans favored building sound up from test oscillators and noise generators; composers such as Herbert Eimert, Gottfried Michael Koenig, and Karlheinz Stockhausen would record electronic sounds onto tape, overlay them, process them through filters and other devices, and then edit them into compositions. The French *musique concrète* studios preferred to start with acoustic sound sources—recorded *en plein air* or in the studio—then followed a similar process of layering, processing, editing, and assembling. By the 1970s, new studios, especially in the United States, had begun to incorporate the analog synthesizers being manufactured by Moog, Donald Buchla, or Arp Instruments. Typically played from piano-like keyboards, these instruments were more conducive to real-time sound production than the manually tuned oscillators and other devices used by the Europeans and reduced the amount of tape splicing needed to produce a finished work.

Alvin's landmark compositions of the 1960s and 1970s depended on electronic devices: *Music for Solo Performer* (1965) used a brainwave amplifier and multiple speakers to resonate drums, and *Vespers* (1969) relied on Sondol echolocation devices, but he regarded these simply as means to ends. He never focused on the technology itself and never spoke of himself as an "electronic music composer." He mastered the tools necessary to execute a specific piece but never had much interest in the principles or potentials of electronic equipment in general. Nor did he have an extensive background in tape-based music: though *I am sitting in a room* (1969) was created with a pair of tape recorders, they were set up in his living room for the process, not in a studio.

So when the time came to make decisions about the new Wesleyan studio, he sought advice from David Tudor. As Alvin told it, when presented with the blueprints for the Arts Center, Tudor zig-zagged his finger back and forth across the whole ten-building complex before landing on the studio and said: "Buy a large mixer and lots of speakers for the studio. Then install microphones all over the Center for the Arts, inside and out, and wire them to the mixer. That's all the sound you could need."

Acknowledging that this was a beautiful and visionary idea (though perhaps excessively surveillant), Alvin knew it was too composer-specific: it would impose stylistic limitations as distinct as those of the European studios, albeit with a different aesthetic tilt. Although Alvin himself had little interest in synthesizers (he used them in just two pieces over the whole of his career), they did represent the latest development in music technology. He knew from the noises in the corner of his office that students liked them, and he thought that they should have a place in the new facility. He also predicted that computers would come to play a role in experimental music. (He had taken a tentative step in that direction himself when he connected Wesleyan's DEC 10 mainframe computer to a synthesizer filter and spring reverb to emulate different room acoustics for *The Bird of Bremen Flies Through the Houses of the Burghers* in 1972.) So Alvin brought in the Boston School of Electronic Music (a company that sold synthesizers, taught classes in synthesis, and included a Wesleyan alum on the staff) to design and outfit a synthesizer-based studio for the Center for the Arts, as well as a computer music studio to be lodged in the Computer Center on the other side of the campus.

When the doors to the studio opened in the fall of my sophomore year (1973), we found:

The old Revox tape recorders and Arp 2600 synthesizer from Alvin's old office;
A second Arp 2600, as well as an Arp 2500, bigger and more sophisticated than its siblings;
A digital-ready, custom-made modular analog synthesizer, waiting for the as-yet-unbuilt computer music facility;
Four Altec "Voice of the Theatre" speakers, each the size of a refrigerator and far too large for the studio's 300 square feet;
Four Altec 604e loudspeakers, almost as large;
Two Lamb audio mixers;
Two Teac 3340 4-track tape recorders;
Numerous Dynaco SCA-80 amplifiers;
Three Countryman phase shifters;
Some Electro-Voice microphones;
Lots of cable.

The equipment was an embarrassment of technological riches, but it was to a proper studio what a delivery from Best Buy is to a kitchen: the room itself was so lacking in infrastructure that we made a trip to buy collapsible lunchroom tables to have something to put the equipment on. There was none of the gravitas of a European facility and no set configuration—a curse and blessing from day one. To use any piece of equipment, you usually had to disconnect the prior user's setup and then figure out how to reconnect it to get what you wanted. Great pedagogic value, to be sure, but frustrating for beginning students and hard on the equipment, which broke down frequently as a result of constant movement. In Wesleyan's benign intellectual-hippie Eden, very little was ever actually stolen, but bits and pieces would go AWOL, borrowed for use in other rooms, for location recordings, or for concerts.

Performance with these objects was now a thing. Machines associated with the production of electronic music in the studio were now being carried onto the stage. An early indicator had been the activity of the San Francisco Tape Music Center, where composers such as Pauline Oliveros, Terry Riley, and Steve Reich had recorded continuous electronic performances rather than splicing together multiple tape fragments—in the studio, but in real-time.[1]

Alvin encouraged his students to go live, as he had with his brain waves and Sondols, and his colleagues Behrman and Mumma with their homemade circuits. For me, music had always been about performance. My earliest image of a composer was the singer/songwriter out in front of an audience—Lennon or McCartney, Jagger or Richards—not someone sitting in a Viennese garret, the Brill Building, or even the studios of WDR.

The opening festivities of the CFA in the fall of 1973 found me performing Alvin's *Queen of the South* (1972), a work based on Ernst Chladni's eighteenth-century experiments using powder to reveal vibrational patterns in the bodies of violins and cellos. In Alvin's piece, transducers—loudspeakers without cones—are screwed to large sheets of metal, plastic, or plywood, which are sprinkled with sand, sugar, coffee, and such. Musicians play through amplifiers plugged into the transducers, moving the powder into shapes in response to different pitches. On Tudor's advice, Alvin had wired electronic capacitors the size and shape of D-cell batteries in line with the speaker cable to protect the transducers from loud signals. A few days before the concert, I was practicing the piece in the studio with the Arp 2600. There was a loud bang, and the Arp sounds vanished as one of the capacitors exploded, sending a stream of mylar ribbon twenty feet across the studio like a chrome party streamer. Thus, I learned how electrolytic capacitors are made: thousands of feet of thin metalized mylar tape rolled up like toilet paper inside a metal can. (How thin is that mylar? A couple of years later, I bought a roll of this mylar for sale on Canal Street in New York; I've been using it for party decorations, children's craft projects, costumes, and Christmas wrapping ever since, with no visible change in its diameter.) Together with Ron Kuivila, a newly arrived freshman, I also assisted in the production of other parts of the festivities, including Charlotte Moorman's performance of Nam June Paik's *TV Cello* (1971), in which she bowed televisions stacked in the rough shape of a cello while wearing two small video monitors as a bra.

Cage came to campus the following February for a series of events, including the premiere of *Etcetera* (1973), a new orchestra piece. Paying a visit to Alvin's seminar, he shocked the attentive students by observing that music wasn't so important and it would be better for us to "study something useful, like environmental sciences." Ron Goldman—an undergraduate in his last year and something of a gadfly—piped up: "But *you're* still composing music."

"I'm an old man," Cage replied. "It's what I do best. You're young, you could still do anything."

Alvin observed that this was a very Maoist attitude, in keeping with the denim suit Cage had adopted after decades in a white shirt and dark tie that made him look more like an IBM salesman than the world's most radical composer.

In addition to *Etcetera*, the concert was to include a section of *Etudes Australes* (1974–5), played by pianist Grete Sultan. I was curious as to why, after pieces like *Cartridge Music*, which brought non-musicians onto the stage, he had returned to demanding virtuosity in his current work. And in a public conversation that week, I raised the question.

"All these talented musicians were asking me for pieces," he explained, "and I thought, if I don't write for them, they'll have to play music by even worse composers."

I may have felt that he had regressed from progressive musical idealism to serving the entrenched music elite, but his logic was irrefutable.

The next evening, a large ensemble combining the student orchestra with master musicians from the World Music Program gathered for *Etcetera*. Violins, woodwinds, and brass instruments joined the gamelan and instruments from Asia and Africa. Ron

Kuivila and I were asked to mix and pan various electronic signals and amplified signals from the instruments, following instructions Cage scribbled on the back of computer printouts. For his piece *HPSCHD* (1967–9), Cage had used the mainframe computer at the University of Illinois at Urbana-Champaign to simulate thousands of tossings of the I Ching, generating a massive stack of line-printer paper that he was still using almost ten years later. Every time he needed to make a chance decision when writing a score, he referred to these printouts, disposing of each sheet after use, like a one-time cipher pad. Still a nervous novice at live electronic performance, my main memories of the piece are that the diverse instruments mixed surprisingly well and nothing blew up.

A network of tunnels connected the buildings in the Center for the Arts, providing a conduit for utilities, temporary storage for all manner of furniture and instruments, and pedestrian passage during inclement weather. The afternoon after the Cage concert, Ron Goldman and I took to these tunnels to present a performance using an Arp 2600 and tape delay recycling in the manner of *I am sitting in a room*. It was not a sit-down event—sound and listeners moved through the tunnels at will, including Cage himself.

At the time he was preparing his lecture "The Future of Music," the opening of which reiterated the sentiment he had expressed in his seminar: "For many years I've noticed that music—as an activity separated from the rest of life—doesn't enter my mind. Strictly musical questions are no longer serious questions." He went on, however, to offer a surprisingly benevolent overview of emerging trends, including mention of our subterranean offering: "At Wesleyan University I met two young men studying with Alvin, Ron Goldman and Nicolas Collins. They gave an electronic concert in the tunnel below the new Arts Center in Middletown. By walking through the tunnels one passed through nodes and noticed (as one does in Pauline Oliveros' work) sympathetic vibrations arising in the building and its furniture." To have my first published review come from the hand of Cage was heartening in the extreme.[2]

When he returned to campus the following year, there was a signing event for his book *M*.[3] I dutifully bought a copy and brought it to Cage to sign. But when Ron Kuivila approached the table, he handed over instead a dog-eared paperback of Paul Hindemith's classic text on harmony, *Elementary Training for Musicians*. Cage, not missing a beat, opened the cover and wrote on the title page, "Needs revision. John Cage."

(I was awed by the hipness of Ron's gesture and envious of the singular Cagean bibliophilic treasure that was its result. A few years ago, I asked Ron if he could send me a scan of the dedication page as a memento. He replied that he had lost track of the book years ago, while in grad school at Mills.)

In retrospect, I realize how extraordinary my access was to the center of new musical invention, and also the astonishing amount of "real world" experiences made possible on a small New England campus. We were tasked with assisting in the production of major works with major artists; we were allowed to present our own pieces as if we were grown-ups, and we were entrusted with actual decision-making. Near the end of my freshman year, Ron Goldman and I applied for university funding to bring musical guests to campus, a program that I continued after he graduated. "Go," as he named our micro-organization, offered tiny honoraria and travel reimbursements to up-and-coming artists as well as our mentors. In exchange for a bus ticket, a pizza dinner, and a couch, Robert Ashley gave a lecture that might have been a concert (the distinction was obscure in his work). Tom Zahuranec arrived with a homemade synthesizer that he hooked up with electrodes to plants borrowed from the Biology Department's greenhouse; as the synth burbled away, he alternately threatened the plants with a blowtorch or misted them gently with water, while the audience listened expectantly for an appropriate sonic response, usually buried in the complicated patterns that the electronics could have produced without plants connected. (Zahuranec hung around the MFA program at Mills College for several years without being officially enrolled before disappearing suddenly around 1976 after federal marshals showed up with a warrant at the house he shared with several students.)

When Alvin was invited to do concerts within driving distance of Middletown, he often struck a bargain: he would bring students to help with the tech if their music could be included on the program as well. By my junior year, this crew consisted of three people: me, Ron Kuivila, and Marc Grafe, a new graduate student who had previously studied with Terry Riley and Robert Ashley at Mills College in California and was brought in to serve as a recording engineer and boost the visibility of Alvin's program within the department.

On these terms, we got to present our own work all around New England—Massachusetts, Rhode Island, New Hampshire. Arriving at the Currier Museum of Art for a concert, Alvin let out a deep sigh and pointed to the stage. "Why is it that every hall in America has a nice Steinway but never a decent set of speakers?" This was where those enormous Altec 604e speakers came in (Figure 4.1).

Each of us was expected to carry one (weighing some fifty pounds) from the studio to Alvin's Volkswagen van, from the van to the venue, and then reverse the process after the concert. (More challenging was installing David Tudor's *Microphone* in Wesleyan's own cavernous art gallery, heaving those four unwieldy boxes up wobbly aluminum ladders to ledges fifteen feet above the floor.) Like weight training for football players, this initiation prepared me for the electronic musician's life of schlepping suitcases full of gear. Nick Bertoni, an ex-Seabee who served as the long-time technical director of the sound studios at Mills College, once told me that the Department of Defense defines "portable" objects as providing a handle for the maximum weight a soldier in full kit is expected to be able to carry (which current guidelines regulate at thirty-one pounds); a radar station could thus be made "portable" by dividing its gross weight by thirty-one and distributing that many handles around its base, so it could be carried out of a landing craft and onto a beach like an enormous coffin. The Altecs, alas, had no handles.

It was a lot of work for what was almost inevitably a small number of ears. (The exception was a concert in the Dartmouth College chapel. Christian Wolff had invited us and explained that the remarkably large audience reflected the absence of any other indoor event within 100 miles that night. It quickly became clear that the concert was welcomed by the local teenagers in the back pews as a warm—if noisy—place to make out on a cold night.)

Figure 4.1 The author carrying an Altec 604e loudspeaker for a concert of Alvin Lucier's *Music for Solo Performer* at Paula Cooper Gallery, New York, 1975. Photo © Marc Grafe, used by artist's permission.

Even at Wesleyan, our audiences were small. Students flocked to attend all-night *wayangs* in the World Music Hall—entrancing music and shadow puppets upstairs, delicious food (and usually pot) downstairs. Gamelan was woven into the very fabric of the Wesleyan experience in the 1970s, and Alvin used it as a standard for our own attempts at concertizing. "Be as good as the gamelan," he would tell his ragtag group of students before each concert. Having conducted the choir at Brandeis before coming to Wesleyan, he expressed disappointment at the meager attendance: "I always had big audiences at Brandeis. There were around fifty kids in the choir, and every one of them had at least two friends. Don't you guys have any friends?" We did, but there were only a handful of us, and we often had to compete with a vibrant film series.

Most of Alvin's music depended on bespoke electronics: the Sondols, a brainwave preamp. Even when he used more generic devices, they were chosen with a specific function in mind. For his early experiments with standing waves (leading to *Still and Moving Lines of Silence in Families of Hyperbolas*, 1973–4) he bought four old-school RCA sine wave test oscillators, each tuned with a big metal dial, like something from a 1950s sci-fi movie. He chose them for the purity of the wave they produced, which was better than any synthesizer at the time. The purity was adjusted with a small screwdriver through a hole in the front panel: turning clockwise reduced distortion, but the tiniest motion past optimum silenced the signal. Needless to say, this was not an easy task to perform in a nervous pre-concert state. Often, by the end of sound check, one or two oscillators remained unusable. Sitting by Alvin's side, helping run the piece, I often heard him singing under his breath the old Second World War weepy, *Comin' in on a Wing and a Prayer* ("With our one motor gone we can still carry on, comin' in on a wing and a prayer . . .").[4]

In the spring of 1974, Alvin was invited to perform at a Cunningham Event. For several years starting in the 1970s the Merce Cunningham Dance Company opened some evening rehearsals in their Westbeth Studio to the paying public. Cage, musical director for the company, would choose composers to present work concurrent with the dance. As always with Cunningham, no coordination between the choreography and the music was expected, so Cunningham Events were a popular way to provide a modest revenue stream for composers while livening up rehearsals for the company.

At the time, Alvin was experimenting with field recordings he had made of "sferics," electromagnetic signals generated by meteorites, the aurora borealis, lightning strikes, and other atmospheric disturbances. He bought three Countryman phase shifters on Tudor's advice for the Wesleyan studio to create Haas Effect spatial panning for these recordings.[i] I was reasonably adept at studio technique and analog synthesis by then, and Alvin asked me to figure out how to automate sound panning between four speakers. I designed an overly complicated configuration of three phase shifters and two Arp 2600s, we loaded all this equipment into Alvin's van (happily, the Cunningham studio had its own speakers), and we drove to New York.

At ten the next morning, the Westbeth studio door was opened by a bleary-eyed David Behrman, then the Cunningham sound engineer. I had met David in the fall when he paid a visit to campus, and he was already one of my musical heroes. The Music of Our Time record series he produced for Columbia Records had included the Terry Riley record that had been my teenage gateway to weird music, he had composed several landmark pieces of live electronic music himself, and was an early advocate of self-made circuitry.[ii]

A big Altec loudspeaker hung in each corner of the space, connected to a wall plate with jacks labeled, "Speaker 1," "Speaker 2," "Speaker 3," and "Speaker 4." Before heading out for coffee, David asked if there was anything I needed to know before setting up.

"Just one thing—Can you tell me *which* jack connects to *which* speaker?"

His face fell.

"You know, in all my years of doing electronic music I've never known which speaker is which."

This was an early reality check: you may never know which speaker is which, even if you're David Behrman.

---

[i] Haas Effect panning uses very short delays to mimic the time difference in the arrival of sound waves between our two ears. It yields a more realistic sense of the location of sound in space than the simple left-right volume shift produced by a pan pot on a mixer or the balance control on a stereo.

[ii] David came from a distinguished lineage: his father was the playwright S. N. Behrman, and David recalled his youthful violin recitals being greeted by relatives with comments to the effect of "that was nice, David, but not as nice as your uncle Jascha [Heifetz]."

Interlude

Multitrack

1

Graduate student Marc Grafe served as the music department's recording engineer. He showed me several smart audio tricks, the most magical being complementary equalization.

When you go to mix a multitrack recording, you usually want to adjust each track independently—rolling bass breath pops off a vocal microphone, adding a little high-end zing to a cymbal. Marc taught me that whenever you boost a frequency in one track, you should dip that frequency by the same amount in another one. For example, if you boost the vocal 4 dB at 600 Hz, balance it by dipping the guitar 4 dB at 600 Hz.

The result is that every instrument suddenly has its own acoustic elbow room. Then later, if you need to shift the relative balance between instruments that have already been mixed down to a single track, you can nudge any one of them up or down a bit by boosting or cutting the frequencies you emphasized for each. This had been a common technique in the days of "bouncing," when you mix multiple tracks down to one to free up space to add more (the painstaking method I had followed with my Tandberg recorder in high school). Irreversible mixing decisions had to be made on each bounce, so using complementary EQ to carve out a frequency-specific space for each instrument was the only hope to "fix it in the mix" later.

Bouncing—like tape itself—is now obsolete, but this EQ trick still amazes my students, who can hear the change in clarity as we punch the settings in and out.

2

Reel-to-reel tape recorders are finicky things that require periodic electronic tuning and mechanical realignment, like an old car, which must be done while the recorder is under power. On one recorder that was popular in the 1970s, a critical setting was made with a potentiometer that lay deep inside the machine between the Scylla of a capacitor whose terminals connected to the power cord and the Charybdis of an exposed aluminum fan that spun to cool the circuitry. This trimmer had to be adjusted with a screwdriver, and if your screwdriver slipped and touched the capacitor's terminals, you would get hit by a 120-volt jolt, causing your hand to jerk up and launch your knuckles against the spinning fan blades. This in turn forced your hand back down, jamming the screwdriver across the high-voltage capacitor again, triggering the next rebound. This painful oscillation process typically continued, like a dribbled basketball, until some bystander intervened and unplugged the power cord, leading to the formulation of what I later dubbed "Zummo's Law," after the sage words often uttered by Peter Zummo, the graduate student overseeing the Wesleyan recording studio before Marc Grafe's arrival: "Kick me off if I stick."

3

I can't listen to music while working or reading, but I love to play music while I cook— mostly vinyl. A well-crafted album side is not only an elegant musical form in itself but also a perfect pace car for the kitchen. My ideal meal takes one side of a record to prep and one side to cook; sometimes A and B from the same LP, sometimes with a change of artist when the *mise en place* hits the pan.

This half-attended-to listening has sensitized me to the differences in musical *thickness* arising from the evolution of recording technologies. My collection stretches back to material originally released on cylinders and 78s, live monophonic performances committed directly to shellac or early tape recorders. By the 1960s, two-track tape recorders made basic overdubbing possible and you can hear studio tricks like "doubling," where one singer is recorded twice, thickening the sound or creating a virtual duet.[i] These tapes had been mixed to mono for their original release, but with the advent of stereo records, companies remixed multitrack tapes in stereo, sometimes featuring absurd panning, with the whole band in the left channel and the lead vocalist in the right. (The stereo re-release of The Shirelles' "Baby Its You" is one stunning example.)

Two tracks grew to four, and engineers expanded what they could record with a single group. The Beatles' records of the late 1960s chart this shift, with a commensurate increase in the density of instrumentation, most famously on *Sgt. Pepper*. As technology advanced and rock became more "progressive," the arrangements grew to fill eight, then sixteen, then twenty-four tracks. The tape went from a quarter-inch wide to two inches. By the mid-1980s, big-budget pop productions would synchronize two machines to provide forty-eight tracks.

Pop music abhors a vacuum, and its musical density (if not complexity) evolved in lockstep with recording machines. Musicians, engineers, and producers utilized every running second of every new track that was added to the towering tape-head block,

---

[i] The sonorities made possible by doubling prompted record producer Shadow Morton to work with pairs of singers who were sisters or cousins—the Shangri-Las, who performed his hit "Leader of the Pack", consisted of two pairs of sisters, one pair being identical twins. The voices were similar enough that when they sang in unison, they would sound like a single vocalist doubled. Using genetic doubling instead of tape doubling, he freed up that second track for things like the sound effect of the motorcycle vroom-vroom in "Leader of the Pack."

like last-minute travel supplies squeezed into the nooks of a car trunk. (After all, they were paying for expensive, wide tape, whether it was blank or filled with music.) The sound of the records in my collection grows thicker as it approaches the present (with occasional contrarian exceptions). I count tracks as I stir my soup.

To a point. A curious thing happened with digital recording: tracks became virtual. Space on a hard drive can be allocated vertically or horizontally—the same number of bytes could be used for a long stereo recording or for a thirty-second jingle built up from dozens of parallel takes. And as memory dropped in price, even budgetary concerns evaporated. With recordings produced after the turn of the millennium, the pastime of counting tracks is too difficult to carry on while minding that the garlic doesn't burn. Now the bandwidth of human attention is the only limit.

5

Playing with Chips

The equipment we hoisted as students now appears comically gargantuan. But things were changing, slowly. Early electronic devices had relied on vacuum tubes as gates and amplifiers to control the passage of electricity; they worked fine, but they were fragile, as big as light bulbs, and demanded massive power supplies whose voltages were high enough to kill (or at least intimidate) amateur engineers. Then came the transistor: the size of a pencil eraser and less lethal but, like the tube, so elemental a building block that you needed a proper understanding of electronic theory to design anything useful. The 1960s saw the introduction of integrated circuits (ICs, aka "chips"), which gathered multiple transistors and other components on a single thin wafer of semiconducting material.[i] This meant that a device like an amplifier or oscillator that once required a dozen transistors soldered to a phenolic or fiberglass board the size of a book could now be bought in a tiny cockroach-size package.

In the 1970s, music synthesizers were still the playthings of pop stars and universities, but ICs—the guts of those costly machines—were getting cheaper every year. These chips contained 90 percent of a functional circuit designed by someone who knew what they were doing; the remaining 10 percent could be filled in by someone relatively clueless if they were willing to peruse geeky magazines and could wield a soldering iron—this was how I built my first oscillator back in high school. The trick was finding the right IC and information in ordinary language on how to wire it up. Those instructions were often hard to come by, and when data did leak down from proper engineers to do-it-yourselfers, it was passed from hand to hand like samizdat literature.

"Circuits are flat," Alvin once opined, "while sound is three-dimensional."[1] But although he had no interest in circuits himself, he did encourage his students to experiment and invited David Behrman to conduct a week-long workshop in building musical circuits. By this time, I had built my Flintstones oscillator, and my dubious high-school proficiency with electronics had been supplemented by one semester of physics and a workshop taught by one of the physics department's technicians. But it was not until

---

[i] A semiconductor is just that: something that conducts electricity some of the time. It allows a small signal to turn on and off and adjust the flow of a much larger signal—like a hand on a faucet. The British term "valve" for the vacuum tubes that preceded the transistor conveys this meaning very succinctly.

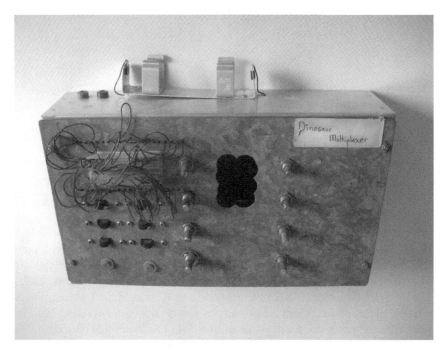

Figure 5.1 The author's "Dinosaur Multiplexer" audio distribution circuit (of which he was remarkably proud), 1975. Photo by Nicolas Collins.

Behrman's workshop that I finally felt comfortable with a soldering iron in my hand. (My father was delighted to discover that I had somehow finally mastered the skill that had eluded us in our summer experiments with license plates—even if at the inflated cost of university tuition.)

David guided us through a couple of circuits and passed out simple schematics photocopied from engineering journals, hobbyist magazines, and drawings by friends and colleagues. He also provided personal introductions to fellow composers—many just a few years older than we were—who had fallen under the spell of homemade circuitry (Figure 5.1).[ii]

Ron Kuivila had two great gifts when it came to electronics: he was good at math (his practice of actually calculating values for resistors and capacitors in a circuit design was an improvement on my method of quasi-random substitution), and he had a gap

---

[ii] Circuitry also had a certain counter-culture cachet. I was still in touch with my high-school electronics teacher, who asked me over one afternoon when I was home in the city. Bob played a series of beeps from a cassette tape and explained that these were the tones an operator hears when you drop a quarter into a pay phone. He asked if I could build a circuit to produce those tones. A week later, I handed off my creation, and Bob successfully placed a quarter-free call to his brother in New Jersey. Many years later, I realized that I had built a crude "Blue Box," the infamous tool of phone phreaks, which was also Steve Jobs and Steve Wozniak's first product before they started Apple.

between his front teeth exactly the right width for stripping the insulation off the wire used to connect components on a circuit board. The latter struck me as a physical blessing on par with Jimi Hendrix's thumb (long enough to reach around the neck of his Stratocaster and fret the lower two strings). On the downside, Ron had no patience for tidily packaging his circuits in little boxes.

During my senior year, ethnomusicologist David Reck invited Alvin to Amherst College to present a concert. As usual, Ron, Marc Grafe, and I supplied labor in exchange for slots on the program. Ron had composed a piece for four musicians playing small keyboards made from pennies embedded in strips of wood connected to a central circuit. As the concert drew closer, he made no progress toward solidifying this circuit—it remained a sprawling concatenation of wires and components poked into a plastic prototyping board.[iii] The night before our road trip, Ron used gaffing tape to adhere his board, cables, and keyboards to the lunchroom table on which he had been working. The next morning, after loading the speakers and various cases into Alvin's van, Ron and I lifted the table while Marc folded the legs underneath, we carried it out of the studio building, and slid it on top of the other gear in the van (like the coffin of a man run over by a steamroller). At Amherst, we shuttled the table onto the stage and popped down the legs. Ron went out for coffee while the rest of us brought in the cases, unpacked them, and patched our cables. At the end of the concert, Ron collapsed his table and returned it to the van. More efficient, if less secure.

Circuits were not only cheaper and more portable than synthesizers, they were also more personal. The same Moog could be used to play Beatles, Bach, Basie or Babbitt. The very thing that made them commercially viable was viewed as a failing by more ornery avant-gardists. I remember Alvin talking in class about a Behrman composition:

> He's making a piece that calls for a lot of oscillators, like forty of them, to make a very thick sound. It would be impossibly expensive, not to mention bulky, to use Moog oscillators—thousands of dollars. So he builds them instead, each using not much more than one cheap integrated circuit. Sure, it takes time, but it also sounds different—less like Robert Moog, more like David Behrman.[2]

By the end of the 1950s, David Tudor had established a reputation as the premier interpreter contemporary piano music, much of it deemed "impossible to perform." By 1960, through his long association with John Cage, he also had become what might be regarded as the first virtuoso of live electronics. His first electronic "instruments" were simple contact microphones and amplifiers, but after some basic instruction from Gordon Mumma, he moved on to building his own circuits. He stopped playing piano, and by the time I arrived at Wesleyan, Tudor was regarded as the "godfather of live electronics." In

---

[iii] Circuit designs are typically prototyped on perforated plastic panels with embedded, conductive metal strips. The metal legs of the chips and other components stick down into the holes, and the metal strips make electrical connections without solder. This is faster to lay out and easier to correct than soldering wires between things, but if the board is jostled, parts can fall out, so these prototypes are seldom considered finished products.

the summer of 1973, he ran a workshop in Chocorua, NH. A group of young composers gathered to learn musical circuitry and to produce Tudor's landmark composition, *Rainforest IV*: a performance-installation-environment in which everyday objects like garbage cans, wrought-iron fencing, and woks are turned into speakers by transducers that make them vibrate with sound. (Alvin used similar transducers to arrange powder into visual images in *Queen of the South*.) The workshop participants (which included John Driscoll, Phil Edelstein, Linda Fisher, Ralph Jones, Martin Kalve, and Bill Viola) dubbed themselves "Composers Inside Electronics" and continued to participate in manifestations of *Rainforest* as well as other Tudor projects. They embraced the concept of "the circuit as score," of looking for musical suggestions within the electronic device, rather than imposing an existing idea—in Tudor's words, "You use the natural state of the components for what they give you, not what they are supposed to do." [3]

I missed out on Chocorua, but like many of my peers, I began designing and building cheap, quirky circuits that did what synthesizers couldn't do, coaxing sounds and forms from what the chips provided. We were not engineers—our circuits were usually noisy and unpredictable, whereas Moog's were smooth and stable. We accepted flaws that a real engineer would have corrected, and we often structured a work around those very defects. (Composer Paul DeMarinis once observed, in awe, that "David [Tudor] will compose a piece based on the reverse breakdown voltage of one specific diode."[4] While incomprehensible to the non-engineer, this observation refers to the death-rattle of a component placed in a circuit backward.)

Performing with such circuits was necessarily an improvisational act, which was a plus for me, since my preference since childhood swung in the direction of music that embraced improvisation—rock, blues, jazz, and, later, Indian music. During his years as the preeminent pianist for contemporary music, Tudor had been known for his meticulous preparation and the unwavering accuracy of his interpretations of complex, unconventional, and ambiguous scores—the very antithesis of improvisation. Yet when he began to incorporate electronics, his approach changed. As musicologist You Nakai explains it: "The nature of this [array of circuits] was such that neither the quality nor the duration of the output could be predicted—as Tudor puts it, 'you could only hope to influence' the instrument."[5]

George Lewis, a pioneer in interactive computer music as well as a brilliant improvising trombonist, has written insightfully about the linkage between circuitry and improvisation. Discussing the work of David Behrman and Gordon Mumma, he noted:

> The late-1960s live electronic music of both composers also drew explicitly on the practice of improvisation . . . [The] "structure" of the piece encompassed both the performance and an interactive environment facilitated by the devices themselves. Unlike conventional scores, the electronics were explicitly conceived as one element in an overall environment that was only partially specified in advance. The composition as a whole, far from allowing a disconnected "runthrough" of a scripted event articulated a kind of dialogue with the outside world. Here, real-time music-making was required to realize the intentions of the work.[6]

British composer and improviser Stuart Jones, a member of the live-electronic ensemble Gentle Fire in the early 1970s, put it more tersely: "You had no bloody idea what would come out of it [the electronics] and that's what we loved."[7]

That said, many composers active in the 1960s and 1970s shied away from the word "improvisation." Cage famously disparaged jazz and rock.[8] Those of Alvin's generation were somewhat more guarded on the subject, but I remember the verbal gymnastics Alvin employed when coaching the performers in *Vespers*—insisting that, although they were free to manipulate their echolocation devices in any manner that served the task of navigating safely across the room, they should *not* "improvise." This convolution undoubtedly had roots in the anti-expressionist ethos of minimalism, with its emphasis on objective phenomena rather than subjective feelings, though it is hard to believe that ingrained associations of class and race did not also play a role in experimental composers' discomfort with the word. Improvisation was associated with vernacular forms generally, and most obviously with jazz, blues, and other Black musical innovations.[9]

Having abandoned so many of the traditional vestments of composition, the post-Cagean generation seemed wary of being dismissed entirely as composers. They still wanted their work to be seen in the context of the tradition they were challenging, rather than as appropriating behaviors from what they regarded as a fundamentally different one. (Susan Tallman points to the long history of this quandary in visual art, where forms that had long existed in diagrams or textiles were suddenly perceived as novel and meaningful when they entered canvases as geometric abstraction.)[10] Some may not have felt competent in genres that embraced improvisation. And others may simply not have recognized that what they were doing was, in fact, improvising. Regardless of the underlying factors, "improvisation was troublesome" for them, as David Behrman has reflected.[11]

As his eighteen-year-old acolyte, I had accepted the distinction Alvin drew between "improvisation" and the kind of performer freedom evinced in *Vespers*, and I partitioned my own rather eclectic musical taste accordingly. I continued to love jazz, rock, and other avowedly improvised music but held them apart from the post-Cagean avant-garde. As the years went by, however, I found it harder and harder to explain to myself *what* the distinction actually consisted of. From my perspective, open-form scores (such as *For 1, 2 or 3 People*) and improvised forms both resemble nautical charts: players and sailors tack between waypoints rather than following a fixed path. Thanks to the vagaries of tides and weather, or the ambiguities of prose and graphic imagery, each run is slightly different, and the pleasure of the process comes from responding to the uncertainty.

Behind the smokescreen of freshly minted terms like "open form" and "indeterminacy," musicians working with circuitry shared common ground with self-identified improvisers. Sometimes new structures were sought out intentionally, and sometimes they were unavoidable byproducts of the available technology. To say that our flawed circuits were imbued with creative, performer-like traits goes too far down the path of anthropomorphism, but they certainly had qualities of resistance and instability that could approximate expected hallmarks of improvisation: these electronic instruments were "designed to stake out territory, assert both identities and positions, assess and respond to conditions, and maintain relativities of distance—all elements of improvisation," in Lewis's words.[12] Or, as Jones says of working with live electronics: "There was no way to organize it. You couldn't function without improvisation, which was a manifestation of the time-honored English methodology of 'we'll muddle through.'"[13]

The distinction between a composer and a performer is rare in most musical traditions, including the majority of those on offer at Wesleyan when I was a student, but it was central to European "art music." Once that division emerged, the question became, how much trust does a composer grant a performer? Since the Baroque, composers have been specifying more and trusting less. Collisions with non-Western and non-art musics in the 1960s triggered a quixotic revival in trust on the part of the composer. Open-form scores, from *Vespers* to *In C,* are designed to cede more responsibility to the player.

I initially regarded alternative scores and homemade circuits as part of larger anti-authoritarian cultural movements, manifest in the harping, common in my circles, against "the conductor as dictator." Over time, I acquired a more nuanced perspective: tasks, tactics, and rules can serve as techniques to evade and avoid too much identity or self-expression being vested in *any* single participant, whether composer or performer. I once asked Christian Wolff where he came down on the balance between a composer's responsibility in the score versus trust in performers, and he replied, "I don't worry about identity as long as the piece works."[14] A player's habitual riff has a parallel in a composer's stylistic mannerisms, and alternative notation can serve to block both. Dutch musician Cor Fuhler explains:

> I find it hard to deal with absoluteness. Who am I to decide what is right? . . .
> For me, modular music aims to incorporate a capacity to rearrange into fresh new forms for every performance, to prolong life expectancy of a work through multiple transformations, and to hand over interpretative power to musicians. It imitates life as I want to live it.[15]

Or as George Lewis puts it: "I prefer to think of conditions rather than constraints, because conditions you can change."[16]

The Infinite Amplification of Silence
(or I Ching for Dummies)

By the end of my first year at Wesleyan, I had fallen so fully under the spell of Cage's credo "any sound can be a musical sound" that I was paralyzed. If any sound could be a musical sound, why even *make* one? Surely, there were enough out there already. I spent hours in front of the Arp but felt no compelling reason to select one configuration of patch cords over another or to sequence my recorded material in any particular order. I yearned for a methodology, something that did not depend on my personal taste, an inherited tradition, or danceable beats. The composers I admired had invented individual solutions to this problem: Cage had the *I Ching*, Reich had tape loops, and Alvin had *a priori* acoustic phenomena. Finally, feedback came to my rescue.

When I plugged a microphone into an amplifier and turned up the volume, feedback's Zen-like infinite amplification of silence generated a haunting whistle with minimal interference on my part. It served as an electronic I Ching for Dummies: I moved the mic instead of tossing yarrow sticks—notes emerged, but I never knew which pitch would pop out next. The results were guided by acoustics rather than by chance or choice. Alvin's exploration of the behavior of sound in space liberated me from my assumption that music had to be rooted in previous music. Acoustics became the glue to unify my disparate interests into a personal musical style. I became fascinated by the ways feedback could give voice to objects and spaces—trombones, tabletops, culverts, concert halls—with minimal composerly oversight.

Feedback happens when the output of a dynamic system is connected back to its input. "Negative" feedback, in which the output is subtracted from the input, is an essential self-corrective property of various cybernetic and machine control systems. The shriek of a microphone in the hands of a novice politician or the roar of an electric guitar held up to an amplifier are examples of "positive" feedback: the output of a speaker is picked up by a microphone and amplified sufficiently to add up and cascade rather than fading away. The politician's voice is drowned out by a loud pitch at whatever frequency the equipment can produce with the least energy. Positive feedback also occurs if you connect a patch cord from the output of an amplifier back to its input and turn up the volume. This was the core technique in some of David Tudor's earliest electronic music, and it had also transformed my Tandberg tape recorder into an instrument.[i]

The pitch of feedback between a speaker and a microphone is determined by the strongest resonant frequencies of all the stages in the signal chain between the initiating energy and the ear, most significantly the hollow space in which the sound is created—an auditorium, perhaps, or an oil drum, or the column of air in a wind instrument. From an acoustic standpoint, a room is basically a big bugle with a very low fundamental frequency (since it is so much larger). The overtones of the harmonic series of a bugle can be articulated by changes in lip and breath; thanks to the behavior of standing waves in a room, certain resonant frequencies are stronger in particular locations, and feedback can be similarly "overblown" by moving the microphone or speaker. As the graphs in their brochures show, microphones and loudspeakers have peaks and valleys in their frequency response that can affect feedback's preferred pitches as well. Given the overtone structure of its acoustical underpinning, feedback is often harmonious—it moves in friendly intervals like octaves and fifths with the elegance of Monteverdi's *Vespers* and the casual aplomb of the Stones' *Satisfaction*.

I had been drawn to modal harmonies as a teenager—they had linked Terry Riley and the Grateful Dead. My affection for feedback's behavior, meanwhile, stretched from The Beatles' *I Feel Fine* to Hendrix's *Star Spangled Banner* and my high-school experiments with the Tandberg. With his *Cartridge Music* instruction that feedback was "to be accepted," Cage had formally designated it as a "serious" musical sound source.

Every electronic musician who came of age in the 1960s or 1970s seemed to have made a piece with feedback. It was a cheap but versatile material at a time when few Americans had access to well-equipped studios. Much of Tudor's and Mumma's early electronic music employed both acoustic feedback between speakers and microphones, and feedback through wires from the output of a circuit back to its input.[i] Performers of Robert Ashley's *The Wolfman* (1964) change the shape of their mouths to articulate very loud feedback between a microphone held at the lips and a PA system.[2] In *Wave Train* (1965), David Behrman scatters loose guitar pickups on the strings of a piano and routes them to a guitar amplifier below; the resulting feedback shakes the pickups, which add percussive accents to the sound of resonated strings.[3]

The Wesleyan studio had a pair of Sony 152SD portable stereo cassette recorders, each slightly smaller than an attaché case. If I poked my pinkie against the erase-protect tongue at the rear of the cassette-well while pressing down the record button, I could trick the machine into serving as a preamplifier that could boost any microphone attached to the recorder loud enough to feed back. As with most tape recorders, you could attach it to an external amplifier and speakers, but the Sony also had a robust internal speaker that transformed the recorder into a self-contained, portable sound system. Its built-in limiter tamed feedback's shriek, reducing it to a mellow sine wave that could be nudged from pitch to pitch by moving the microphone. (A limiter

[i]   Later, it would recur in the "no-input mixing" movement that arose in the 1990s. It's also the central mechanism of many oscillator circuit designs.

presents a good example of *negative* feedback: a portion of the output volume is subtracted from the input signal so that the loudness never exceeds a set threshold, preventing the clipping and distortion typically associated with the *positive* feedback of an out-of-control PA.)

I ran feedback through as many variations as I could invent or discover. I carried the Sony outdoors and "played" culverts with feedback, as if they were huge trombones. I used contact microphones to cycle feedback through solid objects such as tables, walls, floors, and tree trunks (Figure 6.1).[4] I resonated the air columns of wind and brass instruments by embedding tiny lavalier microphones inside mouthpieces and feeding them back with speakers; as performers changed fingering or slide position, or moved the instruments in space, the feedback would break to different overtones.[5] Later I substituted small speakers for some of the mouthpiece-mounted microphones, transforming trombones and tubas into "speaker-instruments," and manipulating feedback between pairs of instruments without the need for PA speakers.

As with my encounters with bathroom resonance, I began to notice feedback everywhere. On a trip home to New York, I visited the Leo Castelli Gallery and saw a Keith Sonnier installation that used telephone lines to connect the New York Gallery with one on the West Coast (the very premise of a long-distance high-fidelity audio connection was then a big deal). Two microphones stood in the center of the room, and a pair of speakers hung on the wall, so visitors in NYC could talk with those in

Figure 6.1 Rehearsing *Nodalings* on Cape Cod in 1974. Photo by George Collins.

Los Angeles: the New York microphones were connected to the LA speakers, and the LA microphones to the NYC speakers. But the West Coast mics picked up a little bit of the East Coast sound coming out of the speakers in that gallery and sent it back to NYC, and vice versa. The sound volume had been set just below the level of feedback, but every sound in the gallery caused a slight ringing as it bounced back and forth between the coasts before dying away. I cupped my hands around the microphone, and feedback slowly blossomed. A gallery assistant walked over to reprimand me, but not before I felt the power of transcontinental feedback.

Back at Wesleyan, I was working in the studio while Marc Grafe was making a long-distance call in the office across the hall. Both doors were open. Marc was unexpectedly disconnected. He called back, and a few minutes later, the line went dead again. After his third attempt, we theorized that some pitch in my feedback must have corresponded to one of the tones the phone company used to control signal routing. (This was the era of the notorious phone phreak John Draper, AKA "Captain Crunch," who discovered that the plastic bosun's whistle that came in boxes of Cap'n Crunch cereal emitted the 2600 Hz frequency that opened a line for free long-distance calling.) We shut the doors, and Marc completed his call uninterrupted.

I began patching modules on the synthesizer to control feedback by imitating electronically movement of the microphone by hand. I cobbled together numerous arrangements of filters and amplifiers, modulated by low-frequency oscillators, before considering a phase shifter. Phase shifters—the devices behind the characteristic swooshing sound of disco era records—introduce very-short-time delays on audio signals.[ii] The studio had three (the Countryman Type 968 I used with Alvin's sferics recordings at the Cunningham Event). When I connected a microphone to a speaker through one of these and raised the gain high enough to start feeding back, changing the phase delay made feedback break to different frequencies. The box effectively "moved" the microphone by altering, ever so slightly, the transmission time of sound between mic and speaker (sound travels at a finite speed, hence increasing the delay time increased the virtual separation). The amount of phase shift was controlled by the loudness of the signal via an envelope follower circuit conveniently built into the Countryman, mimicking the effect of a nervous sound engineer pulling a microphone away from the speaker as soon as it starts to feed back (Figure 6.2).

The resulting feedback tended to seesaw between two pitches, as if the mic were bouncing between two locations. When additional independent audio channels were added—each with its own mic, phase shifter, and speaker—they interacted acoustically to produce more varied and extended melodic patterns. These patterns were hypersensitive to the slightest change in acoustic conditions: taking a few steps

---

[ii] This was some years before the advent of digital delays, in which all frequencies of an audio signal are delayed by the same amount of time. A phase shifter delays the signal by a certain number of degrees of phase, typically from 0 to some multiple of 360 degrees. The absolute delay time varies according to the frequency of the audio: 360° of phase shift on 440 hz = 2.2 ms, while the same phase shift delays a 1 kHz signal by only 1 ms. In this way a phase shifter smears the frequency spectrum in time in a somewhat counterintuitive fashion. The resulting delay is too short to be heard as an echo, but this smear changes the sound in ways that cannot be replicated by digital delays.

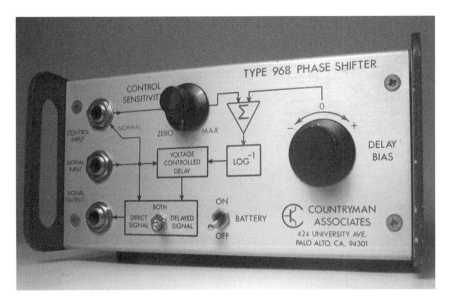

Figure 6.2 The Countryman Type 968 Phase Shifter essential to *Pea Soup*. Photo by Nicolas Collins.

across the room, making a sound, even opening a door or window could cause a note to be dropped from the melodic phrase or a new one added.

I had stumbled upon a remarkably simple, self-stabilizing electronic network that created site-specific "architectural ragas" out of a room's resonant frequencies.[iii] The tempo and phrasing were a function of the reverberation time—bigger halls yielded slower patterns. Perhaps the most elegant aspect was the responsiveness of the sound itself: the performer "plays" this system not by twiddling knobs or pushing buttons, but by moving or making sounds within the field of the feedback. I began to visualize people and objects in a room in terms of their disruption of the movement of sound waves, like blocks placed in the water of the wave tank used in physics experiments. A musician playing an overtone of the sounding feedback on trumpet or flute could induce it to jump to a new pitch; playing a pitch that was heard earlier might nudge the feedback to return to it.

The resulting composition, *Pea Soup* (1974), maps the room with sound. The feedback forms a geography of sound pressure, and the locations of objects within the room are referenced not to fixed points, but to positions floating in a sea of standing waves that, despite their name, do not actually stand still but shift in response to acoustic variables. Stepping back and forth between two spots on the floor might toggle the feedback consistently for the first few moves and then change. You might

---

[iii] Ragas are the melodic frameworks in Indian music. Although similar to modes in Western music, a raga also embeds additional constraints on its performance (i.e., a distinction between notes played when ascending versus descending).

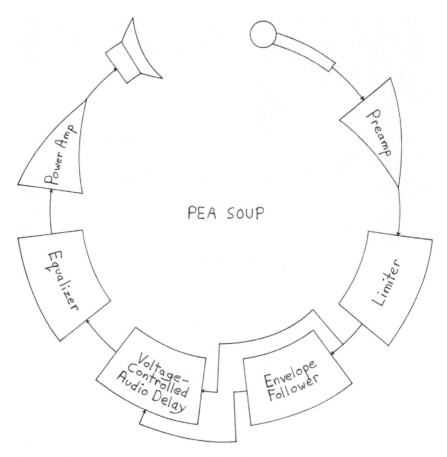

PEA SOUP

Figure 6.3 Author's drawing of the patch for *Pea Soup* in the 1975 score, showing one channel of configuration of audio components.

have stepped back to the same spot on the floor, but the standing waves have shifted a bit to the left thanks to a draft—they don't register you as having returned but as having struck out on a slightly different path. The key to performing *Pea Soup* through movement is to stop *looking* for locations and start *listening* for them, and then wait for the system to respond (Figure 6.3).

It was pointless to "score" a specific set of notes to be played or movements to be made, since the system's behavior and responsiveness changed from room to room and even from hour to hour in the same space. I was content to claim this specific array of modules as my composition—a composition that lay inside the electronics as well as the architecture. I dubbed it *Pea Soup*—a nod to the first letters of the core technology (Phase Shifter) and to the expression "as thick as pea soup," which I thought conveyed the experience of standing within the feedback. It's a silly title, but I'm stuck with it.

The first performance took place in a lunchtime concert in the Electronic Music Studio on October 24, 1974, under the control of guitarist and future Band of Susans founder, Robert Poss, then a freshman enrolled in the Introduction to Electronic Music class Alvin had asked me to teach when he went on sabbatical.[iv]

I presented subsequent performances and gallery installations of *Pea Soup* on campus and in concert exchanges with other colleges around New England. Its site-specific behavior made it satisfyingly portable, familiar yet surprising wherever it was played. I drafted local instrumentalists and dancers whenever possible and supplemented the electronics with verbal instructions that balanced encouragement to "explore" with admonitions to "do less." These common-sense guidelines were eventually collected into an overwrought prose score for my undergraduate thesis.[6]

Pea Soup contributed several innovations to the well-trodden domain of feedback music. Some are utilitarian: the application of phase delays to emulate the physical movement of a microphone; the presence of a limiter to transform feedback's usual shriek into a mellower waveform; and the use of omnidirectional dynamic microphones to produce a wider, less shrill range of pitches than the more common unidirectional (cardioid) microphones.[v] Others border on the philosophical: to the best of my knowledge, this is the first composition to use negative feedback to control audible positive feedback. Working at the Dutch music research foundation STEIM in the 1990s, I encountered many instruments and installations that used ultrasonic fields, video cameras, and other motion detectors to track a performer's movement and control sound in response, but I've never heard another music system in which the sound itself functioned as its own controlling element.[7]

Feedback has an elegant, primal charm. Before they could walk, both my children delighted in waving the microphone near the speaker of their My First Sony™, chortling along with the ensuing squeals. How could I ask them to turn it down? They have moved on, but I have retained and nurtured my youthful obsession. In the decades since *Pea Soup*, feedback has returned to my music with the regularity of a comet: modulated by computer-controlled filters, vibrating guitar strings, eliciting squawks from dead circuit boards, as an aid to transcribing room resonance into staff notation, and generating electromagnetic fields between inductive coils. Feedback's signature sound—the slightly impure sine wave and characteristic envelope of swell and decay—cannot be confused with anything else, electronic or acoustic. I've never heard a convincing synthesis of feedback and can always tell if the feedback is occurring live or played back from a recording. My initial infatuation with the beauty of feedback's skin

---

[iv] Running this class while still an undergraduate was a curious echo of my high-school stint of unqualified teaching, but it would have some profound consequences: Robert would become a close friend and musical collaborator, and when I taught the class again the following year, one of the freshman students was Susan Tallman. Two years later, when I was back at Wesleyan as a graduate student, we began a relationship that evolved into a life: marriage, parenting, and lots of mutual editing—all of which continue to this day and page.

[v] Even the best cardioid mikes have irregular off-axis frequency response, which has a greater impact on feedback behavior than on their coloration when recording.

and controllability deepened with my appreciation of its inner workings. The balance of responsiveness and independence, of implacable science and seductive invitation, is rife with musical implications. It's a natural phenomenon with social, as well as acoustic, overtones, a remover of obstacles whenever inspiration is lacking.

The pieces I came to love most in my four years as an undergraduate under Alvin's tutelage all seemed to spring from sentences that began, "What would happen if . . .?" I knew that what I wanted most was to immerse myself in new situations where people asked that question and to find new ways to finish that prompt myself. I applied to the graduate program in composition at Mills College, the Bay Area hotbed of experimental music, where Pauline Oliveros, Terry Riley, Robert Ashley, and David Behrman were guiding spirits.[8] At the same time, I submitted a proposal for a Thomas J. Watson Fellowship that would allow me to research experimental music outside the United States. And together with Ron Kuivila, I applied for a summer residency at the ZBS Foundation in Fort Edward, NY. All three said yes (Figure 6.4).

   ZBS was first on the calendar. Founded in the late 1960s as a commune on a farm in Fort Edward in rural upstate New York, its members wrote and recorded a radio series in the mold of Firesign Theater. It branched into producing sound effect libraries, and by the mid-1970s, it was being funded by the New York State Council on the Arts to host artists, including embryonic ones like Ron and me.

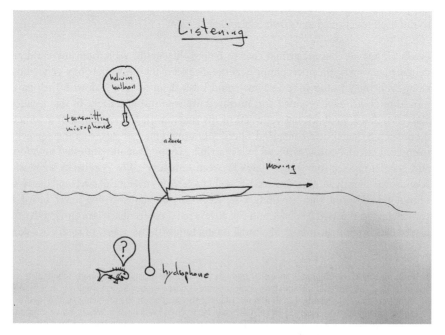

Figure 6.4 Author's drawing of a project proposed during a residency at the ZBS Foundation, Fort Edward, NY, 1976.

Intrigued by the acoustical phenomenon of Doppler shift (the characteristic pitch bend you hear when the blaring siren of an emergency vehicle passes), Ron and I used our residency to conduct a number of sometimes madcap experiments. We strapped compressed-air boat horns to model rocket engines and recorded them as they screamed across a field. We placed four microphones at 100-foot intervals along a country road, wired them to a four-track tape recorder, and asked a commune resident to drive past at high speed, hand on horn, while we recorded the ensuing Doppler effects. Finally, we sent an FM microphone up in a helium-filled weather balloon until the balloon popped and the mic plummeted to earth, where it burrowed one foot into the dirt. (This was unfortunate, since we had borrowed it from Alvin, but prior to its dramatic end, the microphone had transmitted an audio dolly-back that picked up sound from the ZBS property, then the farm across the river, then the nearest town a few miles away, before the bang of the exploding balloon, followed by a classic cartoon whistle as the mic accelerated, ending with a dramatic thud and electronic sputter.)

We left ZBS with a few reels of tape and a handful of photographs. Based on our work, Ron soon developed a technology for translating motion into Doppler-shift sound using ultrasonic transducers, which he employed in a number of compositions and installations. My own investigations never made it into a finished piece. Sometimes the output of experiments rises to the level of a composition, but other times the experience itself is enough.

Old Guard Avant-Garde

The Thomas J. Watson Fellowship was (and remains) a singular grant. It provides financial support for a year of postgraduate travel and research, independent of formal institutions ("Recreating the Voyages of Captain Cook in an Open Sailboat," "Following the Migration of the Arctic Tern from Pole to Pole," "Terrace Farming in Peru, Indonesia and China"). By those standards, my proposal now seems remarkably tame—to find out what experimental music sounded like outside America.

My education at Wesleyan had been global in one sense—tabla, gamelan, mbira—but the World Music Program was, like most ethnographic disciplines of the time, devoted to the study and preservation of traditions that were sometimes viewed as existing outside of time (a Wesleyan PhD student once told me that there's no way to tell by ear whether a gamelan composition was written in 1600 or last year). Alvin's classes, meanwhile, were largely limited to what happened in New York, California, and the occasional Midwest or Canadian outpost in between. Perhaps this was understandable: after two centuries of measuring themselves against a European yardstick, American composers were proud of their own emerging canon.

But I was curious: surely the idea of "the experimental" was universal. In the wake of the catastrophic rupture of the Second World War, it seemed likely that artists in Europe would have had good reason to go back to their own year zero and then to branch out in directions that differed both from past traditions and from American impulses. Given the pervasive under-documentation of the field, however, I could find no books, no records, no local concert series to answer this question. The internet as we know it did not exist. The only way to find out was to do what the ethnomusicologists did: fieldwork.

So in September 1976, armed with a large backpack and a list of phone numbers, I flew a charter to Brussels and then boarded a Russian train for the twenty-four-hour trip to Poland. My plan was to start off by visiting a handful of large music festivals to get an overview of what was being performed and how it was received. First on the list was the Warsaw Autumn Festival.

I had never been to Europe, never mind behind the Iron Curtain, but the Warsaw festival had an unexpectedly familiar vibe, a return to the "Uptown" contemporary music that I had flirted with in high school. It featured knotty, often dissonant music for orchestras, chamber ensembles, and solo piano, performed in formal concert halls, where both musicians and audience arrived in jacket and tie, dress and heels. Here, however, most of the composers came from East Bloc countries or were writing work deemed to be respectful of socialist ideals. Few names were known to me. This was my introduction to the Cold War cultural skirmishes then playing out across European high art. I had arrived ready to detect cracks in the dominant traditions, but in Warsaw, I found almost none.

The concerts were all sold out, and the audiences responded enthusiastically to almost everything. More engaged and appreciative than their New York counterparts, they demonstrated an avid embrace of musical culture that was new to me but, as I learned, old to the continent. The sole exception I witnessed to this happy state of affairs took place at the performance of Morton Feldman's *Two Pianos* (1957), whose tranquil pseudo-tonality, coming on the heels of thorny serialism and booming Prokofiev-ish orchestration, elicited the only boos and catcalls I heard in any concert I attended. (Three decades later, serving on an accreditation panel for the Royal Conservatory in The Hague with the distinguished Polish composer and pianist Zygmunt Krause, I mentioned that I had attended the Festival in 1976 and was surprised at the response to the Feldman. His face took on a stunned expression. "I was one of the pianists in that performance," he told me. "I had been pushing for Feldman's inclusion in the festival. It was years before they would include him or me again.")

Being fiscally prudent, I had booked a room in the official Intourist hotel for only the minimum number of nights required to obtain a visa, naively assuming I would be able to extend the reservation after I arrived. Not so. The Intourist was fully booked, and no other hotels were allowed to accept Western travelers. I threw myself on the mercy of the festival's office staff, one of whom located a friend with a guestroom that was available for coveted US dollars. Off I went.

At eight every morning, when the family's daughter headed off to school and the parents left for work, I would be booted out. A half-dozen men and women would arrive and set up a travel agency in the rooms where the family otherwise slept, ate, and socialized. Reasoning that an empty apartment was a waste of resources, they rented it out during the days as an office.

The only language my hosts and I had in common was French, which none of us had spoken since school (in their case, before the Second World War). Returning from concerts, I would join in glacially stilted conversation while watching television. The imported fare consisted primarily of Westerns, but one night I was surprised to see *La Ronde*, an early Roger Vadim film starring a very young Jane Fonda. Rather than broadcasting in the original language with subtitles or dubbing by a cast of Polish-speaking actors, a single male narrator read translations of all dialogue, male and female, in a dull monotone. This went on concurrently with the original soundtrack, so both languages were heard at equal volume, competing with the usual music and sound effects. The audio track thus presented a bizarre mélange of native French, Fonda's American-twanged high-school French, and a droning Polish voiceover. The plot was further confounded by the excising of the more risqué scenes, of which there were many. When the festival ended, my hosts kindly put me on the same Russian train

I'd ridden east ten days earlier, now heading west to Berlin, with instructions to deposit my rent in a foreign bank in anticipation of their hoped-for emigration West.

Every generation of my mother's Hamburg family has one black sheep who declines to enter the family firms. A second cousin, Joachim von Rosenberg, fled Hamburg to study architecture in West Berlin shortly after the Wall went up and remained there. While visiting my parents in New York as I was mapping my Watson travels, he invited me to stay with him when in Berlin. Since my plans were vague, we arranged that I would telephone from Warsaw to alert him to my arrival date, but this turned out to be impossible, and I headed to Germany assuming I would stay in a hostel the first night and call him from there. But when the train pulled into Zoo Station, there was Joachim on the platform. I do not know how he anticipated my arrival. Years later, it struck me that he might have stood on that platform every evening from the start of the Warsaw Autumn Festival to its end, greeting that day's train until, finally, his young cousin stepped out. You can take the architect out of Hamburg, but you cannot take perfect manners out of the Hamburger.

West Berlin had then been isolated by the encircling Wall for fifteen years, and while its geopolitical significance was reinforced by the presence of American, British, and French troops, it felt like a small town on an island accessible only by an arduous ferry trip. Joachim appeared to know everyone. When I expressed a desire to see Hans Scharoun's Philharmonie building (famed for its acoustics), he telephoned his friend, the concertmaster, and two days later I was wandering about the hall as Herbert von Karajan led the orchestra through a rehearsal. When I mentioned the legendary Neumann microphone company, Joachim rang up one of the engineers, and I got a tour of the factory.

Neumann had just released their new binaural *Kunstkopf,* or "artificial head," microphone. Several companies had developed microphones that could be worn in the ears like backward earbuds, or mounted on a dummy head, to mimic the position of human ears. A recording made this way can be eerily lifelike, allowing a headphone-wearing listener to distinguish not just left/right but whether a sound had originated behind the head or in front.[i] (The classic demonstration is a recording of a haircut.) Since nobody knew exactly which aspects of human physiognomy were critical to binaural perception, the meticulous Neumann engineers began with a complete mannequin customized with anatomically accurate ear canals, in which they placed two of their best microphone capsules. They dressed the dummy in a suit and tie, put a wig on its head, and sat it in a concert hall.

The sound was very good.

"We then asked ourselves, 'are the legs critical for the sound?'" Joachim's friend explained. "We cut off the legs. The imaging was still excellent. 'Are the arms important?' We cut off the arms. Still very good sound. 'Does he have to wear a suit?' We replaced

---

[i] The effect over speakers is not so impressive, but given the prevalence of headphone-listening in the age of smart phones, the technique has come back into favor.

the torso of the mannequin with a felt covered box. Everything still good. 'Does he need the wig?' No, the sound is fine with no hair."

In the end, they were left with a bald head on top of a box whose four felted sides folded up to form its carrying case. In almost every festival concert I attended in Germany that year, there was a screened cube hanging from the ceiling above the audience, and under certain lighting, I could see, suspended inside, a severed head with an aquiline nose.

In his novel *Black Deutschland*, Darryl Pinckney captures the peculiarity of Berlin in those years and identifies a key development: "The conquered city had become the subsidized city." In exchange for remaining on this scarred island, firms like Neumann and their workers received substantial tax breaks, young Germans were exempted from otherwise mandatory military service, and cultural organizations were generously funded. The Künstlerprogramm of the Deutscher Akademischer Austauschdienst (DAAD) offered year-long residencies to international artists, writers, and composers. It had been initiated after the Wall went up as a way to keep the city connected to the world outside, and it had been stunningly successful, bringing luminaries of literature, art, and music to the city and establishing long-lasting networks of artistic exchange. (The list of composers included Iannis Xenakis, Morton Feldman, John Cage, and Igor Stravinsky.) Some recipients stayed on, making the city their permanent home. "The only big business, it seemed, was culture," Pinckney writes. "The students, filmmakers, artists, musicians, actors, writers, and professors were the aristocracy."[1]

Warsaw had one fall festival; West Berlin had two—the Berlin Festwochen and the Metamusik Festival. I stayed long enough for both (cousin Joachim was the soul of generosity). The Festwochen included composers from the New World and Asia but was similar to Warsaw Autumn in its Uptown vibe, dominated by traditional ensembles and well-vetted instrumental styles. It did, however, include a dramatic concert by Karlheinz Stockhausen in the Zeiss Planetarium featuring multi-channel electronic sound. Stockhausen was probably the most visible manifestation of European electronic music, but I had always found myself discomforted by the grandiosity that hovered around him. His music, for all its employment of novel sounds and techniques, remained rooted in the heroic sweep of the post-Mozart canon, and his persona had taken on a semi-spiritual authority that could have given Rudolf Steiner a run for his money. My cocky journal entry after the event read simply: "Not impressive."

The Metamusik Festival was something else entirely. Organized by the composer, musicologist, and journalist Walter Bachauer, it included non-Western music and American minimalism alongside the same kind of contemporary music that appeared in the other festival. The mix brought out a younger, more diverse audience than the Festwochen concerts. David Bowie, then in the midst of mixing *Low* at Hansa Studios, reportedly attended the Steve Reich concert in the Mies van der Rohe Neue Nationalgalerie, probably standing no further than twenty feet from me as I watched two fellow Wesleyan tabla alumni, Bob Becker and Russell Hartenberger, perform in the ensemble. Metamusik was short-lived, running only from 1974 to 1978, but it had an outsized impact on musical life in Berlin: by the early 1980s, other curators were programming a steady stream of experimental music from around the globe. To me, it seemed like an introduction to Europe's Downtown.

Between the foreign armies and state-nurtured exchange programs, West Berlin had an international, multilingual feel that reminded me of New York, but with better public transportation and cheaper, bigger apartments. It had good museums and concerts, and some of the same grubbiness, though for very different historical reasons. It wasn't distractingly beautiful, like many of the cities I would visit that year, and it was infused with a complex blend of guilt, mourning, and pride at having resurrected itself from rubble. I had premonitions that some of the musicians I met in the audience of Metamusik were about to break out on their own distinct paths of musical evolution, but the Parisian Festival d'Automne was next on my roster and I had a train to catch.

In Paris, I had the chance to observe more European responses to American experimentalism, since the program included David Tudor's *Rainforest* as well as the premiere of Robert Ashley's newly completed *Music with Roots in the Aether*, a fourteen-hour video portrait of seven American composers of Alvin's generation. In New York, the audience for contemporary music consisted mostly of other composers, but the European festivals drew crowds similar to those who attended the opera, ballet, or symphony. European culturati generally displayed a broader stylistic tolerance than their New World equivalents, but how far would that stretch?

Rainforest was a "tended installation": the musicians sat at tables manipulating electronic circuits that sent signals to sound sculptures strewn about the cavernous Espace Pierre-Cardin, while the audience wandered about and listened (Figure 7.1). Since I knew most of the participants and my days were largely open, I became an unofficial understudy, filling in when performers needed a break for cigarettes or food, and growing more familiar with the piece and with Tudor. Ashley's *Music with Roots in the Aether*, meanwhile, was installed in the basement of the Centre Culturel Américain on the Left Bank, with TV sets and sofas transforming the gallery space into a comfy suburban rec room. Both the Tudor and Ashley projects were received enthusiastically, unlike Feldman in Warsaw.

Chatting with the Centre Culturel's music curator, Stephen Kleiman, I mentioned that I had assisted in Alvin's contributions to the Ashley project (screen credit!) and added a few comments on my own work. Perhaps I sounded more experienced than I was or maybe, coming off the audience success of *Music with Roots in the Aether*, he was in the mood to take a risk. In any case, he asked if I would like to come back in the spring to present an installation and a pair of concerts. On the off-chance that some such opportunity would arise, I had built and carried with me from New York three tiny circuit-based performance instruments and a fourth circuit for my first audio installation. Of course, I said yes.

Apart from the festival, my other target in Paris was IRCAM (*Institut de recherche et coordination acoustique/musique*), a brand-new music research center headed by France's most visible contemporary composer, Pierre Boulez, whose works had pushed Serialism to its limits and whose furious diktats regarding composition were legendary.

Figure 7.1 Installation view of David Tudor's *Rainforest* at l'Espace Cardin in Paris, 1976. Photo © Ralph Jones, used by artist's permission.

The IRCAM building was still under construction, but Kleiman suggested I call his friend, composer Jean-Claude Risset, who worked there and might be able to give me a tour. I rang and began my introduction.

"First I must ask: do you use computers in your music?" Risset interrupted.

"No, I mostly work with electronic circuitry."

"Ah, then I am very sorry, but I cannot help you. You must speak with Luciano Berio. He is in charge of *electronic* music. I am the head of *computer* music."

"Oh. I also write for instruments."

"Then you should also call Vinko Globokar. What kind of instrumental music do you compose?"

"Mostly for musicians who don't play their instruments very well."

"Then you should contact Michel Decoust, our head of Pedagogy."

"I might mention that many of my electronic instruments are built from logic chips rather than typical analog circuits."

"Well then, I guess you and I should meet as well."

"So I need to make appointments with Luciano Berio, Vinko Globokar, Michel Decoust, and you before I can visit? How does this all get coordinated?"

"Ah, after you have spoken to all of us, please telephone Monsieur [X]," and he gave me an unfamiliar name.

"Who is Monsieur [X]?"

"He is Monsieur *Diagonal!*"

Luciano Berio was so famous that I was too intimidated to make even the first call. As a consequence, I wouldn't pass through IRCAM's doors for another sixteen years. (I did, however, meet Risset on several subsequent occasions, and he proved utterly charming.) Georgina Born's anthropological study of IRCAM, *Rationalizing Culture*, goes into detail about its Byzantine hierarchies, of which my curious phone call was but one reflection.[2] The long drought of freestyle compositional innovation in France is perhaps another.

Still, Paris was Paris, with its infinite list of beguiling attributes. I appreciated the buskers in the Paris Metro—young kids strumming acoustic guitars, Russian immigrants with balalaikas, medaled old men playing accordions—all making fine use of the acoustical reflections off those beveled tiles. One day, soon after my chat with Risset, I encountered a stooped, bewhiskered *mutilé de guerre* holding, with great solemnity, a tin bar tray bearing a vintage Norelco cassette recorder. His busking consisted of rotating three tapes through the machine and pressing "play." *Musique concrète souterraine*—the closest thing to French experimental music I heard that fall.

Newcastle to Narvik

When the Festival d'Automne ended, I took the boat-train to London and headed north to Newcastle-Upon-Tyne to visit Stuart Marshall. In 1969, when he was a student at Newport Art School, Stuart had attended a concert by the Sonic Arts Union in London. Smitten, he applied to Wesleyan for his MA. We had met in 1975 when he returned to Middletown for some events and had performed with me on the Arp 2600 for a recording of Alvin's *The Duke of York* (1971), a weirdly campy outlier in Alvin's otherwise sober repertoire.[1] Talking with Stuart, listening to his work, and reading his Wesleyan thesis had given me insight into what "post-Lucier" music might be.

A pair of early works is representative of Stuart's poignant, unpretentious merger of land art, crowd-sourced performance, and the phenomenology of sound. In *Exhibition on 3 Hills* (1969–70), he set an oscillator and speaker on several hills in West Wales, then mapped the distances at which particular frequencies crossed the threshold of hearing. Another work examined the temporal phasing of "a single, synchronized pulse in a landscape" by having scattered residents of Cwmbran, Monmouthshire, slam their front doors simultaneously.[2]

(The closest thing I had witnessed to this kind of community performance in the States occurred when I spent a month teaching in the summer school at Ohio University before my senior year in college. The university radio station broadcast an appeal to the town's children: if they showed up with a portable radio on a certain downtown corner on Sunday morning at 11 a.m., they'd get a free Big Mac. The kids were met by a grad student who instructed them to tune their radios to the college station, then, while the station broadcast John Philip Souza, a drum major in full uniform led the ragtag marching radio band through town's parade route, wrapping up outside the local McDonald's. What appeared to me to be a charming work of participatory art, however, was an exercise in marketing designed by a professor in the business school.)

Most of the American composers I admired performed their own work, maintaining that most ensembles were not skilled in the unconventional techniques of their novel music (if also, undoubtedly, because established groups were not soliciting it). In Warsaw, Berlin, and Paris, on the other hand, contemporary European composers sat in the audience, waiting for the swanned handwave from the stage at the start of the applause, their cue to stand and take a bow. To me, this suggested an entrenched class structure in which players were the muscle and composers were the brains, no more likely to appear on the stage of a concert hall than to play drums in a strip club. The position of instrument designers and engineers—the people who made the circuits or spliced the tape—was even lower than that of players. (Even in the States there was suspicion that the tinkering behind the circuit-as-score movement was not *really* composing.) As in so many things, England was different.

A number of British composers had also found their trajectories reoriented by Cage. Cornelius Cardew—who started as a chorister singing "Jerusalem" in Canterbury Cathedral and ended up as a Maoist playing workers' songs in pubs— had been Stockhausen's assistant before turning to indeterminacy. A member of the free-improvisation group AMM, he also co-founded the Scratch Orchestra, an ensemble that required no instrumental training or music-reading ability. Building on similar democratic leveling as a means of loosening compositional control, composer Gavin Bryars joined with students at Portsmouth School of Art in 1970 to found the Portsmouth Sinfonia, whose members were discouraged from playing any instrument on which they had competence (Brian Eno, for example, brought a clarinet). Initially a parodic lark, with musicians racing through popular classics such as Beethoven's *Fifth* and Rossini's *William Tell Overture* from memory (both works fit snugly on a single side of the Sinfonia's first LP, with room to spare for Tchaikovsky and Gynt), the Sinfonia would eventually perform at Royal Albert Hall, and their recording *Classical Muddly* (1981) would make it to the top 40 on the British charts.

For an American, Bryars's work seemed to embody a familiar philosophy being put to unfamiliar ends. American phase music, in which repeated motifs slowly move out of sync, was very much associated with the unwavering drum patterns and tape loops of Steve Reich—insistent, majestic, and a bit inhuman. Bryars's *1, 2, 1-2-3-4* (1971) also works with phasing: an instrumental ensemble tries to play along with cassette recordings of light jazz or easy-listening music in a kind of proto-karaoke, but each musician is working with their own cassette player and earphones; variances in motor speed, tape condition, and button-pressing synchronization gradually drive them further and further apart.[3]

Michael Nyman's *The Otherwise Very Beautiful Blue Danube Waltz* (1976) achieved something similar by taking the additive melody process used by composer Frederic Rzewski (David Behrman's classmate at Andover and Harvard) and applying it to Johann Strauss's perennial favorite. Five pianists, beginning together, play the first measure of Strauss's score, then jump back to the start and play the first and second, then the first, second, and third, and so on. Inevitably, however, some lose track of where they are, and everything slides beautifully astray.[i] The result in both cases is a drunken-sounding "phase music," winsome, witty, and elegiac in equal measure.

---

[i] Nyman notes that the title comes from "a derogatory comment of Arnold Schoenberg's of the fact that the first six phrases are rhythmically identical: 'Here one finds numerous slightly varied repetitions, as in the otherwise very beautiful Blue Danube Waltz.'"

Stuart's musical compositions had combined this kind of openness with the pointing-toward-objective-phenomena stance epitomized by Alvin—picked up from, or exaggerated by, his studies at Wesleyan. By the time I arrived in Newcastle, however, he had begun working with video and teaching at Newcastle Polytechnic (later recast as Northumbria University). The Polytechnic's studio art program was divided into painting, sculpture, and "other"; the emergent field of video counted as "other." Stuart also took advantage of the general heading to create what was effectively the first curriculum of "sound art" in the UK, a blend of British visual art pedagogy and the American experimental music ethos. Students acquired the skills and confidence necessary to consider sound as an art material like any other, rather than as the exclusive purview of music. His film and video students began to elevate the role of their soundtracks; sculptors introduced sound to their installations. The Arp 2600 that sat in the school's tiny film editing suite churned out the same boops and beeps one might hear in any music department, only here they were freed from the usual "musical" expectations of timing and form.

Soon after my arrival, Gavin Bryars came up from London for a brief residency. In addition to his work as a composer, he co-founded the Experimental Music Catalogue, which disseminated the scores of like-minded colleagues, and had advised Brian Eno on his post-Roxy Music startup label, Obscure Records. We had met the previous year when he visited Wesleyan. Since Gavin was doing critiques with Stuart's students, I asked if he would be willing to offer me one as well. Ever the gentleman, he agreed, but after listening to an excerpt from my demo tape and looking at a score or two, he announced, "You're not a student anymore—you're a composer." The Watson had provided the first major break in my formal education since nursery school, but Gavin was the first person to recast the negative state of "no longer a student" into the positive condition of "now a composer." (A few months later I finally took the bold, Bryars-sanctioned step of writing "composer" as my profession when registering at a hostel in Denmark, in lieu of the usual "student." Rotating the clipboard, the clerk smiled and remarked, "Welcome to Copenhagen, Mr. Collins. This is the first time we have had a typesetter here.")

Though economically depressed, cold, and damp, Newcastle had a small, vibrant art scene, mostly centered around the Poly. Real estate was abundant and cheap, even if much of it lacked central heating and indoor toilets. Northern Arts, the regional division of the national arts council, was generous so far from London. A group of Stuart's students banded together to rent an unheated warehouse annex built into the side of a hill on the quayside. Modeled on the example of London's Butler's Wharf (an artist-run space established the previous year by a group that also included several former Marshall students), Newcastle's Ayton Basement hosted a mix of performance art, concerts, and screenings, mostly of student work from the Poly and other Northern art schools, augmented by the occasional faculty member or visitor passing through. Audiences were small but stalwart and attentive. I remember a screening of an instructional film on how to thread a 16 mm projector—a piece of found art that begged the elliptical question of how one was supposed to view the instructions without first having mastered them.

Invited to participate in the space's opening run in early December, Stuart opted to revive a low-tech sound performance from his Wesleyan days (*Ideophonics*, performed by Stuart, his wife Jane Harrison, and me) and also to premiere a new piece.[4] The audio facilities at the Polytechnic were pretty basic, but they had two Uher portable reel-to-reel recorders, used primarily for location recording for film and video, but also suitable for tape echo, loops, audio delays, and other forms of signal processing. Stuart set up an ambulatory tape-delay performance, with me assisting. Ayton Basement consisted of two downward-sloping, parallel, windowless corridors, connected through an archway at the lower end. Stuart walked down one corridor while recording onto one of the Uhers, letting the tape spill out onto the floor behind him; once he reached the arch and started back up the other side, I picked up the loose end of the tape where he started, threaded it onto the take-up reel on my Uher, pressed "play," and followed his path as his recording wound onto my reel. Each sound Stuart made (footsteps and talking, as I recall) played back through my speaker at the exact location in the tunnel where he had recorded it a few minutes earlier, like an audio ghost (see Figure 8.1).

I, too, was offered an evening to present my own work. But what to perform? I had the small circuits that I'd been porting around in my backpack, but I wanted to do something that would take advantage of Ayton Basement's strange lugubrious

Figure 8.1 Stuart Marshall (left) and the author performing Marshall's untitled ambulatory tape-delay piece at Ayton Basement, Newcastle-Upon-Tyne, December 3, 1976. Photo by Jane Harrison.

architecture. Feedback was the obvious tool for the job, but my preferred supplies were now an ocean away. Working semi-clandestinely (since I wasn't an officially enrolled student), I made the most of the Polytechnic's modest facilities to fit tiny microphones into a saxophone and a flute that fed back as two students—one per tunnel—crept through the space in a reworking of my earlier feedback pieces.

This was my first concert since leaving Wesleyan, my first in Europe, and the first test of Bryars's benediction. It may have been dark and cold, but I felt like I had arrived. The audience consisted of perhaps two dozen people, half of whom I knew and the other half of whom had been dragged along as their dates. Baffled but supportive, they seemed happy just to witness something they hadn't heard before.

A few days later, Stuart, Jane and I drove down to London where we each presented a night at Butler's Wharf (Figure 8.2). I premiered my first sound installation, *Under the Sun—A Pythagorean Experiment*, in an abbreviated concert-length version. I had designed the piece before leaving the States, and had been traveling with its minimal components tucked inside my backpack ever since: a thin steel wire that could be stretched across a room at a slight incline; a small Teflon loop to hang on the wire; and a little gizmo that would tap the wire every second or so, causing the string to vibrate and the loop to slide down the incline a few millimeters. At each resting point, a different harmonic or cluster of harmonics would be isolated, as on a guitar or harp string lightly touched. A contact mike at the other end picked up and amplified the sound of the string, which came out of a speaker as a metronomic pulse of shifting overtones (see Figure 8.3). The space at Butler's Wharf was far too big for the handful of listeners present, but it smelled wonderfully of the spice trade that had once filled it.[ii]

A month later, I ran the piece in its longer form over a weekend at Spectro, a cooperative arts organization in Newcastle. The upside of installations is that they can carry on making noise while you nip out to the pub, or to another town, or even another country. The downside is that if they do break down, inevitably you're not there to fix it. For this, my maiden voyage into "sound art," I stuck close to the venue just in case, but everything went swimmingly—another rite of passage.

This was 1977, the winter of punk. The Damned came to Newcastle for a gig that lasted around fifteen minutes before one of the many hurled beer bottles connected with the singer's head and brought the set to a snarling close. Inspired by the vitality, if not the violence, several of Stuart's students decided to form a band. My nodding acquaintance with the guitar earned me an invitation to join, along with the request that I at least teach them the chords to *Gloria*. I was happy to help out with guitar rudiments but declined to join up. The road beckoned beyond Newcastle.

In the UK, I had finally encountered a local scene with its own self-grown experimentalist ethos. Cage and his American followers displayed a visceral distrust of popular culture; Boulez, Stockhausen, and their followers still seemed caught up in

---

[ii] Every experimental artist seems to have made a piece with a long string, and this was mine. I had left Wesleyan before Alvin produced his *Music on a Long Thin Wire* (1977). (See Alvin Lucier, *Music on a Long Thin Wire* [Lovely Music, 1980]).

Figure 8.2 The entrance to Butler's Wharf artist's space, London, December 1976. Photo by Nicolas Collins.

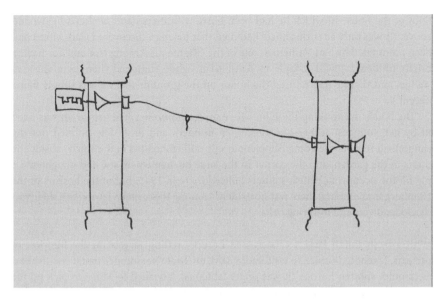

Figure 8.3 Announcement card with the author's drawing for the performance of *Under the Sun—A Pythagorean Experiment*, 2B Butler's Wharf, London, December 17, 1976.

proving something to dead gods, from Bach to Schoenberg. New music in Britain, by contrast, felt curiously free and open. It did not eschew popular culture or the word "improvisation." It abounded with seemingly paradoxical juxtapositions: the mayhem of punk and the roster of the Experimental Music Catalogue, professionals and amateurs, Maoism and Merchant Ivory, bloodless systems and halcyon sentimentality.

I had showed up in Newcastle planning to stay a couple of weeks. I ended up overstaying my visa and got a slap on the wrist when I finally left for points south in February.

The Watson was an unusual grant in that it preferred proposals that were practical but porous. Winging it was part of the plan. I had arrived in Europe equipped with my list of fall festivals, the phone numbers of a dozen people suggested by mentors, friends, and family as potential local informants, and the blithe assumption that people I met on the road would point me to the next festival, club, city, colleague, or relative. I now gave myself over to working those lists.

I traveled to Hamburg to meet my extended family—the prodigal North American son equipped with a crib sheet from my mother explaining whom to kiss, whom to shake hands with, and whom *never* to touch. The grand family houses had not yet been turned into embassies or corporate retreats, but most were broken into (still reasonably grand) apartments apportioned to various members of the extended clan. Joachim's favorite bachelor uncle—a small, sparkling man—happily occupied one floor of the house in which he had been born, with nieces and nephews below and above. (It was only after this uncle had died that Joachim discovered Carl Alfred had been nominated by Yad Vashem as one of the "Righteous Among Nations" for having briefly hidden a Jewish couple in Amsterdam while stationed there as a German soldier, and that he had refused the honor on the grounds that he was simply being decent.)

The house overlooking the Elbe where my grandmother had grown up was lived in by her youngest sister—gracious, open-minded, and droll. She pointed out the cannonball from an invading Napoleonic ship still embedded in the stucco beside the doors to the garden, and the corner in the large kitchen where she had slaughtered a pig for the occupying British soldiers billeted there in 1945. But of the horrors of the Hamburg firebombing, there was no evidence among those green lawns with their vast rhododendrons and towering oaks.

With a fresh Eurail Pass, I crisscrossed Europe, setting targets on the flimsiest of pretexts. I went to Munich to visit Radio RIM, on Tudor's assurance that it was the best electronics shop in Europe (it was pretty fabulous). I headed to Milan to pick up the record of Alvin's *The Duke of York* that Stuart and I had played on, but failed to find the record company at the given address. (A sign of the times, my rail pass, and my own mood: not finding the record company, I simply got back on a train bound for a different city.) In Bourges, I made a formal appointment to see the studios of Groupe de Musique Expérimentale de Bourges, where ranks of tape recorders stood in orderly file and nobody cracked a smile—another world from the fungible chaos of Wesleyan's facilities. In Cologne, I was given a tour of Feedback Studio, a cooperative electronic music facility in what looked like someone's apartment, where casually deployed young composers were at work. Learning of my interest in live performance, they suggested I pay a visit to STEIM, so I hopped a train to Amsterdam.

Founded in 1968 to produce electronic musical instruments for political theater, STEIM was regarded as the most radical of the European state-supported electronic music studios. They designed their own semi-conventional modular synthesizer system as well as *Kraakdoos* ("cracklebox") synthesizers played by direct skin contact. I went by the building several times before someone answered the doorbell. I was given a friendly welcome but told that there was no activity to see at the moment. At IRCAM, there were six gatekeepers standing between me and entry; at STEIM there was just one who often took the day off.

Everywhere, I visited museums—contemporary art, old painting, historic musical instruments, Italian conceptualism, quirky collections of automata. All of it related in some way to things I was thinking about. But after England, the tenor of my Watson project changed. No longer just an observer of new musical scenes, I now saw myself as a participant.

The next proving ground was Paris, where I had accepted Kleiman's invitation for an installation and performance at the Centre Culturel Américain. It was time to try out the ideas I had plotted during my protracted train travels. One involved placing microphones around rooms and corridors on the two floors of the building, wired to a mixer in the concert space. Standing in front of the small audience, I shouted a word (as I recall, just a number identifying one of the microphones), then repeated it louder and louder, while turning up the volume of the named microphone, until the audience could hear my voice as picked up by the mic. It would be heard after a slight delay that depended on distance, its timbre changed by the intervening acoustics. I would then shut off that mic, and fade in one further away, shout another word until my voice came back, a little hoarser, at a slightly longer delay, and more filtered.[iii] On to the next mic, shouting louder, etc., etc.

You get it, right?

And that was the problem: after two or three shouts you got it, and "it" was all there was. There was no aural pleasure, none of the allusiveness that arose from, say, speech dissolving into pure sound, or sound stepping in where vision usually held sway. The experience didn't take you anywhere.

I had spent four years in Connecticut working to emulate the music I admired by making my creations ever simpler and clearer. My task, I thought, was bringing out the *essence* of whatever acoustical phenomenon, circuit, or social gambit formed the core of the composition. (Alvin's most frequent criticism of student work was "too many ideas.") Now I had finally succeeded in rubbing off all the extraneous parts and sharp edges, only to discover that what was left was not really interesting at all. Sadly, I came to this realization halfway through the performance, but felt compelled to carry through to the end, after I had lost faith. (Pity the poor audience!) That night reversed my minimalist momentum and forced me to revise my assessment of how art ideas and experiences intertwined.

While in Amsterdam, I stopped into Other Books and So, a store and gallery run by Mexican artist Ulises Carrión. We were chatting when another customer sidled up, apologized for eavesdropping, said my music sounded interesting, and asked if I would be available to perform in the "Beethoven Music For The Millions Festival" in Arnhem in June.

Despite its ridiculous title and the fact that it was underwritten by a record label devoted to light classical music, the festival was decidedly experimental, even confrontational, in its selections. I was programmed on a long afternoon of performance art, during which every performer left the stage naked, regardless of how they entered. I stood fully clothed for the entirety of my twelve-minute performance, blowing into an inaudible (to humans) dog whistle, while oscillators swooped up and down in response, eliciting odd acoustic artifacts like heterodyning (a psychoacoustical phenomenon of low whistling inside your ear, caused by the interference of two high frequencies). My intention was to use the heterodyning as a kind of navigational aid, but any causality

---

[iii] Only some years later did I realize that this basic mechanism was embarrassingly close to that of a little-known early work of Alvin's, *Quasimodo The Great Lover* (1970). He, needless to say, made better use of it. See score in Alvin Lucier and Douglas Simon, *Chambers*. (Wesleyan University Press, 1980), pp. 55–7.

was completely unclear to the audience. They were far more bewildered by my fully clothed ambling amid piercing glissandi than they were by the naked people lowering their faces into basins of cold water. Once again, I was prompted to rethink the gulf between intentions and perceptions.

I began to understand that the rhetoric of minimalism was just that—rhetoric—an argument that serves a particular time and place, but captures only a narrow thread of what actually makes art work. The conundrum was neatly articulated by a friend and former Wesleyan student, Jack Freudenheim, when he admitted after a performance, "I didn't know if I was supposed to understand it or enjoy it." *I am sitting in a room* is a lastingly beautiful and affecting work not because it is so simple, but because its simple mechanism produces a complex experience that ranges from the aesthetic pleasures of tonality to intimations of mortality. I began to respect, even savor, the presence of grit in an otherwise smoothly running art machine, and my work proceeded to get a little messier with every subsequent year.

With my return to America looming on the calendar, I made my way to Rome, following up a tip from Paul DeMarinis that there was still a record-making booth in the Termini train station. For my two minutes of allotted recording time, I slowly opened the door to allow the sound of the train station to fade up. (A nice but impractical idea: when I finally dropped the result on a record player a few months later, I discovered that the station's ambience was completely overpowered by the surface ticks and pops of the cheap vinyl.)

Getting back on the train, I headed to Narvik, Norway, for the sole reason that it was the longest possible train trip I could make, and that's what you do when you're twenty-three and have four days left on your Eurail Pass and no particular place to go.

The Eden Before the Apple

On receiving the Watson Fellowship I deferred my enrollment in the Mills College graduate program. Eight months later, sitting in a frosty bedsit in Newcastle, where the idea of California should have beckoned warmly, I found myself having doubts. I missed New York, Alvin was encouraging me to return to Connecticut, and there were economic considerations: Mills was unable to provide any financial aid while Wesleyan was offering full tuition plus a stipend.

As regards the non-musical part of my life, the pragmatic choice chanced to be the right one: Susan, my future wife, was still at Wesleyan, now in her third year, and kismet is kismet. As regards my music, I will never know if I made the right decision. At Wesleyan things were familiar but different than they had been. Alvin was achieving greater renown, and his personal life was vastly happier. I was no longer an undergrad in awe of every new idea that came my way, and post-Watson, I was eager to assert my status as a professional, if fledgling, composer. I made regular trips down to New York for concerts at The Kitchen, Phill Niblock's loft, and numerous other small spaces. I engaged in a long-term project with my former advisor, Jon Barlow, producing new recordings of works by Charles Ives that extended Glenn Gould's studio innovations to radical extremes (Jon played Ives's "carillon" voice in the *Three Page Sonata* using the campus chapel bells, over the recording of which we dubbed the main piano part).

But whatever advantages the Eastern Seaboard may have offered me, it was not the Bay Area on the cusp of a computing revolution that was about to change everything for everyone.

To understand how those epochal developments ran through the peculiar niche of experimental music, it helps to dive briefly into some underlying mechanisms. Like many of my electronics-bedazzled peers, I had been drawn to circuits by dumb techno-futurist romance—they were new, and I was young. To begin with, I fell for *analog* circuits (like the oscillator that I built in high school), in which voltage wiggles continuously, waiting to be tamed by turning a knob, just as one would turn a tuning peg to tighten a string.

In analog electronics, a "value" (the loudness of a signal, for example) is registered as a position on the continuous line of fluctuating voltage. Analog computers existed but were used primarily for dedicated tasks that described continuous functions, like tide tables or predicting the trajectories of projectiles. (Gordon Mumma had constructed a singular homemade analog computer—a "cybersonic console" in his lingo—for his 1967 composition *Hornpipe,* where it was employed to analyze room acoustics and control filter circuits, supplementing the sounds of his French horn with bursts of electronic feedback.)[1]

Digital electronics are different: instead of a position on a curve, a value (like loudness, to use our previous example) is expressed as a binary number. Analog signals are fluid and easily converted into sound; digital data is quantized and better suited to arithmetic operations within a device. Digital integrated circuits (chips) were developed to perform a wide range of low-level mathematical operations.

One of the first musical applications of digital ICs was in the sequencers of analog synthesizers, where binary counters could step through a series of notes. At SUNY Albany, composer Joel Chadabe interconnected multiple Moog sequencers to create complex patterns. David Behrman, lacking access to larger synthesizers, built his own sequencer out of the counter chip at the heart of the Moog module: in *Cello With Melody-Driven Electronics* (1974) "pitch sensitive windows" (Behrman's term) trigger a sequence of rich electronic chords in response to specific notes played by the cellist. In Paul DeMarinis's *Pygmy Gamelan* (1972), pseudo-random patterns of binary pulses ring resonant filters to produce pleasing algorithmic music that evokes its Indonesian namesake.

In 1965, Gordon Moore, co-founder of Fairchild Semiconductor, posited that the number of transistors in an integrated circuit could be expected to double every two years for the foreseeable future, and that chips would become ever smaller and cheaper. Each of the early digital chips represented an axiomatic operation in binary arithmetic. A handful of ICs could be combined to build a calculator that could add, subtract, multiply, and divide. With more chips you could arrange a sequence of operations— rudimentary programming—and soon the functions of multiple chips were packed into a single integrated circuit. By 1971, the central processing units (CPUs) of computers had gone from covering several placemat-sized circuit boards in a room-sized mainframe in a computer center to occupying a single IC—the first microprocessor. By the end of the decade, Moore's prescience proved correct, and microprocessors integrating hundreds of discreet operations on one chip became cheap enough for the sufficiently motivated amateur to afford.[2] The Bay Area, long a hotbed of homemade circuitry, was the incubator of what became known as "microcomputer music."

Ron Kuivila had taken the path I spurned and entered the MFA program at Mills the same September I returned to Wesleyan. The following June, I finagled an invitation to crash on his couch for a few weeks. Ron's roommate, the polymathic composer Rich Gold, introduced me to his KIM-1 single-board computer.

A naked circuit board the size of an A4 sheet of paper, the KIM (Keyboard Input Monitor) didn't look like a computer. It had been designed and marketed by MOS Technology as a showcase for the company's 6502 microprocessor and as a development tool for engineers, to encourage them to find ways to incorporate the microprocessor as a control device for devices from lathes to microwave ovens. Unlike modern personal computers, it arrived with no monitor, keyboard, mouse, disc drive, case, or power supply. Programming was done in hexadecimal (base 16) machine code on a small keypad, and the display was limited to a row of six LED alphanumeric digits. DeMarinis likened its appearance to "a friendly autoharp with a calculator glued on top," and at $254 it was cheaper than most synthesizers.[3]

Rich's KIM sat atop a homemade wooden construction that resembled a baby-blue Greek temple and also housed a shoebox-sized power supply. He sat me in his chair, handed me a flashcard with the microprocessor's instruction set, and told me to learn programming while he went off to work.

Machine code had none of the pseudo-linguistic properties of higher-order languages like Basic, the usual entry for novice programmers at the time, nor did it sport the graphic niceties of more recent software.

To add 2 + 3 you would type on the tiny keypad:

1. A9 02 [load the accumulator with number 2]
2. 60 03 [add the number 3]
3. 85 62 [store the result in memory location 62]

You would then enter memory location 62 on the keypad and read off the display whatever answer had been left there by your code (hopefully 5). It was not intuitive, but it was just within conceptual reach if you wanted an elemental sense of how computers operated. After a week of alternating frustration and exhilaration at Rich's desk, I was hooked.

Why bother? Ornery as they were, these early microcomputers offered something intriguing that other musical instruments lacked: memory. Most analog circuits were *instrumental*: they generated sounds. But with a microcomputer, it was possible to lay out a sequence of events—essentially embedding a score. Furthermore, by incorporating conditional if-then decisions made on the basis of incoming information, it could be made responsive—branching, perhaps, to different parts of the program depending on actions taken by the players, a behavior normally the province of players themselves. Thus, instrument, score, and performer could be combined into a single remarkably portable object. It offered a different way of organizing actions over time—less like an oscillator and more like a machine by Tinguely or Rube Goldberg, a goofy marble run chain of events, perfect for my passions.

Rich was a visionary whose career encompassed music composition, game design, performance events, and writing. In 1978, decades before the massively parallel crowd computing used by SETI to sniff out extraterrestrial life, Rich hypothesized that underutilized personal computers (of which there were still very few) could be networked through modems and harnessed to solve complex problems. His *Little Computer People* game for the Commodore 64, created in 1985, was the precursor to *The Sims* (as acknowledged in the later game's credits). While Composer-in-Residence at the Mattel Toy Company, he developed the "Power Glove" tactile game controller based on VR technology—a commercial flop when introduced in 1989, it was hacked by many artists and anticipated the wildly successful Nintendo Wii (2006). In 1991, he helped found the Artist-in-Residence program at Xerox PARC.[4]

Rich modeled rules of game theory to create musical structures and programmed his KIM to generate strategies for human social interaction. His *Party Planner* (1978) calculated degrees of attraction and repulsion between fictional characters and plotted their attempts at maintaining optimum separation (Mary is keenly interested in Seth but hates John; John likes Mary but is jealous of Seth; Seth has taken a vow of chastity, etc.). One performance, on the Napa estate of art collectors Rene and Veronica Di Rosa, had Rich reading data off the display of his KIM while sitting on a dock and passing instructions to his partner, Marina LaPalma, who swam the length of a pond to deliver them to performers ranged over a hillside. "They were meant to then move x number of paces in some direction," Marina recalls. "But of course these were young artists and the terrain was rocky and steep and there were thorns and stuff. So, they moved *somewhere* . . . some just moved closer to a friend or someone they wanted to talk to, thus enacting a de facto *Party Planner* dynamic."[5]

Other composers took to the KIM as well. Behrman updated his *Cello With Melody-Driven Electronics*, with a KIM now controlling his homemade analog oscillators through a digital-to-analog converter (DAC).[i] George Lewis recognized early on the affinity between microcomputer-based music and improvisation. Encouraged by Behrman, he connected a KIM to a Serge modular analog synthesizer and wrote some of the first software for machine improvisation. (His subsequent works, built on the foundation he established on the KIM, set a standard by which interactive music programming is still judged).[6] The League of Automatic Music Composers (Rich Gold, John Bischoff, Tim Perkis, and Jim Horton) interconnected their four microcomputers to create the first networked music performance in 1978, exchanging data between their programs over a tangle of wires, and unleashing a veritable blizzard of raucous drones, swoops, and glitches (Figure 9.1).[7]

In *Guns, Germs and Steel*, geographer Jared Diamond makes the counterfactual assertion that "invention is often the mother of necessity."[8] It can take time to figure out the lasting application of an innovation. The microcomputer was a fine example. Though the musical potential of microcomputers was clear to this handful of Bay Area artists, the notion of digital music remained alien even to most technological visionaries: trademarking its moniker in 1979, Apple accepted the restriction that its products would never be used for any commercial musical applications, lest it infringe on the Beatles' semi-dormant company of the same name. (This led to extended litigation after the iPod and iTunes transformed Apple's business plan and profit line.) Apple's acceptance of the trademark exception seems all the more remarkable given that, in 1975, a music program written by Steve Dompier was the first non-diagnostic

---

[i] A DAC translates the computer's binary numbers into voltages and is an essential glue between a computer and any analog sound-producing circuitry. There were no off-the-shelf DACs to plug into the KIM at first—they had to be built up from rather expensive chips, and the circuit designs were not simple. Happily, at Mills, Behrman was surrounded by like-minded autodidacts who helped solve each other's problems.

Figure 9.1 The League of Automatic Music Composers rehearsing at California College of Arts and Crafts, Oakland, in 1981. From left to right: Tim Perkis, John Bischoff, Don Day, and Jim Horton. Photo credit: Eva Shoshany. © John Bischoff, used by artist's permission.

software demonstrated at the Homebrew Computer Club in Menlo Park, CA—an event attended by the young Steve Jobs, Apple's co-founder.

The BBC Micro was an early (1981) affordable microcomputer produced by Acorn Computers as part of a BBC computer literacy project. Once a week, the BBC would broadcast a late-night radio show reviewing the latest software available for the Micro and offering programming advice. Programs for the computer were stored in fax-like tones on ordinary audio cassettes. Someone at the BBC suggested distributing software by transmitting over the radio the data file normally stored on tape as sound: a listener could simply connect the earphone jack of their radio to the input connector on their computer in lieu of the cassette recorder. Initially, the producers sent images in the form of ASCII art, as a way to test out the practicality of sending software as sound.[ii] Then they transmitted simple programs into which small errors were intentionally inserted and offered a prize for the first person to find the bug and fix the code. Shortly before the program was taken off the air, they sent out non-functioning programs submitted by listeners seeking fixes—an early instance of crowdsourcing software development.

When the Electronic Music Studio opened in the Center for the Arts in 1973, Alvin disconnected the keyboards from the Arps and locked them in a closet to forestall

---

[ii] "ASCII Art" was one of the earliest forms of computer-generated images, in which letters and symbols are mapped into pixel equivalents based on the relative density of the character.

student renditions of pop songs. Deprived of this option, we did other things with the synthesizers, interconnecting various modules (oscillators, filters, amplifiers, etc.) so that the output of one would control the next to create self-governing networks that, left to their own devices, produced complex results—a riff, a melody that repeats, or even repeats with variation, that would never have occurred to our minds or fingers. (The patch I created to pan Alvin's sferic recordings around the Cunningham studio was an example of this approach to synthesis.) Patch cords on synthesizers introduced us to algorithmic thinking. Instead of everything responding directly to the press of a key, like a piano hammer hitting a string, an action could set a sequence into motion. Letting modules control each other exempted me from micromanaging and hinted at what might be possible with computers.

Between my sophomore and junior years, at Alvin's suggestion, I had taken a summer course in programming, but my commitment to live performance rendered Wesleyan's massive mainframe DEC-10 unappealing. Working with a single-board microcomputer, on the other hand, was only one step away from the portable world of circuits. I could stop worrying about it as a "computer," DeMarinis instructed me, and just think of it as "a big, expensive integrated circuit."[9] Its crudeness kept me in touch with the essential nature of the machine: 1s flipping to 0s and back again, electrical impulses flowing through traces and wires—an awareness missing from most of our interactions with computers today. These limitations eased the transition from hardware to software and gave the resulting music produced a gritty, handmade quality.

The unpredictability of analog circuitry had been part of its allure for experimental composers—an improvisational resource or a form of Cagean uncertainty. Digital devices like microcomputers are inherently deterministic, but the limitations of the early interface options—handmade DACs or friends stumbling across Napa hillsides—kept imprecision in play. Small and light, the KIM and its kin were natural follow-ups to the circuit-in-a-box. (Not until the late 1990s would laptop computers approach equivalent portability.)

Back on the East Coast, I ordered, at Rich's suggestion, the newly released VIM-1 from Synertek, another manufacturer of the 6502 microprocessor (Figure 9.2).[10] Basically an upgraded KIM, it arrived with the same 1 kb memory as its predecessor (for reference, a Microsoft Word document containing just one letter currently occupies 12 kb of memory), but the VIM's memory could be quadrupled by inserting more chips in empty sockets—increasing the cost by almost 50 percent, however. Writing very compact code was essential.[iii] With no disk drives or SIM cards, the program vanished from memory as soon as you shut off the computer unless you stored it as a series of fax-like tones on a cassette tape (as with the BBC Micro)—very slow and prone to error. The clock speed of the CPU was 1 MHz—3,000 times slower than

---

iii Virtuosic programmers could free up a little extra space by having their software overwrite a section of the memory in which the program was stored after portions had been executed, like cartoon characters building the bridge ahead by pulling up boards from behind. But this was a risky proposition and meant you couldn't run the program twice without reloading it.

Figure 9.2 Synertek "VIM" microcomputer, in homemade case, built in 1978. Photo by Simon Lonergan.

current personal computers. There were few peripherals available, and expanding the computer's capabilities usually meant picking up a soldering iron. It would be another two decades before personal computers became fast enough to process full-bandwidth audio directly—until then, sound-generating resources were quite limited.

Perhaps most significantly, there was no World Wide Web to search for answers when problems arose—we had to rely on visits, phone calls, and letters from a small group of friends struggling with the same technology. The closest thing to these early microcomputers today would be the Arduino and its ilk: microcomputers the size of a business card commonly embedded in "smart" appliances and widely used by inventors and hobbyists. But the Arduino can be programmed from a full-size computer with a keyboard and display using a higher-order language; your work doesn't disappear when you shut it off, and its speed is much faster than the KIM or VIM. Expansion resources are easy to find, and the Web provides a plenitude of free support.

The early technical hurdles were daunting, but as anyone who has ever tried programming knows, translating ideas into software often helps deconstruct processes and structures in productive ways. Like all machines, these primitive ones arrived with their own built-in talents and preferences. The VIM included a sophisticated "shift-register" chip that could be programmed to output a sequence of 1s and 0s (a "pulse train"). This produced a complex buzzing sound whose timbre could be shifted from bumble bee to dragonfly by changing the sequence of binary bits. It's no surprise that brash drones were a ubiquitous presence in Bay Area computer music as well as early computer games.

Some months before my visit to California and exposure to the KIM, I composed a circuit-based work inspired by Christian Wolff's "coordination" notation. *ANDS* was a kind of pre-computer computer music, using discrete logic chips to detect coincidences in the button-presses of two performers playing small four-button keyboards.[11] This was basic Boolean algebra: *if* player #1 *and* player #2 press the same key at the same time, *then* change something. The sound was generated by digital shift-registers that I had hand wired myself. Those on the VIM came ready to roll and my early computer music made much use of the resulting ambiguous pitch centers (more like a gong than a piano note) and shifting overtones. After beginning work with the VIM, I composed *Little Spiders* (1981), which similarly detected coincidences in the actions of two performers and sound generated by shift-registers.[12] When both players press at the same time the same key on a pair of eight-button keyboards, a single corresponding bit is dropped from the sound-generating shift-registers, gradually thinning the electronic texture until it fades to silence, at which point the program either reloads the shift-registers with new bytes or jumps to the next section of the program. This was the direct sound of data: as the sequence of eight bits reduced from lots of ones to all zeroes, the sound fades away, in loudness, rhythmic variety, and timbrel richness.

Two decades later, I learned that the designers of Australia's first computer (CSIRAC, 1949) had attached a speaker directly to its data bus (the pipeline of information moving through the computer) so that the engineers could track a program's progress by ear since the machine had no visual display. If the software was running smoothly, "the Hooter" (as the speaker was dubbed) emitted a stable drone; when it crashed, the sound would vanish. Paul Doornbusch's book on CSIRAC included a CD of this sound, and I was struck by its resemblance to that of my first computer music (and that of my peers using similar resources).[13]

Despite the complexity of their sound, there was a certain sameness to the buzzing pulse-trains of my VIM's shift-registers. It was difficult to program changes in their loudness, which limited the dynamic range of much early computer music. The sound of data itself had a novel appeal, but like Rich with his *Party Planner*, I wanted to connect the computer to the material world of people and things. Since I remained interested in architectural acoustics, the notion of shaping physical space came to mind.

While visiting my architect cousin in Berlin in 1976, I read an article about the use of interior tents to reduce the imposing reverberation in decommissioned German churches and make them more suitable for secular purposes like conferences. I also knew about the concert hall at IRCAM, completed in 1977 (but hidden from me by IRCAM's doorkeepers), which incorporated motorized acoustical panels that could be rotated between reflective and absorptive surfaces to adjust reverberation time in the space. (Sadly, the mechanism was so noisy that this feature could not be used within performances, only to "tune" the hall in advance of a concert.) I harbored a cheeky ambition to beat IRCAM at their own game by engineering an adaptive acoustical space that could be manipulated in real time.

For *Niche* (1978), I scrounged old canvas sails from sail lofts on Cape Cod and Martha's Vineyard and suspended them from multiple points on the ceiling. A performer would be tethered to points of the resulting tent with ropes and pulleys, so that walking would alter the shape and acoustical properties within. A *Pea Soup*-like feedback system reflected these changes as the tent undulated, and the performer's movement "played" the space like an instrument.

For a performance at a Merce Cunningham Studio Event, I sat in a chair to the side— not competing with the dancers—controlling the ropes like a backward marionette. (The rehearsal was unfortunately marred by one of the sail fittings dropping from the lighting grid onto the dance floor during rehearsal. No one was hurt, but I got a serious glare from Cunningham.)

When the VIM entered my life, I embarked on a mechanized version of this idea, programming the computer to control winches that raised and lowered various points in the fabric, replacing the ambulatory performer (Figure 9.3). The computer-generated ticky-buzzy sounds that would change pattern in response to shifts in the

Figure 9.3 Installation view of *Niche* at Media Study/Buffalo, October 1978. Photo by Nicolas Collins.

acoustics as the tent morphed in shape—two interlocked behaviors, a sort of digital-mechanical *Pea Soup*.

Another early computer piece was sparked by a paper I had read about the use of mercury delay lines for computer memory. In the 1951 UNIVAC (a very early mainframe computer), a single bit of data (0 or 1) would be encoded as a pulse of sound, sent via a tiny transducer down a column of mercury inside a short section of pipe; a contact mic picked up the vibration when it reached the other end, a fraction of a second later, converted it back into an electronic signal, and then played it through the transducer for another run. As long as this recycling continued, the state of the bit (1 or 0) would be retained.[14] This convoluted application of sound for data storage prompted me to consider using architectural reverberation as a kind of forgetful computer memory.

I bought a Speak & Spell, just released by Texas Instruments, and a hobbyist interface that transformed the talking toy into a computer-controlled speech synthesizer.[15] In *The Time It Takes* (1980) I encoded words into Morse code, a burst of which I played into the room and then recorded back into the computer as the reverberation died away; the received Morse signals were translated back into English and sent to the Speak & Spell, which pronounced these words aloud. A Dadaist sentence of sorts would emerge as the original dots and dashes overlapped, garbled, and faded away. The idea was poetic enough, but the actual results were just not very interesting, as John Rockwell pointed out in *The New York Times* when I premiered it at The Kitchen in 1980.[16]

I wasn't a great programmer, but some of my mistakes had charming consequences and carried the 1970s ethos of extracting musical content from aberrant behavior of circuits into my less-than-perfect software. In my 1981 composition *Second State* the VIM controlled two filters that modulated feedback between a pair of microphones and speakers: as a filter swept from its lowest to highest frequency, the feedback skipped through the room's overtone series like the call of a bugler.[17] Thanks to a programming error on my part, the routine controlling one filter took slightly longer to execute than the other; as a result, what would have been a rather predictable sequence of feedback chords devolved into a rich sheering texture of distortion and beating patterns as one filter slipped behind the other.

In May 1979, Susan and I both graduated, she in Wesleyan's cardinal-red bachelor's degree cap and gown, me with an MA hood that none of our professorial parents could figure out how to drape. Susan was San Francisco-born and still carried rosy memories of the city (her grandmother had maintained an impressive rose garden in front of their Pacific Heights house, so this "rosy" view was real). I was itchy to make up for what I imagined I had missed at Mills: a community of musicians working with similar technology, close at hand—instead of a long-distance call away. We loaded up our not-entirely reliable Subaru station wagon and hit the road. I was in awe of the flatness of Nebraska, which induced deep sleep in Susan, who had crossed it too many times as a child. She laughed at my native-New Yorker habit of locking the doors whenever we stepped out of the car, even when taking a photo ten feet into the Badlands of South Dakota. The clutch held on just long enough to get us over the hills of San Francisco and down into the Mission, to the third-floor apartment we had sublet from David Behrman. Floating on the cash cushion of a graduation gift from my grandparents, I crunched musical ideas and spent months programming *The Time It Takes*. Susan sampled various temp jobs while contemplating next steps.

A letter arrived from Stuart Marshall. He had just come out and the idea of paying a visit to San Francisco had fresh appeal. Though now living in cosmopolitan London, he was still agog as we drove down Castro. A muscular man walking along in a T-shirt emblazoned "Deliveries Taken in Rear" inspired shock and awe.

"You could never get away with wearing a shirt like that in the UK!" Stuart marveled. "It would have to be something much less obvious like, 'Tradesmen use postern gate.'"

Stuart was our boon companion for several weeks. Days were spent lugging an anvil-sized video Portapak around, helping him film from the Golden Gate Bridge, the Marin Headlands, the external glass elevator of the Fairmont Hotel on Nob Hill. (Stuart was acrophobic. He was working through a lot of things at the time.) One week, there was a flurry of minor earthquakes. Situated on the top floor of a wooden Victorian building, our apartment would gently lurch. One morning, he was writing in his journal at the kitchen table when a tremor hit. His pen skittered up and down on the page like a seismograph—"the best souvenir I could take home from California!" he exclaimed.

Susan and I enjoyed San Francisco and its surroundings; how could we not? The weather, the city, and the surrounding country were all beautiful. The sushi was better and cheaper than in New York. Reagan had yet to be elected, and the extreme wealth disparity that would come to distort all of this was on no one's radar. We both had friends and family scattered down the Peninsula. Sharing drinks with Rich Gold and Marina LaPalma at the Claremont Hotel in the Berkeley Hills one evening, looking out as the sun set over the water, Rich defined the choice between San Francisco and the East Bay: "Would you rather live in Oz, or look at Oz?" Both were beautiful options. Why would anyone leave Greater Oz?

And yet I felt like I'd arrived at a party just as the washing-up had started. The art scene felt cozy but—compared to New York—somehow complacent. Its participants were enthusiastic, but sometimes in an almost axiomatic way, as if all art was great simply because it was art. We weren't intellectual snobs exactly but we were easily bored. Perhaps I was just too much of a New Yorker to take such comfort seriously. If one of us had been enrolled at Cal, or had started a day job in some energetic startup, we might have found some reassuring measure of stress. But after months of asking "should we stay or should we go now?" we packed up the patched-up Subaru and drove back to the grit and grunge of New York.

A Bright Red Electric Guitar

Soon after returning to New York, I ran into composer William Hellermann. We had first met at a concert by Country Joe MacDonald (minus the Fish) that Hellermann had compèred on the Columbia campus when I was in high school. A serious classical guitarist, he had been pursuing his doctorate when he took a deep dive into minimalism. His 1976 composition *Tremble* was a durational tour de force: a guitarist rattles a slide on the headstock of a guitar, then painstakingly shakes it down the strings and body over the course of forty-five minutes. By 1980, I learned as we chatted through the concert intermission, he was the sound curator for PS1, then a decommissioned, semi-derelict public school in Long Island City in its second life as artists' studios and exhibition spaces. Before we parted, he invited me to do a project there.

The large, second-floor former classroom I was given was perfect for testing out a new iteration of *Niche*, my shape-shifting acoustic tent. My original rope and pulley system had turned out to have reliability issues: sparks and surges from the relays and motors sometimes caused the computer program to crash, which left the winches turning until the ropes snapped and the tent came flopping down. For PS1, I needed an artwork that could run for six weeks with little maintenance or supervision, without hurting people or breaking down. So I began experimenting with hydraulics—hanging buckets from ropes that passed through pulleys attached to points distributed across the tent's surface, linking the buckets with hoses, and using sump-pumps to shift the water from one bucket to another. Instead of winches pulling ropes up, gravity pulling the buckets down did the job.

Borrowing a ladder from the ground floor office, I asked if they had any information about the ceiling structure and its weight-bearing capacity. They didn't have an engineering survey at hand, "But there's a guy on the top floor doing something with the ceiling. You might ask him." I knocked on doors until one opened to reveal a luminous rectangle of blue that might have been mistaken for a light panel until a bird flitted across. James Turrell's assistant was in the process of framing a large oculus that had been cut through the roof. He assured me that the ceiling had not come down without considerable effort. Turrell's *Meeting* took six years to finish, but even in its unmanicured beginnings, it was uncannily beautiful.

In earlier versions of the tent piece, fabric movement had been accompanied by jagged, computer noise. In the new installation, *Water Works*, the only sounds were the rustle of fabric and the creaking of pulleys. It was a neatly closed, zero-sum system and ran untroubled for the duration. (Apart from the time I arrived to find the sails untethered and rearranged for an unauthorized fashion shoot. At PS1 no one would interfere with an artist taking the roof off the building, but neither would they stop a photographer and model from dismantling the art.)

The decision to use old sails to build my mutable acoustic structure had been pragmatic: synthetics were taking over the sail market, and canvas ones—large, heavy, and cheap—were easy to find in boatyards. Only later, standing in the defunct classroom at PS1, did I recognize that their stained and stitched surfaces were rife with associations quite distinct from the blazing white architectural interventions that had inspired me in Germany. The ropes, pulleys, and sloshing buckets were similarly allusive. I had set up what I thought of as a dispassionate acoustic experiment, only to find that it was evocative, improbably romantic, possibly even beautiful. (George Lewis told me that standing under the undulating sails made people feel slightly stoned.)

Two years later and one floor down, I returned to PS1 as a participant in "Sound Corridor," a group exhibition organized by Hellermann.[1] This time I hung a garish red pawnshop guitar on the wall with a pair of transistor radios resonating the strings, a clock motor slowly wobbling the whammy bar, and an amp spilling sound into the room. Where visitors to *Water Works* had experienced an almost imperceptible filtering of ambient noise punctuated by the occasional nautical squeak, those standing before *Killed in a Bar* were assaulted by a foggy approximation of No Wave electric guitar (Figure 10.1).

What had happened? Two words: club life.

Every composer of my generation had grown up with rock and roll and Motown. Whatever we chose to study intentionally, pop music remained an inescapable background soundtrack. Many of us tried to maintain a wall between our "serious" musical work and the stuff we listened to for fun. There were concerts you were supposed to *think* about and others you just enjoyed. There was music that was about ideas and other music that was just about the experience. I loved them both, but differently.

Having returned to New York, I found myself attending concerts in the same lofts I had frequented for years, with the same performers and pretty much the same twenty or so people in the audience. The music could be wonderful, but I knew what to expect. Meanwhile, other downtown venues—the kind with bars—seemed to change personality every week. From my first encounters with punk in Newcastle, I had been sympathetic to its repudiation of musical niceties—a ruder echo of the post-Cagean "year zero" radicalism of experimental music two decades earlier. Three years and an ocean away, safety-pin piercings and beer-bottle dodgeball may have faded, as fads do, but punk's musical repercussions were still playing out at CBGB, the Mudd Club, the Pyramid, and 8BC.

Susan and I were living uptown, in the former custodian's apartment of my parents' building on Riverside Drive. In a basement at the bottom of a sixteen-story airshaft, it was predictably dark, but larger than anything we could afford above ground, so we rigged daylight-spectrum bulbs on timers to imitate the transit of the sun, scavenged vintage kitchen cabinets from a dumpster, built bookshelves (Ikea had yet to cross the

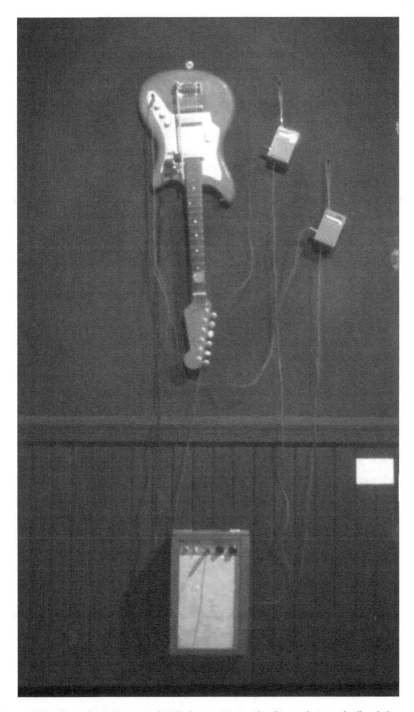

Figure 10.1 Installation view of *Killed in a Bar* in the "Sound Corridor" exhibition, PS1, Long Island City, NY, Spring 1982. Photo by Nicolas Collins.

Atlantic), and settled in. The blessing of our location—a solidly built prewar building with no adjacent apartments—was that I could make noise. The curse was that we were a hundred blocks north of almost everything I wanted to hear: John Zorn, Mission of Burma, Rhys Chatham, Einstürzende Neubauten.

We spent a lot of time on the subway.

It had been five years since the infamous *Daily News* headline "Ford to City: Drop Dead," but not much had changed. Wall Street had yet to receive its full dose of Reaganomic steroids, and most of the city still sported its grizzled *Taking of Pelham 1-2-3* dystopian look. (The *New York Times* recently ran a photo essay about people reading in the city that included a shot of the subway in 1981—grim people bundled up in a car so battered and relentlessly tagged the only legible signage is a lonely advert for Newport 100s.)[2] Rats congregated around the entrance to the 8BC club and waterbugs fell from the weird interior porch roof at CBGBs. Manhattan had none of the beauty or heliotropic pleasures of the Bay Area, but someone was doing something interesting on stage every night, just past the vermin.

One spring evening in 1980, a few days after my less-than-stellar Kitchen concert, I ran into Wesleyan alum Robert Poss, who had performed in the premiere of *Pea Soup* in 1974. "I saw you got panned by the *Times*," he said by way of greeting. "You must be doing something right." Robert was working as a paralegal and gigging around New York with his band, Tot Rocket and the Twins. We began spending time together as he worked to bring my musical tastes up to date with a stack of post-punk vinyl. When Tot Rocket decided to release an EP, he asked me to act as producer. I had no experience recording rock bands, but assumed I was there primarily to serve as an independent pair of ears—someone who could make musical judgments on the basis of what was heard rather than the intra-band social history of how it had come together. We booked time in a cheap eight-track studio with an engineer who sported the then-obligatory Jackson Browne haircut and ended up with the four-song 7" EP *Security Risk* (1981).[3]

Everywhere, it seemed, there was a palpable shift in the ethos of art—a sense that the kind of paring away that had been so fruitful for minimalism and conceptualism may have reached a terminus; an openness to the possibility that maybe there were interesting, worthwhile things to be found in overlooked histories or in jejune pop culture. East Village painters mined the iconography of children's television; architects as patrician as Philip Johnson put silly Chippendale ornaments on skyscrapers. In music I began to see something of the open-hearted refusal of snobbery I had admired in the UK, but this being New York, it took a more abrasive form.

At a Ramones concert a few years earlier, composer Rhys Chatham had an epiphany: the overtone and acoustics experiments he had been pursuing rather clinically as a protégé of composers Maryanne Amacher and La Monte Young were also endemic to the electric guitar. And the sound systems in rock clubs were way better than those in alternative art spaces. Chatham's pivotal 1977 *Guitar Trio* was the result of this realization. It was minimal and maximal simultaneously—three people banging away on the unison-tuned open strings of rock and roll's signature instrument, producing a wall of sound that was to Phil Spector as Richard Serra's Corten-steel slabs were to Louise Nevelson's busy wood constructions.[4]

One of the early musicians to perform in *Guitar Trio* was Glenn Branca. He had come to New York to do experimental theater but threw his lot in with the burgeoning No Wave rock movement and then began composing "symphonies" for orchestras of electric guitars. The first Branca piece I saw live was his *Symphony No. 2*, in which tabletop guitars were played with sticks like hammer dulcimers, accompanied by the percussionist Z'EV flailing away at scrap metal. It was loud. Really loud. I was scheduled to start recording the first LP of my own music the next day, and I was feeling unusually precious about my ears. Noting my discomfort, Phill Niblock handed me two cotton film wipes to roll up and use for earplugs. The sound was undeniably impressive, but I had a negative reaction to what struck me as the most uninteresting, entrenched mannerisms of orchestral music: massed similar instruments and a melodramatic conductor. It felt bombastic—a dramatic experience rather than an auditory one.

Guitars come with a particular kind of aggressive theater, entirely different from that of individuals hunched over tabletops twiddling knobs. Even without antics like windmilling arms, they carry attitude, but they also offer particular sonic properties. Branca and Rhys Chatham exemplified two different approaches to balancing those qualities. Rhys gradually enlarged the size of his guitar ensembles from 3 to 100 (*An Angel Moves Too Fast To See*,1989), not just to make things louder, he explained.

"You know how two electric guitars are twice as loud as one?"

"Yes."

"And three guitars are a little louder than two?"

"Yes."

"Well, a hundred guitars are only a tiny bit louder than four, but they look SO good on stage." In the end, however, Rhys was interested in sound, and theater came second. Branca exemplified the reverse, in my opinion.

A New York native, Rhys had started curating concerts of experimental music at The Kitchen when he was a teenager, but now he shifted his programming to clubland. Since most rock acts didn't go on stage until around midnight, he persuaded the Mudd Club's manager, Steve Maas, to let him book 8 o'clock shows of fringier music. The cover charge and pleasures of a powerful PA went to the artists, Mass got the bar receipts, and, if he was lucky, some patrons of the early show would stick around long enough to be relieved of a second cover when the main act went on. I recall sliding from the thrumming of David Behrman's oscillators to the Japanese New Wave band The Plastics on one blissful night in the early summer of 1981.

Seeing both genres on the same stage made it clear that, however glorious the sounds and structures of experimental music, turning knobs and pressing a few buttons not only lacked the drama of guitar heroism, but also it was opaque. There was no way for the audience to understand the connection between what they saw and what they heard. The music was being performed live, but often might just as well have been a tape in terms of audience perception. This was clearly true of much of my own work: the performers in computer pieces like *Little Spiders* appeared to be touch typing. I knew better than to fancy myself a guitarist. But I thought there might be a strategy that exploited the cultural resonance and sonic vocabulary of the guitar without requiring virtuosic fingers or descending into bombast.

One curious, hidden feature of electronic equipment is that many of its mechanisms are reversible: you can plug a microphone into a headphone jack and hold it to your ear to listen; connect a small speaker to the input of a mixer, and you can use it as a microphone. (Writing my first hacking how-to book many years later, I enshrined "do it backwards" as the First Law of the Avant-Garde.)[5] So I bought a cheap electric guitar and reversed the signal flow: instead of plucking strings whose vibrations would be picked up and sent to an amp, I plugged a radio into the pickup, and let its sounds vibrate the strings. No strumming required.[6]

In my Wesleyan-era befuddlement about how to choose a sound, feedback had come to my aid—the very definition of something from nothing, something that, furthermore, *meant* nothing beyond its own presence. The backwardness of these guitars similarly distanced me from direct control. But perversely, given that the musical application of feedback most people knew came from electric guitars waggled in front of amps, I was now interested in processing found sounds through the strings, rather than generating them directly. I turned to radio—the world's cheapest, lightest, most powerful synthesizer. Like a Cagean jukebox, the dense emporium of New York airwaves offered an infinite variety of sounds—bands, orchestras, spoken words, and (most importantly) things I would never anticipate.

When radio was pumped through the guitar pickups, the listener was enveloped in an ethereal wash of harmonics with hazy traces of the broadcast signal floating free. The effect was similar to shouting into a piano with the sustain pedal down (as in George Crumb's charismatic 1970 composition *Ancient Voices of Children*, in which a performer sings into the piano).[7] In contrast to the completely abstract sonic world created by the long plucked string in *Under the Sun*, I now wanted to use strings to transform sounds that had their own life in the world. Like the old canvas sails, electric guitars were cheap and plentiful, they did the job I wanted, and were evocative of things beyond sound itself.

At PS1, my red guitar was hung like a sculpture, effortlessly responding to the world of radio waves that passed through the building, day after day, week after week. The fact was, however, that it *could* be played, at least with one hand. Chording up and down the neck filtered the resonant frequencies; dampening the strings reduced reverb time; fret-buzz added percussive accents; clamping alligator clips to the strings yielded gamelan-like sounds; adding a distortion pedal emphasized the overtones.

Emboldened by the openness to humor and pleasure that I had witnessed in British experimental music, I expanded the performance possibilities of the backwards guitar by adding a rhythm section of six drumming panda toys (a bargain on Canal Street) and adding switches on the pickguard so a player could select between bears or radio. The bears were absurd but paid lip service to the widely accepted equation "electric guitar + drums = music." Their tinny patterns fingerpicked the strings, while bursts from the radio strummed them (Figure 10.2).

Figure 10.2 Robert Poss performing *Killed in a Bar When He Was Only Three* at The Kitchen, New York, NY, May 12, 1982. Detail of drumming toy pandas in *Killed in a Bar When He Was Only Three*. Photos © Paula Court.

In a quid pro quo for helping with his band's EP, Robert premiered my first composition for backwards guitar, *Killed in a Bar When He Was Only Three* (1982) at The Kitchen in May 1982, concurrent with PS1's "Sound Corridor" installation. (The title of both pieces derived from my older brother's childhood mishearing of the Davy Crockett theme song—the actual lyrics are "killed him a bear when he was only three.") The $100 I gave Robert at the end of the night was, he said, more money than he had ever made on a gig with any of his bands.

I went on to use backwards guitars to process a wide variety of source material in both installations and performances: a swooping oscillator swept the strings' harmonics like a bugle call; drum machines pinged like a cimbalom; spoken voice provided rhythmic phrasing, starts and stops, noise, and pitches. This was analog signal processing with a visceral presence, and served me well for nigh on four decades.

Five months after Robert premiered *Killed in a Bar*, Rhys invited me to open for his band at CBGB. I wasn't sure I was ready for such an auratic venue, but he was insistent. Thirty seconds into my set, I was rewarded with a shout of "get off the stage!" from a large man in front. We were still living uptown, but I had arrived Downtown.

While Susan cataloged Giambologna bronzes and Houdon marbles for an East Side private dealer, I landed a day job with Gene Perlowin Associates (GPA), a small company that designed automation systems to control audio-visual presentations in corporate boardrooms. The concept was way ahead of its time, with a control surface like a paleo-iPad that lit up legends only as needed, so executives could step seamlessly through scripted presentations, even after a two-martini lunch. At the heart of each system was a custom computer. We bought a basic microcomputer board (similar to the KIM-1), then built our own chassis and peripheral circuits to turn on and off lights, close drapes, step through slides, play a videotape, and so on. It was a strange job, but I liked the people I worked with: Gene had been a stage manager for the bespoke corporate theatricals known as "industrials"; Russell Varco was a prescient engineer on the computer-control front; and my friend Jeff Weiss, who got me the job, knew everyone on the downtown club scene (I had met him a few years earlier, when he constituted 33 percent of the audience at a concert I played at Media Study Buffalo). I learned a lot about interfacing computers with the physical world that proved useful in my own work, all while pulling a decent salary from the coffers of Union-Carbide, Bristol Myers, and other Fortune 500 behemoths.

After a couple of years, however, I was lured away to Studio Consultants, a bijou firm run by an older Wesleyan alumnus, Douglas Simon, whose senior thesis had consisted of interviews with Alvin.[8] Studio Consultants designed and outfitted recording studios and, like GPA, appealed to the technologically aspirational—the gear we sold and serviced was the best and was priced accordingly. (Both firms shared the barely secret motto: "we make it cost *more*.") I was Doug's sole employee and thus ran a lot of errands. One of the first was to pick up some speakers from the venerable music emporium Manny's.

When I was a teenager, Manny's had been a temple of desire and humiliation. (Kid to salesman: "Can I try that Stratocaster?" Salesman to kid: "Sure, when you show me $300 in your pocket.") So it was with some trepidation that I entered and asked for the head of pro audio, Doug Cook. Instead of being sneered at or sent back to the loading dock, however, I was greeted with a smile and a handshake. A velvet rope was unhitched. "You're new at Studio Consultants? Come on back. There's something cool I want to show you." The other salesmen and customers in the back room were chivvied out as various wildly expensive gizmos were demoed for me. It was almost an hour before I headed out with the speakers. By this time in my life, I had slept in a room with John McLaughlin, shared undercooked salmon with Claes Oldenburg, and been written about by John Cage, but nothing made me feel more like a member of some elite club than the back room at Manny's.

Other experiences were more sobering. While installing a pair of speakers at A&M Records, I listened to an A&R guy chatting on the phone.[i] While he gabbed on his headset, he was pulling cassette tapes out of a large cardboard box, dropping them one at a time into a boombox, pressing play, listening for five seconds, then hitting eject and tossing the tape into a second box. Again and again and again. Every ten tapes or so, he would fast-forward and listen for another few seconds before adding it to the reject pile. On the phone, meanwhile, he was busy berating program directors at radio stations across Ohio for not pushing a recent single. "I don't understand, haven't I been good to you?" By the time I left, he must have crushed the dreams of a hundred bands.

The Tot Rocket EP joined the dozens being produced by musicians all over Downtown New York. With money from day jobs (many a white-shoe law firm unknowingly underwrote many a struggling band by giving musician-paralegals easy access to copiers and postage meters), bands would rent time in recording studios, send the resulting master tape to a pressing plant in Ohio, get back a thousand records to package in rubber-stamped sleeves, mail them to college radio stations, and drag them to record stores ànd gigs.

If the music you made was something other than pop—something that lay outside the rock/soul/classical/jazz divisions represented by major record labels— there was the added complication of no designated store bins in which to park your record. Then in 1978, Mimi Johnson—whose nonprofit Performing Arts Services managed experimental composers such as Alvin and the other members of the Sonic Arts Union—launched the record label Lovely Music Ltd. For artists, the deal was straightforward: you put up the capital for an initial pressing of the LPs and Lovely handled the job of getting records into stores and the hands of critics. Any royalties that might trickle in were banked against your next album. If the artwork and liner notes were good, the total package could serve as a professional-looking business card with which to impress a concert promoter or reviewer. A half-dozen concerts secured through curators hearing your record would neatly pay off your investment.[ii]

---

[i] "Artists and Repertoire" are the folks in charge of finding new bands for the label.

[ii] Lovely Music had precedent in other artist-run independent labels such as JCOA Records, founded in 1971 by Carla Bley and Michael Mantler primarily as a label for members of the Jazz Composers Orchestra.

In 1982, Ron Kuivila and I agreed to share a Lovely record, one side each. With money earned from building a computer-switching system for Alvin's *Music for Solo Performer*, I bought a Revox B77 stereo tape recorder, which became the heart of a nascent studio for recording my own work. My side of the LP includes *Little Spiders* (my homage to Wolff's coordination scores), the computer-modulated feedback of *Second State*, Robert's performance of *Killed in a Bar When He Was Only Three*, and *Is She/He Really Going Out with Him/Her/Them* (1982), a new piece for computer-automated mixing of found sounds. Ron's side featured one of the first examples of live computer speech processing, pushing the limits of what could be done with slow 8-bit microcomputers, as well as works for a hacked Casio keyboard and the fruits of his ZBS research into using ultrasonic fields to translate movement into sound.

Alternately languid and agitated, the album *Going Out With Slow Smoke* (1982), enjoyed modest airplay on college radio and reasonable press coverage.[9] In a lengthy review for *The Computer Music Journal*, a young Jaron Lanier pointedly observed that while the prevailing approach to computer music was to pursue an "unobstructed channel from musical imagination to actual sounds," Ron and I were "doing the reverse, seeking out the 'corporeal' . . . characteristics of microchips. We do not hear a computer trying to sound like something else, we hear the rarely celebrated intrinsic musical voices of microcomputer technology."[10]

The record stimulated enough concerts that two years later I was able to record a solo LP for Lovely, *Let The State Make The Selection*.[11] In those intervening months, my music became longer and thicker. In *A Letter From My Uncle* (1984), a trio of backwards guitars working with sound sources that included a live vocal performance based on a letter my Chilean uncle had sent in response to my first record. (The performers—Robert Poss, Susan Lyall, and Susan Tallman—would later become three-fifths of the guitar group Band of Susans). Another track mixed multiple recordings from an installation with similar backwards guitars arrayed in the steam room of an abandoned swimming pool at Media Study Buffalo (*A Clearing of Deadness at One Hoarse Pool*, 1983); the shimmer of the sound-resonated strings was now further enveloped in the cathedral-like reverberation of the tiled spaces. A third piece, *Vaya con Díos* (1984), featured my first experiments with live sampling.

Meanwhile, Tot Rocket and the Twins had renamed themselves Western Eyes, and I was asked to produce their first LP in 1984. We recorded the material in professional studios, but to mix the record, I calculated it would be cheaper and more relaxed to buy an eight-track machine and mix at home.[iii] (I was also doing recording and production for a number of other musicians, including Alvin, David Tudor, and improvising cellist

---

iii Hunting for studios in the classified ads in the *Village Voice*, I came across a listing for a twelve-track facility. This was peculiar, as tracks usually came in multiples of eight: eight-, sixteen-, and twenty-four-track recorders were the norm. But I recalled that one company (Scully) had briefly manufactured a transitional *twelve*-track machine. We couldn't afford a sixteen-track studio, but this place was only a little more expensive than the going rate for eight. And it had, in my mind, that "vintage" allure. I visited the studio. At the back of the booth, instead of an obscure relic, stood a standard sixteen-track recorder. The electronics for four of the tracks were blown, I was told, "but

Tom Cora.) Inspired by Martin Swope's adventurous tape manipulations for Mission of Burma, I brought more experimental techniques into the process this time.[12] I called attention to aspects of production normally elided in pop music. A good sounding recording is almost inevitably a fiction: a vocal track recorded on one day, attached to a bass track recorded earlier in the week, in a different room, with a different mic. Reverb is added, voices are doubled, frequencies boosted or diminished, but all to produce the illusion of something that might have happened in another way. On *Western Eyes*, however, noise gates made guitars and voices jump in and out abruptly, adding a jittery insistence to the mix; multiple spring reverbs gave the mix an unreal, spoingy sound; and the balance between instruments and voices shifted disconcertingly. A testament to its time and place, the record's mix of pop sensibility and avant-garde edginess "perfectly reflects the strange ambiguity that is the East Village," according to a reviewer in East Village Eye.[13] And we did it for the cost, Robert pointed out, of a typical record label's pizza allotment.

Not everyone, however, loved guitars. After mixing a record for David Tudor, he suggested I perform at a Merce Cunningham Event but explained rather sheepishly that Cage, as music director of the company, now wanted to hear representative music by composers under consideration.[14] This did not seem like much of an obstacle: John and I had been friendly since my undergraduate days, and I had participated in two Cunningham Events already (Alvin's sferics project in 1974 and the performance of my tent piece, *Niche*, in 1978). I sent over a copy of the freshly pressed *Let The State Make The Selection*, figuring he deserved a proper LP rather than the usual cassette sampler.

Through her gallery job, Susan had contact with an artist couple much in John's thrall, who often cataloged the many forms of his sublimity. "He never telephones at a wrong time," they observed one day. "Whenever he calls it's the *right* time to call." Early one morning, he called while I was in the shower to invite me to come for a chat in the Chelsea loft he shared with Cunningham.

I sat under a small, luminous encaustic Flag painting by Jasper Johns. After some small talk, the conversation turned to music.

"You know, Nic, music can be irritating," John averred.

I agreed.

"Sometimes when I'm in the subway, and someone is playing music too loud, I want to tell them to turn it off."

I sympathized.

"Architecture is not irritating, but music is."

Having been raised by architectural historians, I was inclined to differ, but held my tongue.

"Nic, *your* music is irritating."

This took me completely by surprise. I thought of my work as so amenable compared to his. My music might be boring, or inferior to that of some other composers, or

---

we can still use the other twelve." With a maintenance record like that, I thought, we might start the sessions with twelve tracks but finish with only seven. We walked.

disappointing to those who prefer sweet melodies. But "irritating" seemed excessive, given the diversity of the current scene and John's own reputation.

A bit of prodding on my part revealed the six-stringed culprit. At the New Music America Festival in Chicago the previous summer, John had gotten into a heated public argument over Glenn Branca's *Indeterminate Activity of Resultant Masses*, a work for an orchestra of electric guitars. Later John said, "My feelings were disturbed . . . I found in myself a willingness to connect the music with evil and with power. I don't want such a power in my life. If it was something political it would resemble fascism."[15] For my generation, electric guitars were a default instrument, like pianos for previous composers. But for John, the ease with which they could turn anthemic or bombastic seemed to threaten a dismantling of thought under the power of emotion.

The LP I had sent included two compositions that featured my backwards guitars, but on listening, the instruments are almost unrecognizable—never strummed, they functioned merely as spooky resonators. The cover, however, by the painter Kazuhide Yamazaki, incorporated a red guitar, and the back showed a photo of musicians, guitars in hand. I suspect the damage was done iconographically before the needle ever touched the vinyl. I wasn't tapped for another Cunningham project until both Merce and John had passed away. I sometimes wonder what would have happened if I had sent a white-label cassette instead of that colorful record.

Interlude

33 1/3 RPM

1

Shortly after my first record was released, my father was interviewed at home by the BBC. As the crew was packing up, he pulled the proud-dad card and dropped my LP on the turntable. After several minutes, he noticed that the speaking voices on one of the tracks sounded odd. He went over to his record player and saw that the speed was set to 45 rpm, not 33 1/3.

Hearing this story, I was naturally appalled. "Dad, you didn't really play my record for the BBC at the wrong speed!"

"Yes, but don't worry, it didn't sound so different than it usually does. Anyway, the crew was packing up pretty quickly and this way they could hear the whole record before they left. You should consider this when you have to make a presentation to busy people."

2

Proud of my status as a published composer, I sent a copy of that record to my uncle in Chile, a businessman who managed the family's various agricultural holdings. The post-Cagean avant-garde was hardly his bailiwick, but as a good uncle, he strove to find meaning in my gift. He wrote back thanking me and suggested that I consider making records to increase milk production in dairy cows. His response became the libretto for a later piece, "A Letter From My Uncle," included on my subsequent LP. By the time he received that one, he no longer owned a record player, so I have no idea how he would have responded.

3

Through Susan's first job in New York with a private dealer of Renaissance and Baroque art, we became friends with the eminent art historian Sir Francis Watson, then Surveyor of the Queen's Works of Art. Francis was a delight—generous, witty, and a font of brilliant stories on subjects ranging from the Cambridge spies (most of whom he knew well) to ormolu bronzes. We got along so well that I was moved to present him with a copy of my record. Within days of his return to London, I came to regret this as a social faux-pas—it was unlikely to be the kind of music he would enjoy, but he was far too polite to refuse carrying it across the Atlantic. When he was next in New York, I apologized for saddling him with it.

"Oh no, my boy, I quite appreciated your thoughtfulness."

I was surprised. "Really? You listened to it?"

"Not exactly," Francis explained. "You see, it used to be that when a party had gone on long enough and I wanted my guests to leave I would pull out the Hoover [vacuum cleaner] and start cleaning. Now I just put on your record. It does the trick and it's much less work. Thank you!"

4

With a record under my belt, I joined the music rights organization BMI. Every year I would receive a cursory statement saying there had been "no monitored airplay" and therefore no payment, despite the fact that I had playlists from college radio stations attesting to significant exposure on alternative radio. (Once I actually ranked higher than Mick Jagger's solo album on the charts of a college station in the southwest, though that was admittedly a particularly undistinguished Jagger record.)

So I was surprised when one day an actual check arrived in the mail with a statement attesting to significant quarterly airplay royalties for a track on my first Lovely record. It became apparent that they had confused my composition *Is She/He Really Going Out With Him/Her/Them?* with Joe Jackson's modest 1978 hit "Is She Really Going Out With Him?" (both titled after the memorable opening line of the Shangri-Las' 1960s hit, "Leader of the Pack.")[1] I waited for a corrected statement or request for return of funds, but it never came. Thank you, Joe.

5

For all the convenience of CDs, MP3s, and streaming, I have never given up my vinyl. Like Nick Hornby's sad-sack protagonist in *High Fidelity*, I could happily reorder my LP collection by date of acquisition, tracing the history of my loves from the British invasion, to R&B, psychedelia, Miles Davis, American experimentalists, punk, and early hip-hop.[2] LPs are so much more "thingy" than CDs, never mind digital audio files. A record and its cover evoke all kinds of incidents connected to the history of my ownership (the notes on CDs are in fonts too small to be read for pleasure, more like the warnings on medicines). There are those records I remember listening to in high school, my head in the sweet spot between the stereo speakers or squeezed by heavy headphones, scrutinizing the liner notes closely enough to elevate the activity into an audio-visual experience. Sometimes the surface of the vinyl seemed to contain visual messages. Doug Simon, my boss at Studio Consultants, once told me of a veteran mastering engineer he knew who could *read* the grooves on a record—he could tell by looking what kind of instruments were playing where on the disc, and he had cut enough masters of classical music that he could identify specific Beethoven symphonies by the scribed patterns.[3]

6

In Warsaw in 1976, I met a young Dutch new music fan, my age. He was not a musician; he just loved itchy contemporary music. Sitting together at a sidewalk café, I asked him how he came to be drawn to such esoteric fare. He explained that as a restless teenager in the sleepy provincial town of 's-Hertogenbosch, he would shoplift records. He started with discs he wanted—the Rolling Stones, Led Zeppelin, and so on—and then started taking commissions, stealing on order for risk-averse peers. Finally, he began pulling records at random, just for the thrill. He would compete with his friends to see who could lift the most on a single visit to the store ("we were juvenile delinquents, I think you'd say"). One day his loot included a random LP by Mauricio Kagel—an iconoclastic Argentinian composer who had been working in Germany since the late 1950s. He had no idea who Kagel was when he put it on the turntable that night, lit up a joint, and had his mind blown. The next day he went back, slipped a second Kagel record under his coat, and finally got caught. The cops took him to the station and called his father, who decided to teach him a lesson by leaving him there till morning. All night long, fragments of the music ran through his head. Released the next day, he started paying for records and going to concerts (where others might have shunned the genre for life, lest it trigger PTSD).

7

Doane Perry joined my freshman class at Collegiate School in the fall of 1968, transferring in from another private school in the city. We quickly bonded over shared obsessions with music: I was dabbling with various instruments, still trying to find my place; he was a drummer, serious enough to be playing in a band that made its rounds of church basement dances for high-school kids. Like me, he had been allocated the tiny former maid's room in his family's sprawling apartment. On my first visit, I noticed that he had covered every square inch of the walls with record jackets, cut open and flattened into 12" x 24" panels. Records were expensive, precious objects we handled with care and respect, and the information on the covers—now unreadable unless at eye level—valued as much as the music itself. I was stunned. (Years later, Christian Marclay's *cadavres exquis* of record jackets and floors tiled with LPs brought back memories of Doane's den.)

"There's something I have to play for you. Come here." We went to the living room, and he pulled an LP from the shelf containing his parents' collection and dropped it on the family turntable. The muffled sounds of a party were soon joined by an undulating flute, tuneless and lacking any apparent rhythm, occasionally punctuated by a slap on a bongo drum. After a *long* time (probably no more than thirty seconds), a deep male voice intoned in the grave manner of TV newscasters of the time, "These are the sounds of hippies on LSD . . . ." The record was one of many being produced for nervous parents, harbingers of DARE programs to come. Doane turned to me and exclaimed, "This music is incredible! What is this 'LSD' and where can I buy it?"

11

Devil's Music

Cage may have abhorred electric guitars, but he was not entirely averse to the technology of popular culture. *Cartridge Music,* written in 1960, used a device almost everyone had—the phono cartridge in a record player—and asked performers to *play* it. This recasting of a product intended for passive consumption into an active and adaptive instrument resonated with me. Growing up in an apartment with no piano, my brother and I tinkered with the kiddie record player, and it was through records that my burgeoning musical identity took shape.

On my transistor radio, the disc jockeys had played songs much like museum curators hang paintings: each in its own space, clearly labeled, and selected to serve program needs. Then the "concept album" came along, employing songs as strategic units within larger compositional structures controlled by the band and its producers—consumers and DJs were expected to drop the needle every eighteen minutes now instead of every three. But in the mid-1970s, DJs in discotheques broke up the album and removed the silent trenches between songs, using sequencing and elision to manipulate the dancefloor, shifting the tempo and mood in response to the crowd.

By the end of that decade, hip-hop DJs were elevating the humble record player into a virtuosic musical instrument—not just sequencing tracks, but scratching, back-cueing, and cutting between multiple turntables. Records were now source material for improvisation and composition. "DJs start out as collectors," George Lewis points out, and more explicitly than any other category of instrumentalist; they start from *listening,* rather than playing, and their performances are built on the experience of hearing records rather than by reading scores.[1] Each DJ tailored mass-produced records into something personal—not just to themselves, but to the audience as well. Early turntablists dazzled me with their seeming ability to climb inside my head and replay my musical memories, isolating fragments like I might in a dream, and then creating unexpected variations from overriding, with the skill of jugglers, the default playback.

In *Wildstyle,* Charlie Ahearn's 1983 film on hip-hop culture in New York, there's a lovely scene of Grandmaster Flash (Joseph Robert Sadler) demonstrating his technique. He's standing in his mother's kitchen, with three turntables and an audio mixer balanced on a sheet of plywood over the sink. He back-scratches for a few beats, then crossfades between two discs as he turns his body around 360 degrees. His fade is impeccable, but his rotation is slow and self-conscious. Clearly, this bit of theater was something that Flash—a technically oriented guy who had hacked his mixer with a switch to allow fast cutting between turntables—had prepared for the film shoot. For me, that scene captures the moment when the DJ came down from the booth and became a performer on stage.[2]

The repurposing of a household appliance as a musical instrument, the reimagining of familiar musical material, the development of performance techniques to coax new sounds out of old ones—this is what brought me to the Roxy, a Chelsea roller-disco that programmed hip-hop acts one night a week, more than the rapping or break dancing. As with the electric guitar, I could see that ideas and phenomena I had been smitten with in the niche world of experimental music were erupting across contemporary culture, and I was thrilled. But just like when I was an adolescent failing at electric guitar, it was difficult to see how I could participate, beyond standing admiringly in the crowd at a club. Being a good DJ required innate talent, assiduous practice, pounds of equipment, and a massive record collection—all of which I lacked. Great DJs have an encyclopedic knowledge of recorded music (which I might have managed) but they also have brilliant instincts about what they want to hear at any given moment—exactly the kind of impulse whose absence had governed my path to date. I knew my limits.

So I tried to separate my musical desires from the specific equipment and techniques of DJs and reduced my ambition to finding pathways to three things: self-generating source material (in lieu of records), a means of rapid cutting from source to source (like cross-fading), and techniques for signal transformation (like scratching).

My work with the backwards guitars had reignited my love affair with radio. In the eclectic mood of the 1980s, radio served me much as the physics of feedback had done in my more ascetic 1970s—something already in the world that was amenable to alteration while also telling you something about where you were at a particular moment in time. It could be counted on to provide twenty-four hours of *something*, and weighed much less than crates of LPs. Just as the guitar had bridged the eternal truths of physical acoustics and the hot-moment temporality of club sets, radio offered a way to merge the hands-off detachment of stochastic composition with the hands-on virtuosity I admired in the DJs.

My first solution to intercutting lay in the computer-controlled mixer I had developed for my 1982 composition *Is She/He Really Going Out With Him/Her/Them.*[3] (The title was a nod to the opening line of the Shangri-La's 1964 hit "Leader of the Pack" as well as to the mixer's musical matchmaking.) The computer detected beats in the sound material it was fed—drum machines, tape loops of pop song snippets, cassettes of people speaking—and could cut between sixteen channels whenever two came into rhythmic sync, like a beat-matching DJ with eight times the usual number of arms.[i]

---

[i] I subsequently used this system to mix Robert Poss's *Western Eyes* album (Western Eyes, *Western Eyes* [Trace Elements Records LP, 1984]), as well as my LP of *Devil's Music* (Nicolas Collins, *Devil's Music* [Trace Elements Records LP, 1985]). I built a variation on this mixer for Alvin Lucier for a revival of his *Music for Solo Performer*; the device detected patterns in his brainwave activity and channeled

A route to scratch-like signal processing lay in the emerging technology of samplers and digital delays. Per Moore's Law, the sophistication and speed of ICs had expanded exponentially, enabling by the early 1980s the development of devices that could digitally record sound and play it back later, with some optional modest transformations. Samplers stored the digitized sounds (violins, drums, sound effects, etc.) in computer memory, backed up onto external drives. Using piano-style keyboards, these samples could be played back, transposed across a range of pitches—a digital update to the tape-based Mellotron that gave us the wobbly strings on the Beatles' *Strawberry Fields*. (Salesmen liked to demo their wares by playing *Jingle Bells* with samples of barking dogs.) Samplers, however, were expensive: in 1979 the state-of-the-art Fairlight CMI cost $24,000, almost as much as a fully equipped synthesizer studio. Stevie Wonder and The Residents could afford the $10,000 E-Mu Systems Emulator two years later, but even Ensoniq's Mirage, introduced in 1984 for $1,700, was beyond the reach of many musicians.

Far more reasonable were digital delays, which recorded short snippets of sound to digital memory and spat it out to produce an echo effect. Delays had no keyboards, so they could not be "played" like a conventional instrument, and no disc drives, so the audio sample vanished the moment the power was shut off. The length of the delay was limited by the high cost of memory, and early devices topped out at a quarter-second or so—just enough to emulate the tape-head echo on my old Tandberg tape recorder. If you mixed a bit of the delayed signal back into the input, you could make the echo repeat in a diminishing ricochet, and if you disabled new recording while continuing to play back what was already in memory, the last sounds would repeat endlessly in a short loop. Starting with these basic variations, engineers and musicians invented ways to use digital delays to modulate pitch, approximate reverberation, and produce other effects.[ii]

In 1983, Electro-Harmonix, a manufacturer of guitar effect boxes, introduced its "16-Second Digital Delay" pedal. On a tip from composer Gerald Lindahl, studio director at PASS (Public Access Synthesizer Studio), I knocked on the company's

---

the amplified alpha waves among sixteen channels of percussion resonated by the low-frequency bursts. Alvin gave a few performances using this in the early 1980s but, despite having anticipated a future role for a computer when he scored the piece in 1965, was never really comfortable with it and chose to use a new title for the version released on Nonesuch, so as not to confuse it with his original composition (Alvin Lucier, "Music For Alpha Waves, Assorted Percussion and Automated Coded Relays," On *Imaginary Landscapes* [Nonesuch Records, 1989]) Two decades later I encountered a young British composer almost sharing my name (Nicholas Collins, with an "h") who had written software to perform similar automatic crosscutting on digital music files (see Chapter 21).

[ii] These effects were at once novel and primordial. In the 1950s, recording engineers used tape-head echo to "warm" vocals and instruments that had been recorded in acoustically dead studios, mimicking (crudely) the reverberation heard inside a proper concert hall. Soon after, the rhythmic fake-reverb echo of head-delay on rockabilly vocals became a recognizable effect in its own right, and the band would often match its playing tempo to the echo time of the tape. A few companies saw the market for a tape recorder stripped down to the essential elements needed for the echo effect alone: three heads, a motor, and a loop of tape that circled endlessly (the best-known of these was the "Echoplex"). Early digital delays imitated and eventually replaced those tape-based systems, bringing us to a point where we now have a digital device emulating an analog delay derived from a tape recorder adapted as a substitute for a natural acoustical phenomenon. Whew!

factory door on West 22nd Street, spoke the words "Gerry sent me," handed over $250 in cash, and walked away with my delay. It could loop, reverse, overlay, pitch-shift, and otherwise rework sound material caught on the fly, though the name was misleading: to squeeze sixteen seconds into the available memory, the high-frequency content of the sound was reduced to the point that it sounded like speaking through a wool scarf (longer sampling time and higher bandwidth demanded more memory, which was still expensive). If you ran the box at its maximum (barely hi-fi) bandwidth, those sixteen seconds shrank to one. (This tradeoff helps explain the proliferation of muffled drone music in the mid-1980s.) Electro-Harmonix boxes also had a reputation for unreliability, perhaps because the assembly was often done by young musicians being paid in product vouchers rather than cash—when I first opened up my delay I was greeted with the pong of pot smoke and a sticker with the scribbled message: "Inspected by #7. Rock!" A year later Electro-Harmonix gussied up its 16-Second Delay with some new features under the name "Super Replay," and I returned to the factory door and bought two of those (Figure 11.1).

Devil's Music (1985) pulled my three post-DJ goals together: the performer sweeps the radio dial, sampling sounds, then looping, layering, and de-tuning them. All the material comes from transmissions occurring in the AM, FM, shortwave, and public-service (police, fire, etc.) radio bands at the time of the performance. Nothing

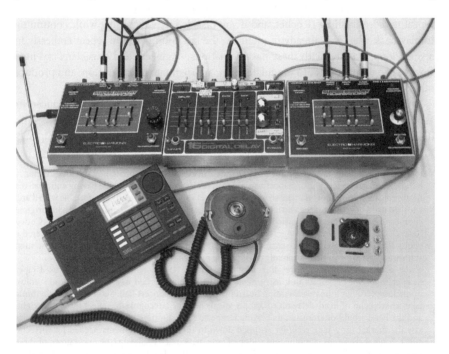

Figure 11.1 The technical setup for *Devil's Music* (1985), showing hacked Electro-Harmonix Super Replays and 16-Second Digital Delay, Panasonic multi-band radio, cuing headphone, and homemade pitch controller. Photo by Nicolas Collins.

is prepared in advance. I bought a multi-band radio with digital tuning, and during sound check, I would assign different types of stations (news, dance, classical) to different preset buttons.[iii] Holding a cueing headphone to my ear, I'd silently preview potential selections while cutting between stations on the radio like a DJ flipping through a bin of records.

When I heard a sound I wanted, I'd grab a second of it with one of the Electro-Harmonix loopers. I modified the boxes with a simple "stuttering circuit" that re-rhythmizes the samples by retriggering or reversing the loops in response to accents in the audio being sampled—in this case the ongoing flow of sound from the radio, which I hear over my cuing headphone but remains inaudible to the audience. The material the audience *doesn't* hear governs the phrasing of the sounds they *do* hear, disrupting the otherwise annoying periodicity of short loops. This erratic gait came to define the core phrasing of *Devil's Music*. A short loop that repeats is instantly (and often annoyingly) recognizable to the ear, but by shifting the start and end points and occasionally reversing the loop, you can obfuscate its brevity and subvert the periodicity—a thrifty solution to the high cost of memory, but also evocative of the signature sounds of turntable scratching and sampler stammering of early hip-hop. Now I had my system for a DJ-manqué, a Discless Jockey (Figure 11.2).

Layering the three Electro-Harmonix boxes produced a jittery mix of shards of music, speech, and radio noise—sometimes phasing languidly, sometimes pulsing rhythmically, sometimes careening frantically—a patchwork quilt stitched from scraps of local airwaves. A typical performance might start with a rhythmic loop sampled from a dance station; after a half-minute or so, I'd add a wobbly chord lifted from an easy-listening station, or a vocal phrase grabbed from a news bulletin or taxi dispatcher. The success of any given performance depended on the number, variety, and character of available stations (New York City was easier than rural Belgium), as well as dumb luck.

Every iteration was different, topical, local. Tours across Europe strung languages together like a charm bracelet, and samples often shimmered with that halo of ring modulation that came as a bonus with mistuned shortwave stations that dominated broadcasts in the East Bloc. I felt the constant tension of searching for the right sound to drop in at the right time. And there was always that transformative moment when the audience realized what was happening: a word from a local newscaster or the score from that day's football match, hinting that this was not off-the-rack electronic noise but made-to-measure out of the here-and-now, just for them.

As a student at Wesleyan I had accepted a rich musical smorgasbord (Stravinsky, Sonic Arts Union, Sharda Sahai, Sam Rivers) heaped on my plate, but, like a finicky

---

[iii] In the 1950s, the automobile industry developed radios with pushbuttons that could be tuned to individual stations. With the advent of digital chips, automatic scanning between stations replaced the manual tuning of each preset. The first car I ever drove with such a radio was a rental we picked up for a trip from New York to Cape Cod. As we left the city, I set it on scan: five seconds of rock, short silence, five seconds of news, short silence, five seconds of easy listening, and so on in an ever-changing sequence of musical bursts. Five hours later, crossing the bridge over the Cape Cod Canal, I commented to Susan how surprised I was that Detroit would include such an avant-garde feature. With a look of infinite patience, she explained, "I think most people settle on a specific station after one sweep through the dial."

Figure 11.2 Performance of *Devil's Music* at De IJsbreker, Amsterdam, November 7, 1985. Photo by Gerda van der Veen.

four-year-old, I worked to keep the lumps separated. In *Devil's Music*, as with the backwards guitars, I played with my food. I was right on schedule. Appropriation and recontextualization were everywhere. John Zorn's *Cobra* (1984) introduced cartoon-like musical quotations evoking his hero, Carl Stalling (house composer for Looney Tunes), to his otherwise austere game-based improvisation. Jean-Michel Basquiat brought graffiti into the gallery. Art Spiegelman and RAW magazine elevated the comic to the status of the graphic novel. *Devil's Music* also defied easy categorization: it snatched material created by others, then reworked it with circuitry that had learned its tricks from hip-hop. Rivaling guitars, it gave audiences the kind of accessible entry point that had been missing from the experimental music I had followed in the 1970s. It even had a beat (of sorts) for the first time in my music—described by Robert Poss as "an intro that never settles into a groove."[4]

I released an LP of *Devil's Music* in 1986 on Robert Poss's Trace Elements label, which gave me expanded access to pop press and radio play (sales profits also went directly into my pocket, instead of being banked by Lovely against my next record).[5] Instead of trying to reproduce a typical live performance with its shifting styles of source material, I focused on two record-friendly genres: the A side was drawn almost entirely from dance music, insistent rhythms disrupted with fragments of radio announcers in multiple languages as vocal jabs; the B side was limited to easy-listening and classical, resulting in a Bryars-esque homage to phase music.

Given the dozens of micro-samples of hot dance music on the A side, I fantasized that DJs might buy it for breaks to drop into dance mixes. I took it to a few specialty shops in Manhattan where break-beat records were sold, but there were few takers. In the 2000s, however, I heard that used copies were changing hands for serious money in German techno swap meets.

Two years later, after the LP was released, for the cassette label Banned, I produced a tape composition that spliced together excerpts from dozens of *Devil's Music* performances across Europe and the United States.[iv] The result was a twisted radio tour from Budapest to California titled *Real Landscape* (a nod to Cage's *Imaginary Landscape No. 4* for twelve radios), and it was packaged in road maps that the label owner extracted from AAA offices throughout southern California under the subterfuge of planning an upcoming road trip.[6]

In 2020, *The Wire* magazine ran an "Invisible Jukebox" with speculative fiction author William Gibson. They played a series of recordings, including the *Devil's Music* LP, and asked him to comment with no information given on what he was hearing:

That music suggests to me the way I would imagine that an emergent sentient AI would be putting its world together, because it starts out sort of purely metronomic. And a minute later, it's becoming actually organic, and it's making echoes within itself. So it's modeling a very interesting kind of complexity that I would assume doesn't actually require human intervention. You could, with the right algorithms—one of my magic hand kind of words—you can have a program that could do that all day.[7]

[iv] There was something perverse about releasing on cassette a work rooted in vinyl fetishism, but this may have been the harbinger of a trend: in 2002, I was a judge in the first Beige World Cassette Tape Jockey Championship in Chicago.

12

Planes, Trains, and Step-Down Transformers

In the spring of 1983, Susan and I grabbed our friends Amy Bernstein, Robert Poss, and Susan Lyall to act as witnesses and eloped to Essex, Connecticut, returning to our basement digs before the day was out. A year later, we moved into a loft on Bleecker Street a few doors from the Bowery in what was then a non-neighborhood wedged between the East Village, the West Village, the Lower East Side, and Little Italy. Local landmarks included a homeless men's shelter, several religious social services, and a seemingly empty warehouse where once a month a dozen black Lincoln Town Cars would pull up and park, each chauffeured by muscle in a shirt-and-tie combo straight out of *The Godfather*. Susan, now in grad school at Columbia, was faced with the reverse commute between downtown and Morningside Heights, but the rest of our life was now walkable: SoHo galleries a few blocks in one direction; the barely business East Village galleries a few blocks in the other; CBGB mere feet from our door.

Occupying half of the second floor of a narrow building, our loft's period charms included a patched and collapsing tin ceiling, unreliable artist-installed plumbing, and wonky interior walls that stopped one foot below the ceiling (perhaps out of respect for building code, or more likely because the previous tenant was too lazy to fill above the eight-foot sheetrock panels). Attesting its prior use in a small garment factory, the floor had a central runway of hardwood and, three-quarters of an inch down to either side, a softwood subfloor where the machines had stood. Both were in poor condition and painted the same dyspeptic yellow as the walls. The kitchen, such as it was, sat on a patchwork of plywood scraps laid loosely over the joists. (The freezer of the ancient refrigerator had solidified into a solid block of ice that took two days to defrost to the point that we could see what it held, which was, of course, a bag of ice.)

Having ponied up our entire net worth for a fixture fee that was (as usual) entirely out of scale with the value of the actual fittings, we set about repairing and renovating to the best of our abilities.[i] We rolled white paint over yellow, topped off the stunted walls, ripped out redundant electrical wiring, nailed down full sheets of plywood and a floor of checkerboard vinyl tiles in the kitchen. I removed yards of gas pipe that crisscrossed the loft (a legacy of the long-gone clothing presses) and reconfigured the scraps to make a more efficient line from the meter to the stove and water heater. Our

---

[i] Fixture fees were a New York institution, whereby incoming tenants paid ostensibly for whatever improvements, renovations, and appliances the outgoing tenant had provided, but in reality, for the right to take over the lease.

upstairs neighbor-cum-building-super, Andy Hetzko, was horrified, but my father had taught me basic plumbing well, and nothing blew up.

Typical of the neighborhood's halfhearted loft conversions, our building had no intercom. Instead, each resident dropped a wire out the front window and connected it to a self-purchased pushbutton haphazardly nailed to a board by the front door, their name scribbled below. The upstairs end of the wire was hooked up to a buzzer or, in our case, a toy ray gun. When a visitor rang (or ray gunned), you'd open the window and throw down a key ring. At some point, our board, with its flaking red paint, peeling labels, and cacophony of wires, caught the eye of German photographer Carin Drechsler-Marx, who included the photo in her 1988 book, *Ich Liebe New York* (Figure 12.1). By chance, the book was printed by a Dortmund firm where German sound artist Jens Brand was working. Jens, who had visited us on Bleecker Street, recognized the doorbell as the book rolled through the press, and put aside a copy for us—our union immortalized in Andy Hetzko's imperfect spelling, "Collins—Tallmen."[1]

The art world of the 1980s was not yet the oligarch-driven glamourfest it later became, but it was already a place where a twenty-four-year-old might find herself (as Susan did) in the back of a limo commiserating with a collector about "how little a million dollars can buy these days" before returning home to repair a hole in the ceiling with duct tape. Without question, we were privileged youth and knew it, but we were also always on the lookout for a bargain: cadging invitations to after-opening dinners at restaurants we could never afford, downing an endless supply of lukewarm vodka in plastic cups (downtown) and *methode champenoise* in wine glasses (uptown).

After an article in *The New York Times* alerted our circle of cash-strapped gallery assistants to the free hors d'oeuvres available during Happy Hour at the classier hotel bars in midtown Manhattan, the list became the founding document of a mobile Friday-night "Hors d'Oeuvres Club."[2] A four-dollar martini at the Drake was a bargain when accompanied by unlimited wontons, empanadas, shrimp skewers, and pigs-in-blankets. Unlike the scruffier downtown musician set, the gallery boys and girls looked like they belonged, and no one ever gave us the stink eye.

Performing around town did not, of course, provide a living wage. Clubs were alcohol-driven business enterprises where performers were paid a percentage of the door, seldom exceeding $100, and the fees at not-for-profit spaces remained frozen at pre-Reagan levels. (In 1979, when I played my first concert at Phill Niblock's Experimental Intermedia Foundation, I was paid $200, which covered two months' rent in Middletown; four decades later, a concert at Phill's still paid $200, not quite covering the weekend's taxis and meals when I flew in from Chicago.) Grants from funding agencies such as the New York State Council on the Arts provided periodic, treasured infusions of cash, but could not be relied upon to cover the base costs of rent and groceries.

To make ends meet, my peers and I combined day jobs (with flexibility and perks weighed against wage—both Gene Perlowin Associates and Studio Consultants balanced the two quite nicely) with touring abroad. European nations, as I had discovered on the Watson, believed the state should play a role in supporting the arts. The kind of art that got supported varied, depending on which side of the Iron Curtain

Figure 12.1 Author's doorbell panel at 17 Bleecker Street, New York, 1987. Photo by Carin Drechsler-Marx.

you were on, but the idea that visual and performing artists represented a nation's values and were therefore worthy of government funds thrived both East and West.

After my casual understudy role in David Tudor's *Rainforest* in Paris, I was invited to join Tudor's Composers Inside Electronics ensemble. Following an audition of sorts at an installation at the Neuberger Museum at SUNY Purchase in 1981, David asked me to participate in a realization of *Rainforest* at the Stedelijk Museum in Amsterdam, in conjunction with concerts in Amsterdam and Utrecht that, in the style of Lucier's road shows during my student days, featured works by the members of the group as well as Tudor himself. This was my first trip back to Europe since returning from my Watson travels in 1977, and I schmoozed promoters wherever I could, though it was clear that most venues wanted to see more of a track record—discography, playbills, and so on—than the Centre Culturel had done.

Two years later, however, the phone rang as we were having breakfast on Bleecker Street. Dutch composer Michel Waisvisz asked if I would be interested in joining in a small tour being organized by STEIM, the music research foundation I had tried and failed to visit in 1977, of which he was now director. In a testimony to the distribution network of Mimi Johnson's Lovely Music label, *Going Out With Slow Smoke* had somehow caught his attention. (Years later Michel told me that if I hadn't picked up the phone, he was going to ring Ron Kuivila, on the B side of the LP, in which case our lives, and those of our children-to-be, would have been substantively different.) No fees were mentioned, but STEIM would cover my flights, hotels, and meals. I replied with an enthusiastic "yes." The tour kicked off with lecture/demos at a music trade show in Rotterdam, followed by concerts in the remote, picturesque town of Middelburg.

Setting up my gear in the spectacular medieval market hall, I discovered that my Electro-Harmonix 16 Second Delay would not turn on. Like all American gizmos at the time, it operated on 120 volts, and Holland, like the rest of Europe, has a 240-volt standard. STEIM had provided a converter transformer to cut the Dutch input voltage exactly in half, but it was delivering an output slightly less than 120 volts, and the delay's poorly designed power supply couldn't handle this shortfall.

Foolishly, I had brought no backup devices and could perform nothing without that one box. But I reasoned that in a small community like Middleburg the electrical grid would rise slightly in voltage as people turned off their lights and went to bed, causing the transformer's output to creep up proportionally. I asked to be put at the end of the program. Sure enough, I watched on a meter as the voltage slowly lifted from 110 to a proper 120 over the course of earlier sets of the evening. I hit the stage at 11 p.m. in a dark town and everything worked.

The rest of the sets featured Dutch artists I would later come to know as core members of Amsterdam's small community of experimental musicians, many of whom had long relationships with STEIM. Here I witnessed an early performance of Michel's "Hands," a gestural controller that became, over the next twenty years, one of the most iconic artist-developed electronic instruments.[3] The audience was small but surprisingly warm. Our friend Susan Lyall—a Canadian with a Dutch mother—had tipped off a cousin our age in Middleburg, who showed up at the gig with a bunch of very punk friends and her pet rat, which walked back and forth across their shoulders during the concert. The STEIM crew were impressed that a New Yorker would know *anyone* in rural Netherlands, much less anyone this hip.

We drove north to Amsterdam for concerts at the IJsbreker, an established venue for contemporary music, followed by a splendid after-party. I felt an instant connection with the STEIM crowd and regretted anew that I hadn't managed to get past their door in 1977, when I was searching for a European outpost of experimentalism just like this, familiar yet different (like the English, but with more electronics). Before leaving for the airport, I shamelessly suggested to Michel that I'd be happy to participate in future events. He laughed. The festival, he explained, was a swan song: STEIM had been notified by the Ministry of Culture that their funding would be discontinued at the end of the year. "We decided that instead of trying to make our grant last as long as possible," he explained, "we'd spend it all on this tour—a big goodbye party." (Despite the budgetary vagueness of Michel's initial phone call, I left the Netherlands with a healthy stack of guilders in my wallet.)

Next fall, however, Michel called again. The ministry had been so impressed by STEIM's tour that they reversed their decision and renewed funding. So he invited me for a symposium and more concerts. Thus began a long, close relationship with the man and the institution that would eventually prompt us to move to Amsterdam. In the short term, I returned every year or so for projects in the Netherlands and as a base for other work around Europe.

It was at a STEIM event in 1985 that I met Peter Cusack. Peter was a London-based guitarist, a few years older than me, who had been a founding member of the London Musicians Collective and Bead Records—an organization and independent label for improvised music, respectively. He was also a keen recordist, spending hours in inhospitable locations recording both wildlife (especially birds) and industrial environments. In the late 1970s he had studied electronic music at the Institute of Sonology at Utrecht University and later worked with STEIM to develop his hardware system for performing live mixing of his environmental recordings, often triggered from his guitar. (This "Gate Crasher" bore a resemblance to the mixer I built for *Is She/He Really Going Out With Him/Her/Them?*, absent the computer.) Peter was the first improvising musician to invite me to perform together, a year later, in a cold, damp room above the vast shed in which the London Underground washed their trains. Given my available resources at the time, I can only imagine that I tried live processing of Peter's guitar through the boxes used in *Devil's Music*, and threw in a solo composition to round out my contribution to the evening. My strongest memory is of the warm, welcoming pub across the street, from which it proved hard to retrieve our small but friendly audience after the interval. Peter and I have continued to perform, record, and tour together to this day (Figure 12.2).

There was an accepted NY protocol for self-organized European concert touring: first, you snare a festival big enough to pay your round-trip airfare; then you write everyone you know on the continent to ask about additional gigs that paid at least enough to cover the train costs from the previous venue and a night in a hotel. Multiple fees added up, even the modest ones, especially if you opted for sandwiches snuck out of hotel

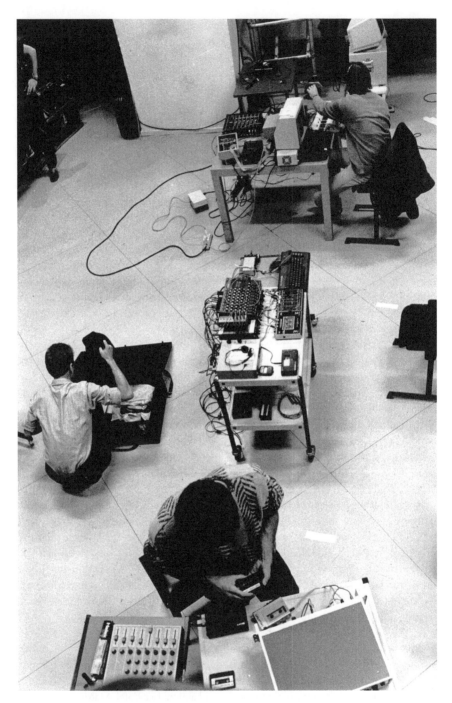

Figure 12.2 Setting up for a concert in the *2nd STEIM Symposium on Interactive Music*, at De IJsbreker, Amsterdam, 1985. From top to bottom: Ron Kuivila, the author, and Peter Cusack. Photo by Gerda van der Veen.

breakfast buffets over lunches at proper restaurants. After sufficient self-deprivation it was possible to come back from two weeks on the road with enough cash in various currencies to cover a month's rent or a new instrument (musicians touring the East Bloc often swapped the unconvertible local tender for musical instruments, utilitarian clothing, or a holiday on the Yugoslav coast). Sometimes my fees were generous enough that Susan—a performer in several of my pieces—could accompany me, often piggybacking her own research and writing projects onto touring destinations.[ii] Any gig in a new city might plant the seed for the next tour or for a friendship lasting years.

No one had warned me that the circuit-as-score ethos meant touring with a lot of gear: every composition required its own boxes, and a full concert sequenced several pieces. I came to define the gigging formula "Nic's Constant": 1 m = 1 pE, where "m" is a minute of music, and "pE" is a pound of equipment.[iii] Even with Lovely Music's network in play, much of the foreign distribution of records fell to the artist: suitcases drooped even heavier with vinyl since the merch table was often more profitable than the gig itself.

Back when I was a student, Alvin had introduced me to the admirably named Fiber Case and Novelty on lower Broadway. It was like meeting the tailor who had clothed the family for generations: FC&N had provided equipment cases for every traveling electronic music composer since David Tudor got wired. But why did it take *so* long to put wheels on suitcases? Porters were a thing of the past, but wheels had not yet made the all-important leap from accessory to integration in the suitcase proper. Collapsible luggage carts were a necessity, for which we got charged extra to have it mangled or lost if checked into the hold, or took it on board for free and put it in overhead storage, where it was either forgotten or fell out onto someone's head. (Composer Elliott Sharp cleverly traveled with a skateboard strapped under his case.)

In 1986, STEIM brokered my participation in the Festival International des Musiques Expérimentales in Bourges, France—a long-standing celebration of the kind of sober, self-important tape music I had encountered in France in 1977. Susan came along, and we planned stops in Paris and Amsterdam for pleasure and work, and in Hamburg, where she would be introduced to the extended family. We were waiting in the loft for our cab to JFK airport when a call came in from John Driscoll, a friend from Composers Inside Electronics. He was in Berlin on a residency with the DAAD Künstlerprogramm and had organized a series of concerts on the theme of "Music with

---

[ii] For one tour that kicked off in Berlin, Susan found ourselves with a couple of hours to kill after landing in Frankfurt before heading by train across still-divided Germany. We made our way to the Hauptbahnhof, crammed our suitcases into a luggage locker, and grabbed an S-Bahn to the Städelsches Kunstinstitut. Floorplan in hand, we found our way to Vermeer's *The Geographer* (one of the few Vermeers we had not yet seen in person), stared for ten minutes, then exited the museum, got back on the S-Bahn, retrieved our luggage, and boarded our train with minutes to spare.

[iii] A tour-derived complement of this maxim is "Nic's First Law of Cultural Economics": for every gig you get in Tuscany you'll have to play ten in Bremen.

Memory." One of his performers—the Texas musician Jerry Hunt—had failed to show up (having assumed the invitation was a joke, Hunt had never bought a ticket).[iv]

"I heard you're heading to Amsterdam," John said. "Any chance you're free to do a concert this weekend?"

Twenty-four hours later we were aboard the same Paris-Moscow train I had taken to Warsaw a decade earlier, our couchette served by a gold-toothed attendant whose sole words of English were the enthusiastically repeated phrase, "Only Russian!" After being awakened in the wee hours by grim East German border agents to affix grandiose transit visas in our passports, we arrived at Zoo Station at 5:30 in the morning. Even my generous cousin Joachim (who had invited us to stay) balked at this timing and asked us not to appear at his flat before 9:00. The festival producer, Matthias Osterwold, dutifully met us on the platform and took us on a three-hour driving tour of the still-walled, still-slumbering city.

Parking near the Glienicker Brücke—the "Bridge of Spies" where prisoners were exchanged between East and West Berlin—we wandered through the gardens of the adjacent Schloss as mist rose over the waters of the Havel, and birds could be heard twittering in both communist and capitalist trees. Matthias made polite conversation, asking where else in Europe we planned to visit. I mentioned Bourges and Paris and visiting German relatives. He asked where in Germany. Hamburg. He asked where in Hamburg. Actually, a small inner suburb on the Elbe. He asked which small inner suburb on the Elbe. And thus we discovered that Matthias had grown up a quarter mile from the house in which my grandmother was born and my great aunt still lived. By the time he dropped us off at Joachim's, we were fast friends and have remained so ever since.

The Berlin festival was produced with understated grace by the DAAD. Guests arriving in the lobby of an otherwise scruffy arthouse cinema were greeted by a mountain of elegant tea sandwiches. I eyed them hungrily at the end of my soundcheck, but by the time I had finished my set, all that remained was a platter covered in small pieces of lettuce. This was three weeks after the Chernobyl nuclear disaster, and everyone in Europe was steering clear of green produce that might have been contaminated by winds from the East. Bread, cheese, and salami, on the other hand, were fair game.

I had been away for ten years, but Berlin still had its unique Cold War grit. As one approached the Wall, even the air changed, made malodorous by the fug of Trabant exhaust. (The iconic East German car contained a two-stroke engine that consumed fuel closer to that used by lawnmowers than by Western cars.) My cousin's partner in his small architectural firm—an enthusiastic East German escapee who had earlier visited us on Bleecker Street—took us on a tour of the hipster Turkish neighborhood of Kreuzberg, repeating in excited broken English, "East Village in Berlin!" I remember

---

[iv] Like David Tudor before him, after a number of years as an interpreter of the scores of others, pianist Jerry Hunt drifted into electronics and composition. His concerts offered an odd mix of high-tech video processing and shamanistic shuffling and dousing with twigs. During her short tenure as the new music reviewer for *The Village Voice*, Linda Sander ended her account of a memorable concert: "When Mr. Hunt started shaking his twig at the ceiling while shouting 'come on down!' I began to question whether I was really cut out for reviewing contemporary music."

little of the other concerts in the festival, except all employed computers in live performance—a rarity in European programs at the time. Speaking with Matthias and musicians in the city, it seemed clear that my earlier sense of Berlin as a place both open-minded and serious—a place where exciting art could happen—had not been wrong.

The annual Bourges festival (now in its sixteenth iteration) had loosened up, ever so slightly, to include some live electronic performance in addition to tape music, thanks in no small part to the inclusion of Michel on the programming committee. The evening on which I was featured consisted of several pieces of the expected tape compositions, played back through multiple speakers, each lit with a differently colored spotlight. *Devil's Music* was the only live performance that night. Pulling from local airwaves, my sampling and stuttering included a fair amount of bad French pop and brought scowls to the faces of the jury members in the front row. The next day, however, as we walked around town, several teenagers flashed thumbs-up gestures and called out, "très cool!"

On a Colombian tour in the 1990s, I flew from Bogotá to Calí. Ahead of me at security was a well-groomed middle-aged man in a beautiful camel hair coat, accompanied by a muscular guy who screamed "bodyguard." The bodyguard placed a very large handgun in a tray on the x-ray belt. He picked it up and re-holstered it, unquestioned, on the other side of the checkpoint whose function was, theoretically, to prevent such weapons from passing. The two men walked ahead of me to the gate for my flight. When time came to board the bodyguard escorted his boss to a seat at the front of the plane and stood in the small galley until the door was ready to close, at which point he exited. When the door opened again in Calí, an identical man strode on to escort the boss off. Concierge security.

In the late 1980s KLM had a flight that left New York close to midnight, which made it easier to fall asleep in cramped seats, and meant that our friends might be awake when we knocked on their doors in Amsterdam. The plane was a 747 with increased cargo space that took up the rear half of the economy cabin. The late start and the smaller passenger load gave the flight a more relaxed, cozy feel. One night, snoozing at the back of the plane, I woke and glanced back toward the bulkhead. The door was open. Inside a cavernous cargo bay were a dozen beautiful horses, suspended from the ceiling in slings, calmly munching from feed bags as a groom strolled the gangway, patting noses and murmuring into ears. The Dutch equestrian team was coming home from the Seoul Olympics.

The touring life.

13

A Computer Walks into a Bar

In 1978, en route to my family in Chile, I stopped in Peru to visit Machu Picchu and Cuzco. Walking through the town one day, I heard a distant brass band echoing off the walls of a narrow alley. As it drew closer, the music resolved into something reminiscent of New Orleans funeral bands but loosened to the edge of breakdown. I assumed my impression of slipping and sliding was the product of acoustics and my own lightheadedness at 11,000 feet.

Vendors were set up in front of the shops along an adjacent street. Behind one table a man was talking into a microphone, heard through a tinny speaker on a wall above the doorway behind him, and wired to a transmitter somewhere inside the building. This was the "studio" of the local radio station, he was the DJ, and most of his patter consisted of greetings and exchanges between citizens in the surrounding countryside—pre-web social media. After a few minutes, he stopped talking and cued up a disc on a child's record player. Instead of routing the turntable through a mixer (as was done in every other radio station I knew), he simply swung his mic over the record player's built-in speaker. When he looked up, I asked him about the marching band. "Huayno," he pronounced, and pointed to the store next door, where I bought an LP record.

A few weeks later, I dropped the disc *Cielo de Tauca* on my own turntable back in Middletown, and the members of the band Primavera de Tauca kicked off with surging rolls on a snare, several false starts by a trumpet that then coalesced into a wobbly hook, joined by a thumping bass drum, and staggered entrances of the remaining brass and saxophones, each repeating a different riff, none sharing exactly the same downbeat.[1] Even indoors and at low altitude, it was outrageous, complex, magical. Loops were endemic in experimental music. But whether created on tape recorders or performed by an ensemble of acoustic instruments, the resulting music was, with few exceptions, unyieldingly metronomic. The players on *Cielo de Tauca*, however, slid patterns against each other like an indecisive form of phase music—looser even than Bryars's *1, 2, 1 2 3 4*. I thought perhaps the band was drunk, but every track sounded drunk in precisely the same way. I listened to the record over and over for months, reveling in its performed instability and asking myself—in the naive pre-post-colonial manner of the time—how can I make something out of this?

This was not a common urge for me. My eclectic record collection reflected a short lifetime logged in pop and jazz, the canon of experimental music introduced by Alvin, and ethnomusicological records from Afghanistan to Zimbabwe. I enjoyed listening to all these things, but I wasn't driven to appropriate. I was still afflicted by the Cagean disapproval of acting on personal preferences. In the short term, I could think of nothing to do with *Cielo de Tauca* besides play it.

Six years later, a lot had changed in my life. I embraced chance in *Devil's Music*, relying on an unpredictable radio-roulette, but after months of touring the piece I had to admit that I sometimes preferred certain samples over others. And our conversation about my guitar music had made it clear that even for Cage, pure disinterestedness was an aspiration rather than a lived reality.[i] Meanwhile, performance spaces were chockablock with appropriation—people using samplers, delays, turntables, and tape recorders to deconstruct and reconstruct found material, mostly pop music, in a flurry of what I called "love songs to pop songs." Los Angeles composer Carl Stone's 1983 *Wave-Heat* transformed Martha and the Vandellas' "Heatwave" with an early French sampling device called a Publison.[2] Under the heading of "Plunderphonics," Canadian John Oswald released a series of radical remixes of pop songs, jazz, and classical music. (The cover photomontage of Michael Jackson's head on the body of a half-naked woman on Oswald's 1989 CD prompted a lawsuit that resulted in the Canadian Recording Industry Association having all unsold discs steamrolled in the clichéd manner of counterfeit watches.)[3] Many of these works used transformations similar to what I had done with the Electro-Harmonix delays: looping and retriggering rooted in turntable technique, pitch changes associated with samplers, post-Reich phase drift.

Around this time, I realized that the stuttering circuit I had designed for *Devil's Music*, which elasticized the modest sample times of digital-delay boxes and disrupted the otherwise tiresome repetition of short loops, produced rhythmic patterns that bore an uncanny resemblance to that of the Cuzqueña band. Now I had a point of connection between my music and that of the Altiplano. But I needed to extend my manipulations beyond the retriggered loops. I wanted to stretch out slices of sounds that normally slip by too fast for perception—to create something that, like Harold Edgerton's high-speed photograph of milk droplets arrayed like a crown, presented you with a phenomenon you've witnessed a hundred times but never really knew was there.

Personal computers were not yet powerful enough to manipulate sound with adequate fidelity, so the engineers who designed early digital signal processors started with the same core circuitry used in digital delays and samplers to move audio in and out of memory, and then added chips to perform the other operations needed to achieve the desired effect (operations we now think of in software terms—add, subtract, multiply, store, retrieve). These ICs were wired together to execute a fixed program with limited variables adjusted with knobs or buttons, rather than being stored in updatable code and controlled by a keyboard, mouse, and pull-down menus.

One such hardware-based signal processor was the "Stargate" digital reverb unit made by Ursa Major, a small firm outside Boston. It emulated reverberation by controlling fifteen short audio delays. Through my day job at Studio Consultants, I became friendly

---

[i] Toward the end of my guitar dress-down with Cage, I asked him what music he did *not* find irritating, what he enjoyed listening to: "Irish vocal music" came his immediate response.

with their engineers, who revealed the various hidden diagnostic functions, like one that "froze" the audio processing so that a cloud of reverberating sound looped endlessly. Cool. Eventually, they gave me a copy of the schematics, so I could analyze what operation each chip in their circuit contributed to the overall process. Even cooler. I bought a Stargate (at a dealer discount), made a few hacks, and was soon able to manipulate sounds with far more finesse than had been possible with the Electro-Harmonix boxes.

I cued up *Cielo de Tauca* on my turntable and went to work.

A few months later, in March 1986, I sat in front of a small audience at the Experimental Intermedia Foundation, where I turned knobs and pressed buttons, gradually expanding samples of the record from micro-slices that buzzed like bees to recognizable chunks of raucous street music, retriggered in imitation of the lurching rhythm of the original. It sounded wonderfully rich but, coming on the heels of the backwards guitars, the performative aspects of knob-twiddling left something to be desired. For the audience, there was no connection between my hand movements and what was coming out of the speakers. Part of the magic of my experience in Cuzco had been the changes in sound as the band marched through the streets. Of this, there was no hint when I sat behind the table.

What I needed was a device played by gestures big enough to be seen from the seats at the back—the equivalent of drawing a bow across a string, or diving to one side of a keyboard in Chico Marx mode, or extending the slide of a trombone. I didn't have a cello or a piano, but I happened to have a battered trombone that I had bought for twelve dollars at a church fair one summer during college.

I pulled the instrument from the depths of our closet, mounted a rotary shaft encoder (essentially half a computer mouse) on its back crook, and coupled it to the slide with a retractable dog leash (very Rube Goldberg). When I moved the slide, the encoder rotated—counting up when I pushed the slide out, counting down when I pulled it in. I attached a keypad to the slide where I could reach it with my right hand, and then linked the keypad and the encoder to a Commodore 64 computer with a ten-foot cable. The computer wasn't powerful enough to process sound directly, but I could program it to read the slide position and the keypad and map them to the settings normally adjusted by the knobs and buttons on the reverb's front panel, via wires between the computer's ports and the Stargate. By pressing keys and moving the slide, I could make sounds longer or shorter, higher or lower, more or less reverberant—and I could do this ten feet away from the Stargate. The trombone became a large, somewhat silly looking remote control.

For earlier feedback experiments with the trombone, I had coupled a compact speaker to the mouthpiece. I connected the Stargate's output to this speaker, so the electronic sounds played back through the instrument and out the bell, for further *acoustic* alteration by a plunger mute and the slide position, like with any ordinary brass instrument. I mounted a Yamaha breath controller on the back of the driver so I could articulate the sounds by blowing.[ii] Now the trombone was both a controller for manipulating sound digitally and a performance device for scattering sound around the room acoustically.

[ii] A breath controller is a device that translates breath pressure to a control signal for a synthesizer. It was developed to give wind players a familiar point of access to electronic sound.

The limited low-frequency response of the mouthpiece-speaker combined with the acoustical characteristics of the trombone to imbue this hybrid instrument with a quaint, gramophone-like character at odds with the digital textures. When I wanted a bigger, bassier sound, a button on the keypad redirected the audio signal to the PA.

The net effect was less infantile than the drumming pandas but still pushed back against the idea of dignity. With its dog leash and long cable dangling behind, it suggested an instrument on life support or an astronaut on a spacewalk. But I could play while standing and pacing, using large actions that were both visible and audible, instead of sitting passively behind a table, twiddling (Figure 13.1).

When I first opened the Stargate's metal case, I was greeted by a large circuit board swarming with integrated circuits. Each one executed some operation in the signal processing path that simulated reverberation (the equivalent of a few lines in a computer program). I could remove any of these ICs and wire its empty socket to an interface port on the Commodore 64, on which I could program variations on whatever it was that particular chip did. If I emulated the *correct* behavior of a chip that counted up from 0 to 254, for example, the reverb performed as expected. If my program counted *down* instead, the audio would play backward. As I explored the functions of the various chips and replaced them with ports on the computer running alternative instructions, I gradually rewrote the hardwired Stargate program and built up a collection of tools that ranged from familiar effects (sample recording, looping, reversing, pitch shifting) to stranger ones: retriggering a loop from random locations, internal feedback, or raspy time-stretching.[iii] This hybrid approach meant I could let the Stargate hardware do fast things the computer could not (like digitizing and playing back the audio), while my Commodore software handled slower operations (such as changing the direction and limits of a counter) and offered the flexibility and seemingly infinite updatability of software.

As a New Yorker I abhorred wasted space and there was a lot of it inside the Stargate's chassis, so eventually I extracted the Commodore motherboard from its bulbous plastic case and mounted it above the reverb's main circuit board (Figure 13.2). Whenever I wanted to revise my software I'd remove the chassis' top plate and hook up a keyboard, monitor, and disc drive to the computer motherboard. When I finished, I'd burn a programmable memory chip (EPROM) with the new code and connect it to the Commodore so the software would run automatically when the computer turned on.[iv] Live computer music at the time usually required bulky desktop machines and monitors; performers typed and looked at screens as if in an office cubicle. On the trombone, however, every parameter of my program was mapped to a specific key, so every change was "manually knowable," like the keys on a conventional musical instrument, and immediately reflected in sound. (Years later, a younger Swiss composer told me how influential this goofy instrument had

---

iii The latter technique subsequently became popular in academic computer music circles under the name "granular synthesis."

iv EPROMs are similar to USB flash drives or the game cartridges of early video game consoles, enabling a computer to run a fixed program without needing a disc drive, monitor, keyboard, or external prompt.

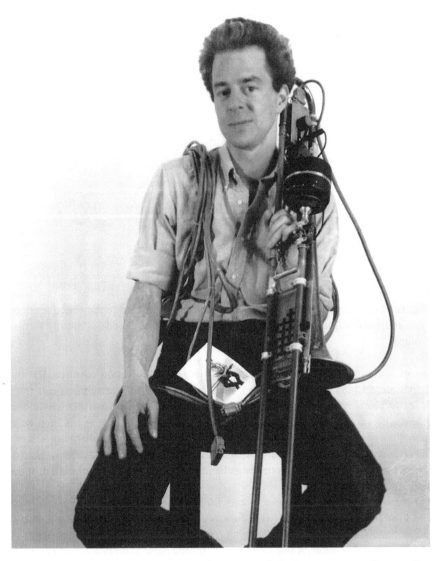

Figure 13.1 The author with his trombone-propelled electronics, Vandoeuvre-lès-Nancy, May 1991. Photo by Claude Philippot.

been on his generation, not because they understood exactly how it worked but because "it showed that such a thing *could* work.")[4]

I spent the better part of a year designing and soldering the interface circuitry, programming the Commodore in low-level assembly-language and adapting the mechanics of the trombone—all in order to process found material for a ten-minute

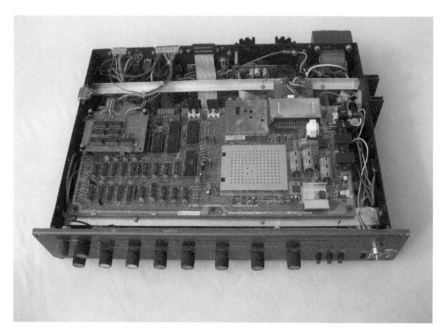

Figure 13.2 Hacked Ursa Major Stargate digital reverb, opened to show modifications with inserted Commodore 64 processor board and interface circuitry. Photo by Nicolas Collins.

composition, *Tobabo Fonio* (1986).[5] As in the precursor version performed at the Experimental Intermedia Foundation, the Cuzqueña music gradually emerges from a sea of abstract buzzes, but the trombone provided a new visual dimension and physicality, as well as acoustic variety: moving the slide and mute engendered wah-wah filtering effects, and pointing the trombone's bell hither and thither elicited sonic reflections within the performance space (an oblique reference to Lucier's *Vespers*). There was a poignancy to an entire brass band emerging from that battered bell at the end of the performance.[v]

    In most of my previous compositions, the score and the circuit were one; seldom did I use the same electronics (with the exception of generic devices like mixers and microphones) in two pieces. My "trombone-propelled electronics" (as I dubbed it) was different. It was versatile. A few months after *Tobabo Fonio* I composed *Real Electronic Music* (1986) for the same instrument, stretching out tiny bursts of sound from a

[v]   There can be a comical aspect to hearing recorded brass instruments emerging from a speaker inside a trombone, but similar technology was employed some two decades later for the most somber of purposes. In the early 2000s, there arose a shortage of military buglers for graveside services for veterans. In 2003 S&D Consulting introduced a modified mute containing a digital audio player and a speaker that, when inserted in the bell of a standard bugle, would allow a non-musician to play back a recording of *Taps* in "a dignified manner" at the press of a button. See https://www.ceremonialbugle.com.

scanning radio.[6] More compositions followed. And importantly, like a well-adjusted toddler, I was now able to play with others.

In his 1980 book, *Improvisation*, British guitarist Derek Bailey coined the expression "non-idiomatic improvisation" to describe unscripted music that did not follow traditional guidelines of how to improvise, such as those central to Blues or Jazz.[7] Within a few years, it became apparent that nothing stays non-idiomatic for long: get a group of players together and an idiom grows itself.[8] Various pseudo-non-idiomatic idioms proliferated across Downtown New York.

"Free improvisation" players consciously tried to avoid references to any other music—melody, functional harmony, and a steady pulse were typically shunned. The emphasis instead was on texture, on unfamiliar techniques, on extended durations of sound and silence, and on spontaneous interactions between players.

The players I called "loose-formalists," on the other hand, merged elements from established musical forms (rock, blues, jazz, contemporary classical music) with aspects of improvisation drawn from outside those styles. At one extreme, you had rock-band-wannabes, happily acknowledging adolescent musical influences but often not quite up to the standards of a proper rock club. At the other lurked conservatory-trained instrumentalists shifting their sights and sites from Uptown to Downtown. Between them roamed a host of musicians and ensembles who, immersed in the postmodern mood of the 1980s, mixed unfettered free improvisation with, well, something else. Elliott Sharp's variable ensemble Carbon incorporated elements of hardcore and blues. Mixing musicians from NYC and the South, Curlew brought strains of bluegrass and R&B into their sets. Third Person, a trio founded by Samm Bennett and Tom Cora, rotated guests into the third seat, guaranteeing unexpected elements to offset funk-tinged drums and what Tom dubbed "folk cello." And there was tactic-based improvisation, most conspicuously represented by John Zorn, using rules derived from sports and board games to discourage players from falling back on personal habits (riffs) or conventional musical models. (An antecedent for Zorn's strategies lay in Christian Wolff's coordination pieces of the 1960s.)

As a composer I felt I shouldn't repeat the same composition in the same city, and since a given piece might take ten months to create, the frequency with which I could perform a fresh concert program was pretty limited. In improvised music, however, there was no repertoire, which meant musicians could play out as often as a venue was available and the audience was not yet bored with what you had to offer stylistically. Variety was ensured by permutations of participants, factorial variations on a cluster of regulars such as Zeena Parkins, Tom Cora, Shelley Hirsch, Elliott Sharp, Ikue Mori, Ned Rothenberg, Christian Marclay, and many others. The onus on the player was to find something new to say—spontaneously—in every performance.

A fluid scene thrived on the efficiency and richness of open, usually unrehearsed collaboration. It found homes in clubs with liquor licenses; in oxymoronically labeled "established alternative art spaces" such as The Kitchen, Roulette, and Experimental Intermedia Foundation; and in pop-ups of various flavors (galleries, record stores, bookstores, living rooms, bowling alleys, laundromats). Just as guitars on rock stages had seduced me earlier, I began looking for means of engaging with this active (and popular) community. My trombone-propelled electronics opened the door.

The trombone-propelled electronics had no voice of its own but I could grab snippets of whatever sound was connected to the Stargate. A dub of an old LP for *Tobabo Fonio*, a scanning radio for *Real Electronic Music*. But that sound could also come from a microphone aimed at someone else's instrument. I could grab a moment of whatever it was playing and return the sound transformed: speed a note up, slow it down, chop it, stretch it out, loop it, re-trigger it, filter it, let it reverberate or feedback. And I could perform these transformations instantaneously, like any other musician engaged in call and response. Sounds played through the bell of the trombone merged neatly with acoustic instruments on the stage. When amplified instruments drowned me out, a tap on a switch sent my signal to the big speakers of the PA.

For years, I had sought out musicians to perform my compositions, but classically trained players were often suspicious of prose scores, alternative notation, and electronics. Musicians who styled themselves as "improvisers" were more amenable to experimentation, and I was making friends with many of the players in the Downtown scene. Now, when I invited them to come by our loft and interact with my trombone, they replied "sure" and often added, "are you free next week to play at [insert name of sketchy bar here]?" And thanks largely to Peter Cusack my pool of musical collaborators soon spread to England and Europe.

My transition to improvisation was facilitated by the presence of a familiar instrument at the core of my trombone-propelled electronics, which gave my system an unthreatening appearance. George Lewis once said I was the first person to take a computer onto a bar stage, but I smuggled it on disguised as a trombone.

The trombone's responsive alteration in real time was a fresh and provocative presence at a time when electronics beyond amps and a few effect pedals were rare in improvised music. Players and audiences alike responded enthusiastically. Though I could not initiate a sound, I contributed a distinctive additional voice to a performance. I might grab my very first sample while musicians were still tuning up (though if paired with a tentative player, the set might get off to a delayed start, frozen by the "after you" deference of two polite people stalled at a doorway). Since I could easily spin a few minutes of variation out of one captured second, the effect of my presence was often to slow things down. For better or worse, I had a hand in introducing elements of minimalism—the drawing out of fleeting sounds for closer listening—into a scene that had been growing increasingly prone to, as George Lewis observed, "too many notes."

Roulette, one of the longest-running spaces for improvised music in the city, was founded in 1978 on West Broadway in Tribeca by musicians David Weinstein and Jim Staley. A Chicago-born composer and pianist, David, had moved to New York in the late 1970s and was active as a keyboard player in Downtown ensembles. Jim was a conservatory-trained trombonist who had been radicalized by new improvisation while stationed with the US Army in Berlin from 1971 to 1973 (apart from the Berliner Jazztage festival, the annual Total Music Meeting supported more experimental work and Free Music Production operated as a record label and management for improvising artists). From the start Roulette distinguished itself in its shoestring hosting of European musicians as well as local players.

The Knitting Factory opened on Houston Street a decade later, and it was soon the busiest venue in town. They programmed multiple sets most nights of the week, so it was easy to play regularly in shifting configurations of musical partners. It was just two blocks away from our loft, and the ray-gun doorbell would sometimes buzz during dinner when their soundman, Bob Appel, needed some odd adapter cable to finish his sound check. He'd yell his order up, I'd drop the cord out the window, then pick it up at the end of the show (the loaned cable securing me complementary admission). Where Roulette was a not-for-profit organization in the tradition of other alternative spaces like The Kitchen, the Knitting Factory was very much for-profit, as bars are wont to be.

It was actually a pretty horrible place to play. The room was long and narrow, with a small stage. Things got worse when the club opened a second venue, the Knot Room, in the basement. There was no sound insulation between the floors, and upstairs sound checks would drown out the early show on the Knot Room's even smaller stage. But thanks in no small part to its liquor license, the club drew a regular and substantial audience that went beyond musicians and their friends.

John Zorn played the Knitting Factory frequently. John had been a unique figure on the Downtown scene since the late 1970s. He was extraordinarily generous in his engagement with musicians across multiple genres of music in NYC and worldwide, while retaining an obsessive certainty of exactly what he wanted to hear. He was insanely productive, highly influential, and often abrasive—the quintessential 1980s artist. His early game-based ensemble strategies tended toward the abstract playing styles common to free improvisation, but he would name Carl Stalling as an influence (composer of memorable soundtracks for *Looney Tunes* and *Merry Melodies*) on par with Cage or Ornette Coleman, pointing to Stalling's jump-cuts and quotations. (The timing and mood of Stalling's cuts arose, of course, not from the desire to disrupt audience expectations of standard musical forms, but from the narrative demands of the cartoon. Stalling's decision to use pastiche in what now seems a proto-postmodern way was similarly pragmatic: he had been told he could write his own music, use anything already owned by Warner Brothers, or otherwise free of copyright restrictions—the latter two options were obviously more efficient.)[9]

By 1984, when he composed his best-known work, *Cobra*, Zorn had bowed to the precedent of Stalling and opened his instructions to accept a wide range of musical references. The result was a frenetic collage that drew from the players' divergent specialties—pop, jazz, classical, and so on. One unusual feature of *Cobra* is its use of "memories": at any point in the performance, any player can signal for the current musical activity to be preserved as a memory (leading to furious scribbling on notepads); later on, a player can signal for a memory to be recalled, prompting the musicians to reconstruct that earlier moment—the band now quoting itself rather than Strauss, The Sex Pistols, or Stockhausen. The performance unfolded from a to and fro of the various signals between the players and a mediating conductor—typically Zorn himself in those years.

I participated in a few recordings and performances with Zorn, including *Cobra*.[10] One night I signaled to save a memory while the band was still waiting to play its first notes. Zorn looked at me like I didn't understand the rules (I did), then as though I was trying to sabotage the piece (I wasn't). He protested by gesture and word, but begrudgingly entered the memory as valid. That expectant silence was called back several times by various players in the course of the performance to what I thought was fine effect, inserting momentary calm into an otherwise unrelenting freneticism. I was not, however, surprised when he never invited me back—he was not a fan of quiet. (Some years later, cellist Tom Cora, long a mainstay of Zorn ensembles, told a similar story: "One night I figured out how to create a silence in *Cobra*. Zorn didn't like it and never asked me to play with him again.")

At a 1990 festival in Munich, Alvin Lucier and I participated in a panel discussion where a young German composer asked why American composers chose to work with such small forms—writing shorter works for soloists or small groups rather than full orchestras. It was one of the few times I saw Alvin get angry.

"You Europeans have no idea what it's like to be a composer in America," he objected. "Orchestras almost never perform our work and when they do there's never enough rehearsal time. In Europe you have commissions, subsidies, ensembles specializing in new music, as many rehearsals as you need. Small forms are all we have."

Whatever the cause, American experimental composers had taken small forms and made them grand. Minimalism was an exercise in extracting the greatest impact from the most modest of material, and Alvin's best works are shining examples of this principle. New York's Downtown improvised music scene was another triumph of the small form.

My first CD release, *100 Of The World's Most Beautiful Melodies* (1989), was rooted in that ideal. The borrowed title notwithstanding, the CD encompassed forty-two short duets between me and fifteen improvising musicians (they ranged in duration from a 36-second duet with Anthony Coleman on electric organ, to 5'30" with George Lewis against a backing track of our loft's noisy radiators).[11] The liner notes encouraged listeners to re-sequence the disc into playlists of favorite tracks, or to use the curiously Cagean shuffle option to surprise themselves with forty-two-factorial variations. I've no idea how many people did this, though one college radio station sent me the track sequence of a broadcast played in shuffle mode.[vi] *100 Of The World's Most Beautiful Melodies* merged several of my favorite small forms.

[vi] The interactivity of the CD format was heavily promoted in its early days. Compared to LPs and cassettes, it was easier to jump from track to track on a CD, and most machines included modes for playing back a random sequence (shuffle) or programming a specific set of tracks. I encouraged buyers to take advantage of these features to personalize my disc. But having plonked down the exorbitant price of a CD, most listeners expected to be entertained, not to have to work for their music. The primary appeal of the format at the time seemed to be freedom from having to turn over a vinyl or cassette at the end of the A side.

We Were All Seated Around the Campfire

Now consigned to the media mulch pile alongside eight-track cartridges and VHS tapes, the compact disc was briefly a rising star. It promised a playback medium with lower noise, wider frequency response, and greater durability than LPs or cassette tapes, plus you didn't have to turn it over.[i] For the record companies it was a win-win: cheaper to manufacture than LPs and an upgrade that prompted consumers to replace music they already owned, meaning the label could sell the same content twice. Distributors extolled the lower shipping expense of lighter media and the fact that a broken CD case was easy to replace, whereas a damaged LP jacket rendered a record unsellable. Soon enough, however, listeners began to question the vaunted audio quality: subjective adjectives like "cold" and "brittle" were inveighed against measurable metrics like signal-to-noise and bandwidth.

If CDs were never as lovable as LPs, there were nonetheless artists who were intrigued by their potential as a performance medium. Yasunao Tone, an early member of Fluxus and co-founder of Japan's Group Ongaku, is considered by many the "grandfather of glitch" for the music he made by doctoring CD surfaces after buying one of the earliest players in 1984. He capitalized on a critical difference between the CD and its analog predecessors: the digitized audio goes through a circuitous decoding before it reaches our ears, and damage to the disc surface causes that intervening circuitry to do strange things in its struggle to extract a legitimate signal from the noise. A tick or skip on a vinyl record leaves the surrounding music intact, but a scratch on a CD shatters coherence into a thousand confetti-like fragments. Through trial and error, the judicious application of Scotch tape, and toggling the >>| and |<< buttons, Tone learned how to nudge the sound in specific directions. That said, the machine still produced wild variations of its own, and his control was indirect at best, more like surfing than driving a car.[1]

I saw the CD as another path to the lightweight DJing I had pursued with the radio sampling in *Devil's Music*, but potentially with more direct manipulations akin to turntable scratching and cueing. I was curious as to what was going on inside the player. Unlike the random-access behavior of CD-ROMs and hard discs for computers, the audio on a CD is encoded in a continuous, linear track of microscopic dots and

---

[i] The CD format was introduced in 1982, but the first commercial music release on CD manufactured in the United States was reputedly Bruce Springsteen's *Born in the USA*, in September 1984.

dashes etched on the surface of the plastic, mimicking the format of the groove on a vinyl record. A laser traces a spiral path around the disc, from the center inside out to the edge (the inverse of a record), reading the reflections from the surface. But when a disc is paused or advanced from one track to another, the laser is not lifted like a turntable's tonearm: it just freezes in place (in pause) or jumps to a new location (track advance) while the disc continues to spin and the player's circuitry silences the audio output. If I could locate the source of that silence command, I might be able to disable it and hear the not-music as well as the music.

In 1989, I finagled a service manual for a portable D2 Discman out of Sony's service center. Buried in the largely incomprehensible schematic was a signal labeled "mute."[ii] I traced its origin to a pin on a large chip that controlled the overall behavior of the player and, armed with a soldering iron and a sewing needle, disconnected the pin from the trace on the circuit board, releasing a flood of hitherto unheard sounds. Starting and stopping the disc was now accompanied by a brief loud squawk. Pressing "next track" in shuffle mode evoked John Zorn's frantic stylistic jump-cutting, while "pause" sustained a short fragment of sound in a lilting loop.

Unlike the familiar metronomic repetition of a skipping record, the paused CD *swings*, interrupting its default tempo with occasional off-beat accents that impart a distinctly musical rhythm. If I briefly un-paused the CD or pressed the "search" button, I could slowly progress through the disc, drawing out the track in a step-wise sequence of off-kilter loops, extending thirty seconds of recorded music to ten minutes of tranquil playback. In other compositions, I had gone to great lengths to defeat the periodicity of looped samples (such as the stuttering circuit in *Devil's Music* that re-trigger loops quasi-stochastically). The removal of the mute connection in the Discman produced automatic variations on any compact disc.

Testing out every CD in my modest collection, I found to my surprise that the most magical results arose from recordings of Baroque and Renaissance music. The pause-loop froze the flow of the counterpoint into modal chords reminiscent of certain 1960s jazz piano accompaniment, or of student counterpoint exercises where adherence to the rules takes precedence over melodic invention.[iii] The glitches that the machine frequently threw onto a loop's joint contrasted with the lush sound of the acoustic instruments, adding floating accents that evoked the snap of Latin percussion—"digital claves."

Endearing in its own right, the skipping CD also mixed beautifully with live instruments, especially those similar to the ones recorded on the disc being used. My first composition for a hacked player, *Broken Light* (1991), written for the Soldier String Quartet, pitted the musicians against a disc of Baroque *concerti grossi* by Arcangelo

---

ii   In the days before the online profusion of user manuals and other technical resources, I was quite adept at convincing equipment manufacturers that I was an authorized service technician for their products, and they would quite freely part with detailed documentation.

iii Well-written contrapuntal music emphasizes the interplay of several separate horizontal melodic lines. In the early stages of learning counterpoint, students follow a set of rules about the vertical interaction of the voices (i.e., what notes are sounding at the same time, as in a chord) and often sacrifice melodic character in deference to harmonic order.

Figure 14.1 Hacked Sony D2 Discman with footswitches for remote control in *Broken Light,* 1991. Photo by Nicolas Collins.

Corelli, Giovanni Torelli, and Pietro Locatelli played by a string orchestra.[iv] Controlling a hacked portable CD player through a set of footswitches that duplicated its buttons, the quartet scratched across the disc to trigger noisy rips, nudged the paused disc ahead through a series of looped phrases that moved the harmony along, and called up specific tracks for each of the composition's three movements. The loops provide the rhythmic and harmonic underpinning for instrumental variations that the players improvised according to guidelines specific to each movement. At times it's hard to distinguish the live strings from the recorded ones (Figure 14.1).[2]

Until the advent of personal computers and music programming languages, most compositions that combined electronic sound with live acoustic instruments featured the playback of a tape, prepared in a studio, over which the musicians performed, like karaoke.[v] By the mid-1980s, a number of composers, such as David Behrman and

---

[iv] Founded in New York in 1984 by David Soldier (the musical nom de plume of neuroscientist David Sulzer), the Soldier String Quartet specialized in music by composers outside the domain of classical quartet repertoire. They were especially supportive of works by improvisers and artists making use of non-standard electronic technology.

[v] Well-known examples include Karlheinz Stockhausen's *Kontakte* from 1958 and the eight compositions for instruments and tape in the "Synchronisms" series by Argentinian-American composer Mario Davidovsky, written between 1962 and 1974. Works like Gordon Mumma's *Hornpipe,* for French horn and live "cybersonic" electronics, were the exception.

George Lewis, were writing programs that "listened" to players and responded in real time with electronic sounds. The hacked CD player provided an inexpensive, portable compromise between the backing tape (technically simple, but always the same) and interactive computer music (flexible, but expensive, bulky, and technically daunting for many musicians). Instrumentalists working with my CD system could familiarize themselves with each track in advance and even have a score of the recorded music in front of them, but their control over how far things moved forward with each press of the "next track" footswitch or toggle of "pause" was imprecise. As a result, performances had the tension and uncertainty associated with improvised music while being set against the knowable harmonic roadmap of an underlying form. The hacked player turned every disc into a chart through which musicians plotted courses, like members of a swing band, and the result evoked the presence of a composed core.

Individual CD players display unexpected idiosyncrasies. The skip rate, tempo irregularities, degree of swing, and glitchiness vary from one machine to the next. The first tracks on any disc skip at a faster rate than later ones, so track number effectively determines the tempo when paused (a useful means of differentiating sections in a multi-movement composition). Once, while searching for the mute signal on a new player, I tapped a test probe to a pin on a chip and was rewarded by the playback slowing to half-speed and all the sounds dropping an octave in pitch, but this feature seemed to be exclusive to the Sony D121 and was not present in other machines. As with those 1970s handmade circuits, each player seemed to contain, if not a score, at least a style of its own. I designed each composition around the behavior of a specific model, and substitutions usually changed the character of a work.

Sadly, with each improvement introduced to a product line (especially in areas of error correction and shock protection), the glitch artifacts grew milder, and the trend toward integration of more functions onto fewer chips made players increasingly difficult to hack. I was driven to seek out obsolete models, and my instruments—once so modern—became anachronistic.[vi]

Concurrent with these CD investigations, I had been pondering new relationships between players, acoustic instruments, and electronics. The 1970s mantra of "circuit as score" seldom extended beyond the horizon of the object itself: it was enough that the composer let the chips follow their own lead. But the longer I worked with electronics, the more interested I became in extracting the score from the circuit and realizing it by other—preferably non-electronic—means. If there was a score inside that circuit,

---

[vi] Eventually, companies began producing CD players designed for DJs that incorporated cuing functions similar to my mute-removal hack, and by the early 2000s, using software such as Max/MSP and SuperCollider, one could write programs that looped and stepped through any music file in the style of my modified CD players—as I did when my favorite Discman, long out of production and impossible to find even on eBay, finally stopped working in 2007. The artifacts of CD looping and errors entered mainstream pop music through electronica and "glitch music," which in the late 1990s introduced audiences to sounds previously the purview of the avant-garde (e.g., Oval's *94 Diskont*, Mille Plateaux CD, 1995, or the *Clicks & Cuts* CD series on Mille Plateaux). By 2000 CD-derived glitches even featured on a Madonna album ("What It Feels Like for a Girl," on *Music*, Warner Music, 2000).

it should be possible to arrange it for other instruments, like those Baroque sonatas that can be performed on anything that fit the range of the written parts, or Webern's expansive orchestration of Bach's fugue from *The Musical Offering*. Historically, much electronic music had focused on the creation of novel sounds, but I was equally, if not more, intrigued by the various structural and formal innovations that the technology fostered and how those might be mapped onto more conventional musical resources. (I was not alone: Steve Reich had moved from tape loops to instrumental realizations of phase patterns in pieces such as *Piano Phase*, and Terry Riley's landmark loopy ensemble composition *In C* grew out of his earlier experiments with tape in *Mescalin Mix*.)

Tobabo Fonio—already a hybrid of electronic processing of indigenous music played on brass instruments imported from Europe—struck me as an apt test subject. The structure of my piece is simple: a drone of varying timbre descends in steps of large pitch intervals, followed by a mashup of musical fragments that briefly resolve into a tune. The opening digital loop of Cusqueña music is short enough (125 microseconds) that it sounds like a pitch (roughly B four octaves above middle C). I periodically reload the loop with a new sample to change the timbre of the waveform, then slide the slide and waggle the mute to emphasize different overtones. After two minutes, I lengthen the loop by 50 percent, dropping the pitch a perfect fifth. A minute later, I extend the loop another notch, dropping to B an octave below the first pitch, and fade in the PA to add bass and volume. Thirty seconds on, I drop to the G below, then stretch out the loop to its maximum length, so the buzzing pitch becomes a metronomic tick interrupting two seconds of silence. I gradually fill in the silence with a jumble of random snippets of music that eventually cohere into a recognizable passage from the record. Then I fade out.

This descending pattern of sustained pitches, with its prevalence of wide intervals like fifths and octaves, reminded me of guitarists and violinists checking their tuning, so I began to experiment with instrumental patterns that cycled through the open tunings of various stringed instruments. For the changes in timbre that arose from the micro-samples or the slide and mute, I isolated the harmonics of these open strings.

A 1989 commission from the New York State Council on the Arts and The Kitchen encouraged me to dig into this *Tobabo*-redux as an expanded experiment in orchestration and structure. Over endless cups of tea in the Mitropa buffet car of a train slouching through East Germany (the tea was execrable, but the china beautiful), Susan and I winnowed down the myriad options. We discussed the peculiarity of reworking a composition (*Tobabo Fonio*) that was already a remake of (and commentary on) another piece of music (*Cielo de Tauca*). We considered the different flavors and nature of loops and repetition—"Droste effect" image-within-image recursions, the many stories of fakes and forgeries that Susan had studied as an art historian, an old routine of my father's from when I was a child:

It was a dark and stormy night and we were all seated around the campfire. John turned to Mary and said, "Mary, tell us a story." And Mary proceeded as follows:

"It was a dark and stormy night and we were all seated around the campfire. George turned to Luke and said, 'Luke, tell us a story.'" And Luke proceeded as follows . . .

By the time we arrived at Zoo Station in Berlin, I had a structure—a cyclical form that could play out through text, instruments and electronics alike. I began embedding stories about copying into the looping "it was a dark and stormy night" format to build a spine for the composition. The texts came from art history, literature, mystery novels, and critical theory, linked together into a continuous narrative. I added a voice-driven backwards electric guitar whose open strings were resonated by the spoken words in parallel with the played open strings of an electric guitar and a string quartet. A hacked pitch-to-midi converter triggered percussion samples in a drum machine in response to the rhythm and inflection in the voice.[vii] To deliver the spoken text, I invited David Moss, who had a reputation in the improvised music community as both a vocalist and a drummer. I explained that this was the perfect piece for him: "you drum by talking, no need to carry any kit."

The performance moves through several iterations of the descending sequence of open strings on guitar, string quartet, and a second cello, with instruments added with each repeat and the harmony thickening as their different tunings are superimposed. The players sneak in short quotes from the Peruvian music, played in natural harmonics of the open strings, mimicking the tuneful snippets that break through the abstract drones in *Tobabo Fonio* from time to time. A trumpet, trombone, and accordion enter, one at a time, to reinforce the string overtones and contribute additional quotes. The filling-in and clearing-out of the *Tobabo Fonio*'s longest digital loop is emulated by the guitarist moving from isolated choked chords to rapid tremolo and back, by fragmented ensemble playing, and by Moss's improvised cut-up variations on the text. Finally, the band comes together on a rollicking transcription of one of the tracks from the Cuzqueña record.

Tobabo Fonio, which clocks in at a little over nine minutes, generated the core of *It Was a Dark and Stormy Night*: the descending melodic motif, the prevalence of loops, the shifting timbres and, of course, the source music. Over its thirty-minute duration *Dark and Stormy* extends these elements through repetition and variation. The players introduce materials and techniques only possible with acoustic instruments, but I would never have conceived of even these non-electronic additions without the example of its electronic predecessor.[3]

Since developing the trombone-propelled electronics, I have performed with a lot of improvisers at many venues in numerous countries. The hours spent together in sound checks, concerts, and recordings formed a master class in orchestration. I am always impressed by improvisers' approach to "extended technique." Classically trained

---

[vii] MIDI (Musical Instrument Digital Interface) is a technical standard developed in the early 1980s as a means of interconnecting and controlling synthesizers and other electronic equipment, including computers. A few companies manufactured "pitch-to-midi" converters that translated sung or played notes into MIDI data, so musicians who did not play keyboards could nonetheless control electronic sound.

musicians typically apply the term to anything that lies outside the realm of "normal" tone: multiphonics on a flute (playing more than one pitch at a time), harmonics (those whistly overtones) on a violin, or bowing a cymbal like a musical saw. When a score calls for them, well-trained musicians can often execute these eccentric effects competently, but the transition from their normal playing style is often awkward and disruptive.

By contrast, good improvisers seem to regard all instrumental sounds as existing on a continuum. The journey from a cello tone befitting Bach to one mimicking the screech of subway brakes can be accomplished in one draw of the bow, and many players delight in that sweet spot where one stable sound breaks into another, as when reed players hover between two overtones. It's easy to get lulled into a belief in the inevitable progress of one domain (electronics) and the inherent stasis of another (the trumpet has remained unchanged for over a century). Spending time with improvisers dispelled this myth. I'd walk off the stage at the end of a night humbled, with increased respect for familiar instruments and their players: I might have spent a week programming a filter routine, while a "real" trombone player could just waggle their toilet plunger to mimic me mimicking them.

When preparing the parts for *It Was a Dark and Stormy Night*, I asked Tom Cora to listen to the Cuzqueña melody and figure out how to play it using only natural harmonics of the open strings on his cello. He did so in one evening and performed it beautifully in concert and on the eventual recording. Other cellists have subsequently struggled with the part for hours without coming close to Tom's execution.

It Was a Dark and Stormy Night was presented for two nights at The Kitchen in February, 1990, with an ensemble consisting of Moss and Cora, the Soldier String Quartet, Robert Poss on electric guitar, Ben Neill on trumpet, Guy Klucevsek on accordion, and me on backward electric guitar. It was shockingly well received by the audience. Kyle Gann wrote glowingly about it in *The Village Voice* and maintains that the CD we eventually released remains one of his favorite recordings from that decade.[4] Given the daunting logistics of getting all these busy musicians together in one place, however, it was only performed by the original ensemble once again, and it would be another two years before it could be recorded.[5] Fortunately other groups stepped into the breach. The Relâche Ensemble performed it at the Pennsylvania Academy of Fine Arts in the fall of 1990; a Dutch language version was commissioned by the Korzo Theatre in The Hague in 1992 and performed in three cities by the Barton Workshop with Jaap Blonk as vocalist; and in 2002 the Emit Time festival in Bern, Switzerland, commissioned a quintilingual version (Schweizerdeutsch, French, Italian, Romansh, and English).

As a composer I am most comfortable working on a modest scale ("small forms"), but I have long embraced a parallel activity in which I bring larger groups together under amorphous rubrics—what usually gets called "curating." I loved the social and musical outcomes of arranging low-budget concerts at Wesleyan, and when Bill Hellermann asked if I wanted to take over as Sound Curator at PS1 in 1985, my reply was an eager "yes." My responsibilities included organizing sound art exhibitions at PS1 as well as a concert series at The Clocktower, its satellite on Leonard Street in lower Manhattan. In both venues, I saw an opportunity to bridge performance and installation and to tease out the relationships between experimental and minimalist work of the 1970s, the appropriationist ethos of 1980s visual art and music, as well as the busy improviser scene.

For two years I produced events at both sites, co-curating first with Jerry Lindahl and then Susan Stenger. Takehisa Kosugi—a founding figure in Fluxus and a pioneer of Japanese electronic music—created a quietly sublime installation that featured old-fashioned earpieces from portable radios buried under sand. We mounted an exhibition of the prose scores that Christian Wolff wrote while in residence at an art school in London in 1969. In the Clocktower Gallery, Christian Marclay tiled the floor wall-to-wall with LP records—the first iteration of his LP floor pieces—through which the spiral staircase leading up to the clock itself emerged like a giant turntable spindle (Figure 14.2). In our "New Solo Virtuosos" festival, Ben Neill gave his first New York one-man concert, Shelley Hirsch—the diva of downtown—ululated as she descended the staircase, and free jazz musician Jerome Cooper performed a mesmerizing percussion set.

In 1987 we organized a night of music by Christian Wolff played by local improvisers. Given the obvious similarities between John Zorn's game pieces from the 1980s and Christian's "co-ordination" scores from the 1960s, I asked John to participate. Acknowledging that Wolff "was once a big influence on me," he led a performance of *For 1, 2 or 3 People* with Wayne Horvitz and David Weinstein on keyboards and Zorn on alto sax. Elliott Sharp's band played some of the bluesier parts of Wolff's *Wobbly Music*, a work from the 1970s that incorporates songs by Joe Hill and others associated with the Industrial Workers of the World (Wobblies). The most poignant set of the night was Arthur Russell's delicate interpretation of a few of Wolff's songs arranged for cello and voice. Given the improvisers' somewhat casual approach to rehearsal, "some of the performances were wobblier than others," as Christian observed as he left to drive home to his farm on the Vermont-New Hampshire border. Apologizing for his prompt departure he explained, "it's lambing season" (an excuse seldom heard in Downtown New York).

In 1987, we also presented the world's first concert of remote-linked computer music, performed by the Hub, a networked computer sextet that grew out of the League of Automatic Music Composers. Our budget would only stretch to two airfares from San Francisco, so I persuaded Phill Niblock to co-produce an event in which three Hub members would perform at the Clocktower and three at Phill's Experimental Intermedia Foundation, ten blocks away, linked by modems. Mitchell Kapor (founder of Lotus Development Corporation and the Electronic Frontier Foundation) contributed $800 for the final two tickets. Computer networking was then so primitive we needed two separate phone lines to connect the two sites, one to send data from Niblock's to the Clocktower, and the other to return it. A single ticket gave admission to both spaces, and a leisurely intermission facilitated strolling between the two venues in warm spring evenings. Wide stereo.

In 1988, The Kitchen asked me to produce a two-week festival of live electronic music I titled, in a nod to Cage, "Imaginary Landscapes." Participants included both esteemed

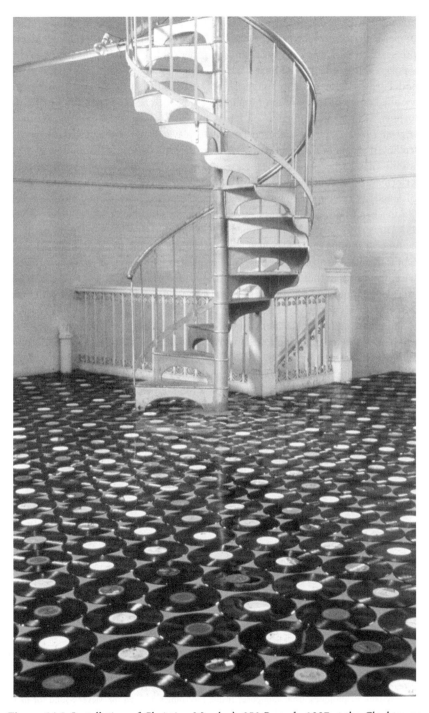

Figure 14.2 Installation of Christian Marclay's *850 Records*, 1987 at the Clocktower, P.S.1, New York, Spring 1987. © Christian Marclay, used by artist's permission.

veterans of experimentalism (Alvin, David Tudor, Maryanne Amacher) and younger composer-performers such as the Swiss duo Voice Crack, presiding over a table strewn with small circuits, and Laetitia Sonami, a former student of Robert Ashley, who gave a spoken word performance in which her French-intonated voice was chopped and modulated by homemade circuitry. Three sweaty buff figures twirled loudspeakers in Canadian composer Gordon Monahan's epic *Speaker Swinging*. Baritone Thomas Buckner sang about abduction by UFOs in "Blue" Gene Tyranny's *Somewhere in Arizona 1970*. A computer-driven Disklavier player piano spat out variations on a Beethoven sonata in Anglo-Indian composer Clarence Barlow's contribution.

Phil Glass, who was on the board of The Kitchen, underwrote recording the performances and persuaded Nonesuch Records to release a CD of the festival, which still stands as a testament to how listenable (and diverse) experimental music can be.[6]

Amacher, who was both famously loud and famously difficult, had not given a New York concert for years. I programmed her as the sole act on the opening night. In the months leading up to the event, I spoke with her regularly by phone, answering technical and logistical questions. She requested floorplans of the performance space, which I sent, but when we came to discuss her staging a few weeks later she professed ignorance of the details. "I'm a very busy person," she explained with some exasperation. "I can't be expected to open my mail!"

She moved into The Kitchen two days before her concert, filled every hour, but by 9 p.m. on the opening night she was ready. Multiple Meyer speakers were strewn asymmetrically about the space, with a sub-woofer the size of a phone booth near the center.[viii] The sound was oceanic. One dreadlocked audience member embraced the sub-woofer for the whole night, coupling the thunderous low frequencies directly to his groin.

Reviewing the concert in *The New York Times*, Peter Watrous compared this wall of sound to "bass-heavy reggae sound systems or a high-volume Sonic Youth concert at CBGB," while acknowledging how transformative the experience was.[7] Maryanne was irate over the pop-cultural allusions, but Kitchen curator Scott McCauley was sanguine: "I don't see what's wrong with this, they mention The Kitchen twice."

[viii] Meyer Sound Laboratories produced one of the best (and most expensive) loudspeaker systems for live concerts, which The Kitchen rented for the festival, a sign of their commitment to sound quality. The company's founder, John Meyer, had been one of the engineers behind the Grateful Dead's infamous "Wall of Sound"—a massive speaker array often credited with being the first truly "HiFi" PA system. Ralph Jones, from Composer Inside Electronics, worked for Meyer Sound for many years.

Interlude

Sound Check

1

In 2009, Matt Rogalsky, a former Lucier student, organized a retrospective of Alvin's music in Kingston, Ontario. He invited two fellow exes, composer Ben Manley and myself, to help with some of the pieces. On the first night, Matt programmed a concert of our music in a local club. I flew from Chicago that morning, changing in Toronto to a tiny plane for the last leg. My suitcase didn't arrive. The ground personnel in Kingston told me this was quite common, that the baggage hold was so small that it usually couldn't fit all the suitcases, but not to worry, it was sure to arrive on the next flight. Or the one after that. Very Canadian.

Matt finally retrieved my bag from the airport and brought it through the club door at 9 p.m. on the dot, the publicized start time of the set. I somehow managed to set up under the cover of the last sounds of the (slightly delayed) opening act and was ready to play when they ended. Subsequently, Alvin would comment, "Nic Collins can soundcheck a concert in no minutes."

2

At the end of a soundcheck in preparation for a shared concert in Germany, David Tudor commented, "Nic, I don't like your performances, but I love your soundchecks." I was reminded of my favorite card in Monopoly: "You have won second prize in a beauty contest! Collect $10." But better a soundcheck than nothing. My pieces in those days were short (five to fifteen minutes) and tightly structured, while Tudor luxuriated in more free-form forty-five-minute blocks, often with the Cunningham dancers providing visual distraction. Soundchecks, however, opened my material into looser timeframes, which he preferred. Periodically, I reach a point in the composition process when I ask myself, "should this sound more like a soundcheck?"

3

In 1991, Christian Marclay invited me to participate in his *100 Turntable Orchestra*, a project sponsored by Matsushita in Tokyo. This was at the nadir of turntable culture, when the public had fully embraced compact discs, so Panasonic (a subsidiary of Matsushita) had to pull back its Technics turntables from distributors all over Japan to populate a huge spiral table constructed in the center of Tokyo P/N, the company's showcase building in the Ginza. Performance responsibilities were shared by Christian, Otomo Yoshihide, Perry Hoberman, Jazzy Joyce (a young hip-hop DJ from the Bronx), and myself—twenty-five turntables per DJ.

A few of my hacked Sony Discmen lay on my table with the rest of my performance setup. Competition between Panasonic and Sony was fierce. When we came back from dinner after soundcheck, I discovered that the stage crew had placed a tiny strip of black gaffing tape over each Sony logo to prevent the possibility of the competitor's name being visible in any photo or video documentation of the event.

4

A year later Christian and I shared a concert at Fri-Art in Fribourg, Switzerland. Christian set up his turntables on one table, and I stacked my gear for the trombone-propelled electronics on another, several feet away. To sample his sounds, I plugged a long guitar cord into the output of his mixer and ran it across the stage to my table. Before connecting it to my equipment, I tapped the sleeve of the plug against the metal chassis of my amplifier—an unconscious habit I'd developed over the years to discharge static electricity. There followed a large spark, a bang like a starter's pistol, and the theater went completely dark. When the circuit breaker was reset and the lights came back on, I noticed that my plug was stuck to my amp. Evidently, the grounds were crossed between the electrical outlets on the two sides of the stage. Christian had plugged into one, I into another. When the plug bearing his ground touched my grounded chassis, 240 volts rushed down the wire, welding the sleeve to my metalwork. Had I plugged in without my precautionary tap, that voltage would have surged through my circuits instead, laying waste to several years of work.

15

Still Lives

In 1987, I did a two-week European tour with Elliott Sharp and Christian Marclay. The transatlantic tickets were paid for by the Captured Music festival in Karlsruhe, Germany, one of the first festivals to be organized around sampling. We reached out to our various contacts and strung together a series of dates that traced a wiggly line from Hungary to Switzerland.

Touring Eastern Europe was still difficult: visas could be hard to obtain, and the local currency was valueless once you returned to the West, so you had to spend all your earnings before you left. I sought out electronic oddities, while Christian hit flea markets and thrift shops in search of regional records to insert into the evening's concert. During sound check at a club in Budapest, he auditioned some material he had bought that morning. One spoken word disc triggered muttering among the crew. Eventually, a guy came up and suggested that it would be better not to play that particular one. "Why not?" It was a record of Stalin addressing a party congress in the 1930s. "Not a good thing."

Two years on, Peter Cusack and I were invited to play a series of concerts in Poland. Susan came along. I had not been back there since the Watson, and we arrived just weeks after the first non-communist government in a Soviet satellite had been installed. The rest of the East Bloc had been in turmoil for months. In East Germany, summer protests had been followed by a sharp clampdown, and the train platforms in East Berlin when we passed through were patrolled by guards with machine guns. In Warsaw, our host, composer Marek Chołoniewski, picked us up at the train station and drove us along a wide boulevard to the gig. Gesturing at an endless wall of drab concrete apartment blocks with his rolled-up Solidarity newspaper, a smiling Marek proclaimed, "We are no longer a communist country, but we still *look* like a communist country!" There was a giddiness in the air.

In Poznań, Peter commented on the minimal street lighting compared to Western European cities, which felt to him—a child of bare-bones post-war Britain—nostalgic. Shop window displays also had a non-Western paucity to them. At our venue, the sound system consisted of a home stereo that used multi-pin DIN sockets for which we had no matching plugs. I hadn't seen this type of connector since the 1970s, when it was still popular in Germany, but evidently, it never went out of fashion in the East. The Poles had lots of experience in making do, however: when I pointed out the problem to our local handler, she pulled a few bobby pins from her hair and asked, "Would these help?" I cut the end off of a patch cord, wrapped the bare wire around the pins, jammed them into the sockets, and we had sound.

After the concert, she asked if there was anything she could get for us. Peter and I replied that a beer would hit the spot. Her face fell.

"Oh, that's a problem—it's Friday."

The connection was lost on us. "No one drinks beer on the weekend?" Peter asked.

"Of course they do! But the beer goes on sale on Monday, so by Thursday it's sold out."

Poland was no longer a communist country, but the inefficiencies of a centrally planned economy did not disappear overnight. In Kraków, Peter's desire for a bath set off a two-hour scavenger hunt for matches with which to light the boiler. Our host returned triumphant, with two bars of soap. He explained that one bar of soap (unavailable in the shops at that moment) could be traded for matches (also unavailable in the shops).

Where Warsaw and Poznań bore scars from the War and blight from Soviet-style reconstruction, Kraków was architecturally epic. We played in a former synagogue (a slightly chilling experience, given the proximity to Auschwitz), assisted by an enthusiastic group of local musicians organized by Marek to improvise with us. A street near the venue was crossed with bright red banners proclaiming support for Solidarity. (When I returned almost ten years later for the "Audio Arts Festival" the same street was again festooned with red banners, this time announcing, in Polish, "Windows 95 is here!")

We returned to Berlin, where we spent several days visiting friends, including Matthias Osterwold and artist Barbara Bloom, his girlfriend at the time. We were having fun, and they urged us to push our return tickets back by a few days. We were tempted, but I had a concert in New York, and a home test had revealed that Susan was pregnant and she had yet to see a doctor. So we rode the train through East Germany (armed guards at every station), West Germany, and the Netherlands, where we caught our flight to New York. We were awakened by the phone early the next morning. It was Barbara. "Boy did you fuck up!" she shouted over the din of a city-wide party. "Turn on the news!"

The Wall had fallen while we were in the air.

Any regrets we had about missing the fall of the Wall were softened by the fact that we were indeed expecting a child. And whatever panic we had about being completely unprepared to be responsible adults was soothed by the pragmatism of our own parents. "Think of it as one of your little projects," advised Susan's mother, "like building bookshelves together." "It's really only a commitment of eleven years or so," offered my mother. "After that, kids are pretty independent" (an interesting insight into my own New York City upbringing).

Seven months later, on a clear morning after a dark and stormy night, we became parents ourselves.

Of course, I planned to take a long time off from touring once the baby was born, but a few months before the due date my friend Herb Levi telephoned to invite Peter and me to a festival he was producing in Seattle in July. As it happened, Peter and his partner were expecting a baby the same week we were. I explained we would both have to beg out. Then Herb quoted the fee.

I called Peter, who also demurred until he heard Herb's number.

"Blimey! That's what I earn in a year of gigs. Let me talk to Anna and I'll call you back."

Per the Anglo-American "special relationship," while many European artists could count on fairly generous state support, British artists were in the same leaky fiscal boat as Americans. When Swiss composer Thomas Kessler apologized for the modest (but unspecified) fee when he invited Peter and me to his annual festival in Bern, Peter laughed. "When the Swiss say they have a 'very small budget' you'll be paid more than you'll be paid anywhere else." True enough, with the apparent exception of Seattle.

A month after we welcomed two new people into the world, Peter and I rendezvoused at the Seattle airport. Every minute we weren't on stage found us back in our hotel room, sound asleep.

Susan and I had assumed that parenthood might push us toward a new fiscal pragmatism—a realization that my tech skills could be applied in a more remunerative domain, or that Susan should finish off that pesky PhD and hunker down in academe, or that both of us would feel a sudden yearning for the suburbs (or at least an apartment with bedroom doors). Instead, we looked at the baby and agreed, "We need a cottage of our own in the country!"

It was January 1991. Bush Sr. had just invaded Iraq. Getting out of the city seemed like a sensible idea, so we drove up to the family's summer house in West Falmouth. The real estate offerings in beach communities in winter are pretty thin, but the local paper featured an ad for a weirdly affordable property. We figured that either the address (in a village I had known since infancy) or the price must be a misprint since it was about a third of the cost of the next cheapest thing in town, but at dinner that night a friend assured us he knew the place—one of a quartet of small old houses tucked back along the disused railroad tracks.

The black-and-white photo in the paper had failed to capture the chromatic hysteria of the pink siding, lime-green trim, and Astro-turfed porch. Beneath the festive cladding, however, hid a solid, well-laid-out, century-old house on a stone foundation. There was a good climbing tree in the backyard and a claw-footed tub in the upstairs bath. The owner was the widow of the town's long-standing postmaster (a grouchy PT-boat veteran who had annoyed my father to no end by persistently addressing him as "sonny"). They had bought the house in 1946 and must have been the traveling salesman's best friends—the siding and Astroturf were complemented by Florida-style jalousie windows entirely unsuitable to New England winters—but it was clearly much-loved.

A couple of months later, and a half an hour after closing (made possible by a ludicrous new financial instrument offered by our bank: the "no income verification mortgage"), we were on the porch with a crowbar on the off chance the original Victorian porch posts were hiding behind the hammered-up plywood (they were).

Holding our baby in front like a Russian icon, we then introduced ourselves to our elderly, year-round neighbors, who took us in with subdued Yankee goodwill.

The plan was to rent it out for eleven months of the year, and spend August rehabbing—a rhythm we followed for some three decades. That first summer, Matthias flew from Berlin to visit Barbara in New York, and, being a serious gardener, he attacked the invasive plants encircling our yard while Susan and I ripped out knotty-pine paneling, wallpaper and carpeting, and slapped up paint around our son's nap schedule. Hurricane Bob hit the same day as the August Coup in Moscow. Christian Marclay arrived expecting an idyllic New England weekend and spent the time clearing downed tree limbs with me and teaching our toddler soccer.

A significant part of our income came from my touring, but being apart from the family for weeks at a time sucked. (It's both sweet and distressing to learn that your child started walking while you were 3,000 miles away.) Susan was now writing regularly for museums and periodicals on both sides of the Atlantic, so we began to romance the idea of renting a small apartment in Amsterdam as a base for European concerts. I wrote to Michel at STEIM for advice. He called back to say that he couldn't help us with an apartment, but would I like to take over his job as Artistic Director at STEIM?

Our peers were getting squeezed out of Manhattan—musicians and venues were moving to Brooklyn or departing the city altogether. Guns were on the rise. Our Bleecker Street block was sealed off for several hours one day as SWAT teams clambered over our fire escape yelling, "Get down! Get down!" Tuning in 1010 WINS, the local news radio (in those pre-web days), I learned that a neighbor across the street had gone up on his roof with an Uzi and sprayed the street in a factional dispute with members of the Jewish Defense League; he had missed his intended targets but hit a plumber sitting in a van eating his lunch, and was now holed up in the building with an arsenal of weaponry. After a standoff of several hours involving the theatrical intervention of a bomb-detonating robot, he surrendered. The plumber survived and New York being New York, the next day Susan passed a guy walking up and down the Bowery hawking "Jewish sniper bullets, five bucks!" Typical New York mayhem, perhaps, but it feels different when you're pushing a stroller.

Born and raised in Manhattan, I was a terrible snob about the outer boroughs. If we were going to cross a body of water, it might as well be a big one. "Artistic Director" had the ring of grown-up stability. In Amsterdam, we might be able to afford two bedrooms. Our baby would learn to speak Dutch! The prospect of good, free education glittered on the horizon. We sold off furniture and most of my recording studio, held a goodbye party at Roulette, then loaded everything that was left into a U-Haul truck and drove to Cape Cod. Since the house was rented out for eleven months of the year, our possessions went into the attic, whose floor joists we had reinforced in anticipation of ninety-seven boxes of books and records. We spent the summer chasing our toddler up and down the beach, and in September 1992 flew to Amsterdam.

Through a friend of a friend, we sublet the upper two floors of a seventeenth-century house on a narrow alley off the Nieuwendijk, a pedestrian shopping strip that runs from Central Station to Dam Square, offering an endless supply of spandex clothing and energetic pickpockets. The house was tiny—400 square feet split between an open-kitchen-living-room floor and the two bedrooms tucked up under the eaves, accessed by a spiral staircase of remarkably slippery metal. (I have never understood why the world's largest people built the smallest houses.)

Six weeks after we arrived, the *Vreemdelingenpolitie* (immigration authorities) informed me that my job was illegal and we could be deported because STEIM had never bothered to apply for working papers. STEIM's lawyer eventually submitted the appropriate documents, but not before some tense interactions down at the immigration hall.

One of the great things about toddlers is that they don't yet know what they're supposed to be interested in and, as a result, can find fascination in anything. One day we took a father-son train trip to The Hague to visit Radio Twente, a wonderfully funky electronics shop. Susan needed quiet writing time, I needed parts for a project, and I figured a two-year-old might have fun exploring the bins of colorful components and picking something out to take home. Nothing in the shop cost more than a few guilders.

Back in Amsterdam, the new toy was enthusiastically brandished for maternal admiration. Susan looked at me and sighed. "You bought a two-year old a telescoping radio antenna? Did you never hear the expression, 'you could put someone's eye out'?" Sensible response, but the antenna remained, as did all our eyeballs.

The following fall we moved into a larger apartment on the Palestrinastraat, a short, quiet street named for the sixteenth-century composer, close to the Vondelpark and the Concertgebouw. The movie star Huub Stapel lived a few doors down, flustering our normally unflappable babysitter. (Susan and I were less au fait with Dutch cinema, but nonetheless smitten with his beautiful spaniels.)

TV brought in Dutch, Belgian, French, German, and British stations, each broadcast in its original language (this immersion from childhood is undoubtedly a major factor in the polylingual competence of the Dutch). We'd surf the news channels with the sound muted, trying to guess the language by the movement of the lips and hands. Every nation had a characteristic labial and manual choreography, with the pursed French moue being perhaps the most distinctive.

Many young children have obsessions: a stuffed animal or doll, blocks, a favorite food, trains. With our son, it was cars. Cars were coveted, hoarded, played with, carried on planes in a small but heavy vintage suitcase that always drew attention when it passed through security scanners. His play often took the form of set theory: placing three cars (it was almost always three) in a line on a chair or sofa, he would stare at them for a few minutes, then replace one from the stock down at his knees; there would be another episode of study, another exchange—this could go on for an hour.

At the time we moved to Amsterdam, every stroll was accompanied by his small voice calling out the make and model of every car we passed, reminding me of the Guastavino-vault-spotting of my own childhood. I'm not sure how such encyclopedic knowledge was acquired in the days before Google and with parents who neither owned nor cared for cars, but it never failed. One night we sat outdoors at a neighborhood restaurant with friends, while our three-year-old identified everything driving by or parked on the block. This continued until our friend Tom Demeyer, a programmer at STEIM, interrupted:

> "No, that one's not a Citroen."
> "Citroen."
> "Sorry, you're wrong."
> "Citroen."

The bickering went on until it was suggested that the two of them take a walk down the block for a closer look. Our son was smiling when they returned. The telltale sign, he informed us, was that the rear wheel well was cut straight across rather than arched.

(Tom, however, proved an important mentor. When the car-obsessed, mathematically-precocious child was four and observed, "Infinity must be an even number because $\infty/2$ = infinity," Tom asked, "Okay, but how much is $\infty + 1$?" A moment's thought and a broad preschool smile. "Infinity is a special number because it's both even and odd! Like zero!" A sign of things to come.)

We had always heard, and believed, that small children pick up languages easily. As with so many truisms, however, it depends on the kid. After a year of semi-participation in a Dutch preschool, ours was standing in the corner saying, in English, "I don't speak Dutch." There was no problem with comprehension—mention *ijs* (ice cream), *cadeautje* (gift), or *pindakaas* (peanut butter) and the little hand shot up. But speaking was another matter. Susan consulted her sister, a child psychologist. "Well, in the long run, which do you think is more important—Dutch as a second language or social skills?" Our dreams of free Dutch education were doomed the moment we walked through the doors of the British School of Amsterdam. It was the kind of school you'd move 4,000 miles just to enroll your kid in, and it was walking distance from our house.

We now had a nice place to live, a great school (albeit far from free), friends both expat and native, a regular income, a wonderful babysitter, and soon enough, a second child born in record time at Onze Lieve Vrouw hospital. I enjoyed my job, and even a difficult day was capped by a bike ride home through fairy lights that arced along canal bridges and reflected, dancing, in the water. I could even carve out time for my own music.

Spoken word had figured in my compositions before, but the ritual of reading to my children made me acutely aware of the power of prosody: I learned how to inflect any text, from *Goodnight Moon* to *The New Yorker*, to entertain or lull to sleep. We may have been overly indulgent in the way of bedtime rituals. At its most elaborate, my evening routine consisted of

1. Inventing a story that functioned within one of several established franchises—the bed that became a magic boat and the evildoings of the Pasta Monster were the ones I remember best.

2. Improvising a poem featuring characters from the story. The last syllables have to rhyme, and the opening phonemes of successive lines have to be alliterative as well. (Video artist Steina Vasulka later informed me this was a traditional Icelandic poetic form.)
3. Reading a story from a book.
4. Loading a cassette of Prokofiev's *Romeo and Juliet* into his red-and-yellow My First Sony™ and press play.

In Amsterdam, speech acquired a significance that reached beyond bedtime: all around me as we settled into polyglot Europe, I heard words. Sometimes I understood them, most often I sort of understood them, but sometimes they were pure sound. Hearing my own voice, speaking English, now evoked a bittersweet sense of sonic *Heimat*, like whistling to oneself in the absence of a radio.

It Was a Dark and Stormy Night had been a landmark in my musical development and would go on to be performed in various languages. But it was not as portable as my solo or duo repertoire. So I set about on yet another round of adaptations that had started with *Tobabo Fonio*, now extracting the core innovations of *It Was a Dark and Stormy Night* and mapping them onto a reduced set of resources. This became *Sound For Picture* (1992).

Read aloud, a text by South African poet David Wright describing his experience of going deaf as a child resonates the open strings of a backwards lap-steel electric guitar, as voice did in the ensemble piece. The performance follows a similar descending voice-resonated pitch pattern, and once again vocal inflection triggers drum samples. There is an optional part for an acoustic musician. From a big brass band to small form electronics to not-so-small form ensemble and back to small again—a derivative of a derivative of a derivative.

Sound For Picture became the starting point for *Sound Without Picture*, a series of compositions that would carry me through the next decade.[1] Each piece extracted sound and form from the inflection of spoken word and was built around a text that invoked the heightened presence or traumatic absence of a sense—sight, hearing, taste, touch, smell and "sixth sense." The rhythm, inflection, and timbre of the spoken voice were translated into sonic accompaniment by means I had used before—resonating the strings of backwards electric guitars, triggering drum or piano samples from a pitch-to-MIDI converter, digital signal processing—and with new forms of technology as I developed them over the course of the series. The texts came from books, interviews with friends, newspaper stories, or were penned by Susan or myself. Composing the series formed the musical and linguistic spine of my years in Europe: the first emerged as we arrived in Amsterdam, and I recorded the last one (*The Scent of Mimosa*) while we were preparing to move back to the States eight years later. This musical output would never have happened without the commonplace experience of negotiating the threshold of sleep with my children.

Parenting also triggered an increased awareness of the fragility of life. I had experienced all sorts of emotions before—from love to bliss to heartbreak—but I had never been interested in making work "about my feelings." The non-pop music I most admired was about (I thought) things like physics, and biology and other objective phenomena made present in new and affecting ways. (The notion that a work like *I am sitting in a room* contained intimations of mortality and the erasure of self would have struck me as completely wrongheaded.)

The delights of parenthood, however, brought with them a new sense of precariousness and of the relentlessness of time. And within a few months of our arrival in Amsterdam we were hit with a number of losses: my grandmother in Chile died, followed by my father. They were both elderly and neither death was unexpected. But then in May we lost our close friend Stuart Marshall. Although Stuart had been diagnosed with AIDS some years previously, the end came unexpectedly and left me reeling.

Now the skipping CD material I had understood so dispassionately ("interesting textures" etc.) revealed itself to me as a gesture toward stopping time. I wrote a new piece, *Still Lives* (1993), as a memorial to Stuart. (In art history the correct plural for pictures of apples in a bowl is "still lifes"; the use of a "v" in place of the "f" in my title allows for a double reading as a verb that is entirely intentional.) A hacked CD player steps through skipping loops of a recorded canzone by the sixteenth-century Venetian composer Giuseppe Guami. A live instrument (usually trumpet) anticipates and suspends pitch material from the pulsing harmonies, while a narrator reads a passage from Vladimir Nabokov's memoirs in which he recalls, with preternatural detail, a moment from childhood that was unremarkable but for his retrospective observation that "everything was as it should be, nothing will ever change, nobody will ever die."[i]

---

[i]   The piece evoked the uncanny so well that it later assumed the role of representing sixth sense in my sense series.

16

STEIM—IRCAM with a Human Face

In 1986, STEIM relocated from the Red Light District to a stately building on the Achtergracht canal, steps from the Amstel River and the iconic *Magere Brug* drawbridge. The main building was spacious and connected to a narrow residential building on the street behind that could be used to house visiting artists, soon dubbed the "STEIM Hotel." A single-story concert space linked the two buildings. This real estate coup was engineered by Michel, who had been tipped off that the cultish commune run by Adelbert Nelissen that was squatting the building was about to relocate. Michel called the building owner (tour boat mogul Ab Kooi) with a proposition: STEIM personnel would move into the building while it was being vacated by the commune, before any new squatters could arrive, if Kooi would give the organization a below-market, long-term lease. Evicting squatters was difficult and expensive, and some income was preferable to no income. Although central Amsterdam real estate values later skyrocketed, Kooi remained true to his word and STEIM held onto those facilities until after Kooi's death. (In 1998, Nelissen, an early advocate of a macrobiotic diet, was brought up on quackery charges in the deaths of four cancer patients he persuaded to refuse standard medical care in favor of his alternatives.)[1]

The main building housed the engineering facilities, offices, studios, a concert space, and an apartment for Michel. The STEIM Hotel, meanwhile, meant the organization could now invite artists from all over the world to come and work. The first American guests were George Lewis and California composer Joel Ryan, who arrived from residencies at IRCAM in Paris soon after STEIM's move.

Despite ostensibly similar missions, IRCAM and STEIM could not have been less alike in character. I had failed to get in the door of either organization during my Watson year, but at IRCAM this was a result of its Byzantine gate-keeping, while at STEIM everyone was out, probably because it was a nice day to sit outside a café. (As one expat, long-resident in the Netherlands, explained: "The Dutch spent centuries working every hour of every day to keep the water out. Now they're enjoying a long weekend.")

For all STEIM's casual demeanor, however, the musical technologies developed there were remarkably prescient. Their pragmatic approach of piggybacking bespoke inventions on the back of commercial products stood in marked contrast to IRCAM's insistence on building the best from the ground up. STEIM's "Lick Machine" program, developed in the 1980s, manipulated MIDI data as if it were sampled sound—

speeding up note commands, slowing them down, looping them, changing their start and end points—inspiring the German software company Ableton's commercially successful "Live" software, launched in 2001. The SensorLab—a paperback-sized computer that converted switches and other sensors into MIDI data for controlling commercial synthesizers and samplers from homemade electronic instruments—demonstrated the utility of embedded computers for creative use, leading to Arduino's development of compact, affordable single-board microcontrollers in 2005. Both of these STEIM innovations emerged in response to technical requests from Michel for use with his "Hands" gestural controller: the SensorLab converted sensors on two hand-mounted miniature keypads into MIDI data, and Michel used the Lick Machine to play back and transform musical riffs that played on his synthesizers. Todd Machover started the "hyperinstrument" project at MIT's Media Lab "with the goal of designing expanded musical instruments" a few months after returning from the 1985 "Symposium on Interactive Composing in Live Electronic Music," which highlighted STEIM's technological developments and artistic outcomes.[2] And, to this day, many of the presentations at the annual "New Instruments for Musical Expression" (NIME) conference, founded in 2001, can be traced back to STEIM's innovations.

STEIM's best-known product was probably the Cracklebox (*Kraakdoos*), also inspired by Michel. His father, a ham-radio buff, had removed the back panel of his receiver to help cool the machine, which is how a young Michel discovered that if he touched the exposed circuit boards with his fingers, strange sounds flowed from the speakers. He played for several minutes before his hands brushed against the 240-volt power supply, knocking him across the floor. When he awoke, the radio had been nailed to the wall, but the vision of an electronic instrument that could be played by skin contact stuck with him.

Working with engineer Geert Hamelberg, Michel designed an instrument whose circuitry and speaker were packed into a wooden case the size of a box of kitchen matches. The circuit board was exposed for direct touch, like his dad's radio but safer (powered by a 9-volt battery): the player's skin created the essential feedback paths by which the circuit went into oscillation, and changing the position and pressure of one's fingers shifted the sound from swoops to glitches. Touch contacts had been incorporated into keyboard controllers by maverick synthesizer designers Donald Buchla and Serge Tcherepnin, but the Cracklebox was the first mass-produced electronic musical instrument that used the player's skin as a variable electrical component in a sound-generating circuit. Four thousand would eventually be sold.

STEIM served musicians like myself, who were accustomed to making their own devices with whatever skills they had, but also those who had an idea but not the means of realizing it. This was a symbiotic relationship: Artists arrived with concepts for bespoke instruments; STEIM engineers started from these prompts and developed technology that in turn inspired other artists to do new things. Both the originator of the idea and those who came later to work with the hardware or software results profited from cumulative user evaluations and feature requests. Unbundling innovations from the individuals behind them, STEIM developed resources that could be more broadly used. This model of crowd-sourced niche technology became a distinctive trait of the foundation's activities.

The engineers (mostly young) offered advice but expected the artists to do most of the work themselves. They often disappeared to the nearest herring stand when most needed, taking a tough-love approach to uncramping the visitor's maker-mind. They occupied that sweet spot between hiring a proper contractor to do a job and phoning a handy friend for help hanging your kitchen cabinets.

My own experience as a repeat artist at STEIM was a lesson in both perseverance and failure. On the heels of trombone-propelled electronics, I had an idea for a new instrument that would extend the polyphony of sound manipulation. The trombone slide could only move along one axis, which meant I could only change one parameter at a time. At a festival in Quebec in 1988, the image of a concertina popped unbidden into my head: if I replaced the reed-buttons on each face with pushbutton switches, I would double the size of the trombone keypad and make it accessible by two hands. I could map the flex of each of the six sides of the bellows to a different sonic parameter, and I could embed a speaker inside, hook the whole thing up to a signal processor, and squeeze away on a compact, six-slider trombone. Or so went my vision.

STEIM's SensorLab device—then under development—would be perfect for translating all those switches and sensors into data, so I pitched a proposal to STEIM, resulting in a three-month project residency in 1988. And another in 1989. And one in 1990. The problem, I eventually realized, was not technological; it was my approach to playing. The old trombone was "sticky": the slide moved smoothly enough for my purposes but stayed in place when I removed my hand. The bellows of the concertina, however, were floppy, and I had to hold my hands perfectly motionless to keep the data output from jittering. It was more of a "free-air controller" like a Theremin or Michel's Hands. Such free movement works well for some performers (Michel was a former boxer), but not me.[3] There are limits to technical cleverness when it runs up against the human body.

Despite the disappointing outcome, the effort was not without benefit. In 1994, en route to a concert in London, a taxi ran over my trombone at Schiphol airport. Several hours later, I played duos with Peter Cusack on a curiously bent instrument, and continued to perform with it for several months until, seconds before beginning a live Dutch radio broadcast, it died, dramatically and permanently. In the wake of the taxi trauma, I heeded the inner Boy Scout motto, "be prepared," and began designing a second trombone controller, this one based on the SensorLab and the coding I'd developed for the concertina. In lieu of the cute but clattering dog leash, ultrasound measured the movement of the slide with precision. The SensorLab generated MIDI (rather than the homebrew protocol of the first version, dubbed "NICI"), which was sent to a commercially available multi-effects unit that replaced the hot-wired but now stone-cold Stargate. This gave me most of the basic looping and sampling effects of the original system, minus a few of its quirkier ones, but with new options and the potential for upgrading and expanding as new MIDI devices became available. In

February 1995, I was shedding tears over the loss of my long-time companion, but by March this merry widower was seen in public with rev.2. Over the next four years I extended the SensorLab code and hardware, as I adapted the instrument for several composed works and improvisational strategies.

In part because of the failure of my concertina project, I brought to the STEIM job a useful range of experiences in the nascent field of "alternative controllers" (devices for controlling electronic sound that were not based on the usual piano keyboard) and extended instruments. The job entailed four main areas of responsibility: guiding research and development of hardware and software; supervising the artist-in-residence program; organizing concerts, symposia, and outside events; and general administration. The first three activities were closely linked: most residencies were tied to adapting some form of STEIM technology to an artist's personal project, and concerts provided a platform for demonstrating what had been accomplished. We brought in around fifty artists each year for residencies that ranged from one-week orientations to month-long visits spent constructing their inventions. (These were capped at one month shortly after my three-month visit because, as Michel explained, "After four weeks the artists lose concentration and spend most of their time in coffee shops [Amsterdam's legal pot vendors].")

Some projects (like my concertina) did not live up to expectations, but others were brilliant. Laetitia Sonami's "Lady's Glove"—finger flex sensors from a Virtual Reality controller sewn into an elegant evening glove—provided a powerful, intuitive link between hand gesture and sound, which she incorporated fluidly in her works for spoken word.[i] Jon Rose's "Space Violin" used a deceptively simple mechanism—an ultrasonic transmitter that measured the distance between the tip of his violin bow and a receiving sensor some feet away—to add an electronic voice to his acoustic instrument, generating a burbling, semi-autonomous counterpoint from both small bowing gestures and more dramatic fencing motions.

Visiting artists were given tiny private studios on the top floor of the main building, whose quiet isolation was sometimes the high point of a visit (Ben Neill spent his whole stay in his studio, scoring on paper a new piece for solo trumpet). There was a SensorLab Lab equipped with scraps of wood in various shapes and sizes and an array of sensors covered in Velcro so artists could quickly assemble prototype instruments in a Lego-like fashion: drumsticks that detected the upper limit of your stroke instead of its impact; a tennis racket that translated the speed of your swing into a musical glissando.[ii] The basement was outfitted with a workbench, a drill press, and hand tools needed to fabricate physical instruments or boxes for circuits (it also housed twenty-five years of damaged or abandoned instruments, as well as what passed for STEIM's archive). There was a concert space with adjacent recording studios on the ground

---

[i] Her first instrument used sensors from the Mattel "Power Glove" game controller designed by Rich Gold.

[ii] Design of this lab was outsourced to BMBCon, a Dutch media performance trio with a long-standing symbiotic relationship with STEIM. I had met them in Middleburg at my first STEIM concert in 1984.

Figure 16.1 Ben Neill (left) and the author rehearse *Still Lives* at STEIM, Amsterdam, October 1993. Photo by Stéphan Janin.

floor. (See Figure 16.1.) Almost everything needed for a project (not including pot) could be handled in-house. (One of the recording studio spaces was hung with hinged panels that could be opened and shut to vary the acoustics. The design was borrowed from the concert hall at IRCAM but while IRCAM's were motorized STEIM's had to be adjusted by hand. Modesty has its rewards: IRCAM's eventually froze in place, while STEIM's remained operational until the foundation moved out in 2017.)[iii]

In the 1990s, STEIM's research focus shifted from hardware to software when advances in personal computers made it possible to process sound and video without additional, special-purpose hardware (eliminating the bottleneck that prompted the Commodore-Stargate hybrid of my trombone-propelled electronics). In 1993, Tom Demeyer wrote "Big Eye," one of the first image-tracking programs for translating movement into MIDI data. A few years later, he programmed an inverse of sorts, "Image/ine," which manipulated video in response to MIDI commands (inspired by discussions with video artist Steina Vasulka, who succeeded me as Artistic Director in 1995). Frank Baldé programmed the first version of "LiSa," software for live sampling, in 1995 in response to Michel's growing interest in incorporating that technique into

[iii] STEIM's pragmatism grew out of a long Dutch tradition of fiscal frugality. When Susan and I were expecting our second child in Amsterdam, our midwife and friends encouraged us to opt for a home birth, since having a child at the hospital (as we had with our son in NY) was "much more expensive," even with insurance. Digging deeper, Susan discovered that the difference was less than $100.

his Hands instrument.[iv] This became one of the most widely used STEIM innovations since the Cracklebox.

With funding from the city of Amsterdam, we ran a concert series every Thursday night for three months each spring. (Thursdays had been picked by Michel because he maintained there was never anything good on television that night.) I would stand up at the start of each concert and announce the forthcoming events in my best Dutch, which never got very fluent. One night a friendly drunk collared me: "We love it when you try to speak Dutch, but it really doesn't matter who's on the bill. There's a saying in Amsterdam: 'If you're not doing anything else on Thursday night, go to STEIM.'" The bar in the foyer certainly didn't hurt our popularity, though it may have diminished the quality of our video documentation: shunning the usual camera tripod, STEIM had a monopod on the assumption it was easier to move around, but after a thirst-quenching intermission, the second set often entered the archive with considerable wobble.

We had some wonderful concerts: Jon Rose performed badminton-controlled music from his opera on the life and sado-masochistic loves of Percy Grainger; the eighteen musicians of Laboratorio di Musica e Immagine drove up from Bologna in a big van for a night of music and silent film, cooked dinner for everyone in the STEIM Hotel, and returned to Italy the next morning. Performance artist Stelarc showed slides of an event in New York in which he suspended himself, completely naked, from pulleys connected to hooks embedded in the flesh of his back and shuttled like a gondola between the upper stories of buildings on either side of a street in the East Village. Crawling in through the window at his destination, he was greeted by several burly New York cops demanding identification. "Can you imagine?" he chortled. "Identification? I was NAKED! Where was I going to carry my passport?"

STEIM had its supportive scene in Amsterdam, but elsewhere in the Netherlands, audiences for adventurous music were often small and cool in their response, despite the quality of the venues and production. I commented on this to the director of the Royal Conservatory of The Hague, Frans de Ruiter, a high-up in Dutch music funding circles. "This is quite normal," he assured me. "The Dutch have an understanding: We will pay taxes to support culture, but don't expect us to enjoy it."

This belief in the value of culture, even if underappreciated, ran deep. In 1990, as the American National Endowment for the Arts was under fire for funding exhibitions of "obscene" artists such as Robert Mapplethorpe, Susan interviewed a spokesperson at the Ministry of Culture for an article in *Art in America*. Perplexed by these American controversies, he observed that in Holland, "the government considers culture a kind of infrastructure of the country. Like roads and sewers."

This largesse led to policies that were often hard for Americans to get their heads around. One day, composer Maarten Altena walked into the office with a poster for a

---

[iv] Many of LiSa's core features are similar to techniques I implemented a decade earlier, in cruder form, in my trombone-propelled electronics, which had been presented at STEIM on numerous occasions since its inception—another example of the symbiotic relationship between artists and developers at STEIM.

ten-city Dutch tour marking the tenth anniversary of his ensemble. I was baffled. Most of the towns were less than an hour apart by subsidized public transportation. I had attended concerts in every one and returned to my bed in Amsterdam by midnight.

"Wouldn't it make more sense to play four concerts in the Netherlands and spend the rest of the budget on gigs in other countries like Germany or France?" I asked in my innocence.

Maarten laughed. "No Dutch person would travel more than twenty minutes for a concert, and besides, the funding agency only supports performances in Holland."

Things were vibrant and comfortable inside the country but sometimes curiously disconnected from the external world in a way that had not been the case in the 1960s and 1970s. Many artists and composers were content within the borders of the small nation that nurtured them, with the result that Dutch art of the 1980s was not often seen abroad. The few internationally visible Dutch artists, such as painter Ger van Elk, were often critical of what they saw as coddling. Ger was a good friend of ours, having met Susan when she was working for his New York Gallery and introduced him to the classic egg cream at Dave's Luncheonette on Canal Street. His work was deft, humorous, and conceptually complex, and he had an abiding interest in odd music. To me, he was unfailingly generous and invited me to perform at several of his museum openings in the Netherlands and Germany. Partly educated in Los Angeles, where his father was an animator for Hanna-Barbera, Ger was enough of an outsider to regularly slam Dutch cultural institutions in public media, and enough of an insider to be tapped to do a portrait of Queen Beatrix.

The Dutch music fan with the sticky fingers I had met in Warsaw once visited us in New York, where he spent hours on long-distance calls to the Netherlands, appealing a planned reduction in the government stipend for the pirate radio station he had been running. Susan thought that perhaps something in this story had been lost in translation and explained that in English "pirate stations" were actually illegal. "Just because something is illegal there's no reason the government should not fund it!" our friend fumed. It took me years to understand the many shades of gray in the Dutch legal code. Recognizing that once you declare an activity illegal you lose control of it to criminals, the pragmatic Netherlands developed a kind of purgatory (*gedoogbeleid* or tolerance policy) whereby things like pot dealing, prostitution, and euthanasia are not actually legal, but won't be prosecuted if regulations are followed. Susan used to say that life for an American in the Netherlands was confusing because superficially everything looked so familiar, but with critical hidden differences it could take decades to intuit.

For example, I was never able to break into the Dutch granting network, in part because of my lack of instinct for how things were divided up. The Dutch tradition of *zuilen* (pillars—a term originally used to designate the country's parallel Catholic and Protestant cultures) meant that even artists were quickly and rather rigidly categorized. Soon after moving to Amsterdam I was given the advice, "Whatever you do, don't play at the Bimhuis [the major venue for jazz and improvised music] or you'll be labeled a 'jazz artist.'" As I discovered in the course of several unsuccessful applications for grants to support instrumental compositions, my STEIM position had marked me as an *electronic music* composer (moreover, one year the panel added the criticism that my music "sounded too American").

Nonetheless, the Netherlands showed me how a society could de-marginalize its artists. We raised our young family in a nice apartment in a nice neighborhood, down the block from a famous actor. If Dutch grants panels did not smile on me, increasingly musicians and ensembles both inside and outside of Holland did. Shortly after inviting the multinational Barton Workshop to perform in the Dutch version of *It Was a Dark and Stormy Night*, Jim Fulkerson, its American director, asked if I would join the group as co-director.

Essen-based flute player Lesley Olsen commissioned *Shotgun* (1995), which involved embedding a tiny speaker in the end-cork of her bass flute and connecting it to a hacked CD player that skipped through a recording of shakuhachi music—a hybrid of my trombone-propelled electronics and my CD hacks. Her fingering not only determined the flute note that sounded by blowing, but it also filtered the recording of the shakuhachi as it played back through the air column of the instrument. The two sound sources modulated each other acoustically. Listening to the pitch bends of the shakuhachi drawn out to half a minute, Lesley observed, "these days a semitone is a hell of a big interval"—a timely observation, given that microtonal music was all the rage in the 1990s, with Amsterdam as a major center of composition, performance, and archiving.[v]

The Nederlands Blazers Ensemble requested a new work that would adapt the skipping CD and solo trumpet of *Still Lives* to a brass ensemble, to be premiered at their New Year's Day concert at the Concertgebouw in 1997. For *Die Schatten* [Shadows] (1996) I burned two audio CDs with twenty-two iterations of Schubert's five-minute-long elegy *Eine Kleine Trauermusik* (the ensemble director had specified the composer to use). One modified CD player steps through the first track on one disc, while another plays the last one. The eighteen musicians play against these two versions of the same recording, each looping at a different tempo, creating rich, shifting polyrhythms.[4]

The Concertgebouw New Year's concert was a nationally televised event, and as it happened, the opening piece on the program was Prokofiev's *Romeo and Juliet*, the lullaby of choice for our son. As the horns boomed their loping refrain and the crane-mounted television cameras swooped low over the front rows, the nation saw Susan with a blissfully snoozing blond head in her lap. Prokofiev meets Pavlov.

The most ambitious project I organized in the Netherlands was *Stroomgeest*, a weekend-long event that filled an abandoned wing of an old manor house with installations and performances that touched on experiences of haunting (the title was a neologism combining the Dutch words for spirit or ghost and for current or flow). Dutch visual artists Ger, Christiaan Bastiaans, Mirjam de Zeeuw, Felix Hess, and Jo Heijnen shared crumbling spaces with video pioneer Steina Vasulka (Iceland), musicians Matt Wand (England) and Matthijs de Bruine (Netherlands), British expat photographer Annie Wright, and myself.

---

[v] "Microtonal music" generally refers to any form of music that utilizes pitch intervals that deviate from the standard semitone tuning of the piano and most orchestral instruments (often known as "equal temperament"). It can be applied to the alternate tunings of the same twelve named steps, but is most commonly associated with scales that utilize more steps and smaller intervals, such as quarter-tones.

Some years earlier Susan had become interested in the Pre-Raphaelite painter and writer Anna Mary Howitt (1824–84), an ancestor who in mid-career had turned from painting to Spiritualism. Feminist historians were just starting to recover the overlooked or fragmentary careers of artists like Howitt, while in other corners of academe, Spiritualism was being reconsidered in the context of a historical moment in which invisible phenomena like electromagnetism, radio, and the subconscious were just beginning to have names.

You cannot work with radio or feedback without becoming aware of their occasional spookiness, and there is an obvious affinity between the post-Cagean desire to outsource decision-making and the methods employed by mediums, Freud and frauds aside. The planchette or wineglass used in séances to point to letters on a table can be seen as a kind of "alternative controller," though who was controlling what was open to question.

I had pulled these elements together in a 1991 performance at Roulette under the title *Truth in Clouds*. (The phrase was taken from Howitt's hero and nemesis, John Ruskin.) Singers Shelley Hirsch and K. J. Lang sat at a table with fingers on an inverted wineglass, singing and speaking texts from Howitt's writing; an ultrasonic sonar system extracted from a Polaroid SX-70 camera tracked the movement of the glass and channeled sound through props strewn around the space in emulation of the sonic trickery or (for believers) true revelations of séances. STEIM's Big Eye software offered improvements on my technology, allowing me to recast *Truth in Clouds* as an interactive installation where visitors' fingers could activate the wineglass and the dislocated sonic banquet.

With this in mind, I sought out other artists and projects sympathetic to the slightly spooky rubric. Through a gallery connection of Susan's, I met a Dutch art collector who not only was interested in my curatorial concept and its participants but happened to own one of the oldest country houses in the region, once grand, now fallen into disrepair. While he waited to restore it, he was happy to let a bunch of artists construct installations in the abandoned rooms.

Although less than an hour from Amsterdam, Groot Bentveld was considered remote by Dutch standards, and the opening took place at midnight during a thunderstorm on Ascension Day (one of those religious holidays when all retail in the defiantly secular Netherlands shuts down by law). STEIM hired a bus whose seats sold out quickly, leading people to carpool and borrow vehicles to get to the event. The experience prompted one of my truisms about curating: produce an event that's easy to get to and some people will come; produce one that's difficult to get to and no one will come; produce something that's *impossible* to get to and everyone will come. Foot traffic over the run of the show was impressive, although many locals came simply to walk through the house, which had been abandoned and sealed for many years.[vi] (The funding for this project came in part from the Thuiskopie Fonds, a new agency set up to distribute proceeds from a recent tax on blank cassette tape.)

[vi] The site requirements of *Stroomgeest* prompted my technical director to turn to me at the end of one phone call and utter the words, "You know you're a festival producer when you rent chemical toilets."

Interlude

Silence

1

When selling high-end professional audio gear, sometimes the best pitch is the most minimal one. The big trade exhibitions are usually held in cavernous convention centers, where everything is loud even before salesmen start demonstrating speakers and effects. In the 1980s, a welcome respite was provided by Sonex, who made nubbly foam rubber sheets for mounting on walls of recording studios to absorb sound and cut down reflections. Their sales team assembled Sonex panels to form a tunnel, eight feet high, four feet wide. The moment you entered, the din of the convention center would subside into a gentle murmur. You'd have your checkbook out by the time you strolled out twenty feet later. Professional audio gear? Expensive. Silence? Priceless . . .

2

Acoustics in a concert hall change with the size of an audience. Clothed bodies absorb sound, so a full hall always sounds warmer than an empty one. A clever engineer invented an auditorium seat whose bottom panel has the same sound absorption factor as the average adult: when unoccupied, the cushion flips up to a vertical position, exposing the absorptive material underneath, minimizing the sonic difference between an empty and full hall. Which works fine until winter: bulky winter coats soak up more sound than a seersucker suit (and I've never heard of such seating coming equipped with interchangeable summer and winter baffles). The acoustician Cyril Harris had a clause in his contracts that mandated that all overcoats must be checked before entering a hall of his design, lest his signature sound shift seasonally. This triggered consternation among patrons: Harris seemed disinterested in the fact that audience members don't wear fur coats to check them at the door, they wear them to be seen wearing them.

In 2017, I was a guest in a residency program in Madeira. The dining room of our hotel felt quieter than it should have for its size, even off-season. One evening, I absent-mindedly ran my fingers under the lip of the table and recoiled from the sensation of what I assumed were wads of bubblegum placed there by younger guests. I bent down and noticed instead a sheet of nubbly Sonex-like absorptive foam inset into the bottom of the table. This material took the edge off the typical din of a restaurant by trapping the noise of conversation and clattering dishes as the sound waves bounced up off the floor. A clever, invisible solution to a common problem.

3

Around the corner from our apartment in Amsterdam and across the street from the Concertgebouw's stage door stood a comfortable café that had changed very little since the turn of the century. It was one of the only bars in Amsterdam with no background music and, as a result, was popular with musicians. According to legend, shortly after it opened, the concertmaster of the Concertgebouw orchestra paid a visit. "If you promise never to play music, I will bring the orchestra here after every performance."

4

In the early 1980s, the back pages of magazines like *Guitar Player* and *Keyboard* often contained small advertisements for the "Thompson Vocal Eliminator." This was some years before karaoke became a popular pastime in the United States, but working musicians—especially singers—often needed to produce backing tracks for popular songs requested at weddings, bar mitzvahs, and anniversary parties.

The (entirely analog) circuit in this device was simple but clever. Vocals on stereo records are usually mixed so they appear in the center of the stereo field (equally loud in left and right channels), while instruments and backing vocals are panned a little to one side or the other to create the illusion of players distributed in a space. By inverting the phase of the left channel (electronically turning the signal upside-down) and mixing it with the right channel, any sounds that exist in both channels at the same level cancel each other out—centered mono signals vanish, but the stereo backing band remains intact. The result is usually a familiar song minus its vocals. (A similar technique is employed in noise cancelling headphones: a microphone picks up the surrounding sound, inverts its phase, and mixes it in with whatever you're listening to, so the electronic and acoustic versions of the airplane cabin thrum cancel each other out.)

Like the X-Ray glasses advertised in the back of comics, the Vocal Eliminator seemed too good to be true, so Thompson would send a free demonstration record upon request. The narrator on the blue vinyl LP addressed the listener directly, guiding them through the application of the Vocal Eliminator on snippets in various genres of music, concluding each style with a statement along the lines of "The Thompson Vocal Eliminator is 91% effective with folk-rock." Clever dodges were employed when the device performed less than optimally, none better than the caveat after processing a clip of an Elvis Presley ballad. The dry vocal track vanished from the mix, but traces of his voice could be heard floating like a ghost in the lush stereo reverb that surrounded his band: "The King is gone, but his reverberation will accompany you." Could any wedding singer ask for more?

5

A limiter is a common signal processor found in most studios, either as a standalone piece of hardware or as a plug-in for digital recording and mixing software. The user sets a "ceiling" level, and the limiter ensures that the audio coming out never exceeds it, preventing distortion from unexpected loud sounds.

In the late 1980s, Britain instituted regulations limiting noise exposure in the workplace, including music venues. To help clubs comply, one company introduced a novel kind of limiter, according to a product announcement I read in *Studio Sound*, a British magazine for recording engineers. A built-in microphone measured the absolute sound level in the room. When the official threshold for hearing damage was exceeded, the box turned on a yellow lightbulb that could be seen by both the engineer at the mixer and the musical act on stage, warning them to turn down. If the sound remained above this level for one minute, a *red* lightbulb lit up. After three minutes of excessive loudness, the box actually cut the electrical power to the PA and stage, shutting off all amplification. The ultimate limiting.

6

When the Sonic Arts Network (UK) invited me to curate a CD/book hybrid for distribution to its members, I spent fruitless weeks puzzling over possible rubrics. In helpful-psychiatrist mode, Susan asked what I would actually want to listen to. "Nothing!" came my testy reply. "So make it happen," she suggested. I contemplated absences of sound, not-quite silences, homages to the unnoticed: the crackly grooves between songs on a record, the hum of a guitar amp, audience anticipation, a memorial minute of silence. This was not long after 9/11, and the hole in the skyline at the tip of Manhattan was a visceral reminder of how absence can be more powerful than presence. Cage's 4' 33" and Rauschenberg's *Erased De Kooning Drawing* were exercises not in nihilism, but in sensitivity to traces of things past or passing. I chose to organize the project around audible absence. Starting from the old roué's quip "a drink before and a cigarette after are the three best things in life," I solicited the ellipse.

"A Call For Silence" attracted over a hundred submissions, from which I selected thirty-three.[1] The tracks range from contemplative (Valerian Maly's twelve-second recording of an apple falling from the tree under which Isaac Newton once sat) to disquieting (Matt Rogalsky's computer-processing of Bush's speech declaring war on Iraq with all the words edited out, and the resulting whir of camera shutters and roomtone elevated to ear-splitting loudness). Clearly, artists are still wrestling with the Cagean conundrum of whether there is such a thing as silence.

Whistling in the Woods

Meanwhile, back in Berlin, Matthias Osterwold had been named music curator at Podewil, a Baroque palace off Alexanderplatz in the heart of former East Berlin that had been converted into a venue for contemporary music, dance, and theater. He was asking various artists to guest curate concerts in their area of expertise (a singer proposing "extended voices," an improviser programming a long night of improvisation, etc.). After years of arranging concerts and festivals of electronic music, but fresh off the rather wacky *Stroomgeest* rubric, I proposed a festival of whistling instead.

I have always whistled for pleasure or out of boredom while doing the dishes or home repair or, to paraphrase Fountains of Wayne, when the car radio was broken, but Peter Cusack had sensitized me to the musicality of human whistling (he often whistles in his performances), as well as birdsong (he is also an avid ornithologist).[1] I had composed one piece that drove a sampled string quartet from pitch-tracking birdsong (*Les Plus Beaux Chants d'Oiseaux*, 1985), and another in which a recorded bird resonated the strings of a backwards guitar (*Pet Sounds*, 1988). I began to see whistling as a shared interspecies sonic activity, a historical bridge between music and the not-yet-music that came before (like the clicks of the bats that so beguiled Alvin).

Once you start listening for it, you realize that whistling is everywhere: film, sports, animal husbandry, linguistics, ornithology, navigation, public safety, poetry, communications, epistemology, and more than 500 years of music. As a festival rubric, it offers space to be both erudite and broadly popular, appealing across age and education. Everyone I spoke with—musicians, film buffs, scientists, parents picking up kids from school—had suggestions for what to include.

The festival title, *Pfeifen im Walde*, is the German equivalent of "whistling in the dark." For nine days in September 1994, we presented concerts, installations, films, and site-specific events. There was Renaissance recorder music for training songbirds. British pianist Peter Hill performed pieces from Olivier Messiaen's *Catalogue d'Oiseaux* (a set of thirteen compositions based on transcriptions of birds native to France). We screened movies with whistling soundtracks (*The Good, the Bad and the Ugly*, with its famous whistled theme by Ennio Morricone; Fritz Lang's *M*, in which the murderer betrays himself through a whistled melody). Two dozen amateurs competed in our International Whistling Competition, won by Sheila Harrod, a self-described housewife from the Midlands. Lino and Maria Rodrigues, teachers of Silbo, the whistled language of the Canary Islands, carried on a rooftop-to-rooftop conversation across the Podewil complex. Dutch border collies herded German sheep in the courtyard in response to the whistled commands of their handlers (Figure 17.1).

We invited Alvin to perform his *Tyndall Orchestrations* (1976), based on the acoustic experiments of nineteenth-century Irish scientist John Tyndall, who discovered that a Bunsen burner's glass chimney will whistle when the flame is adjusted correctly and, conversely, the flame will flicker in response to the high-pitched twitters of birdsong, providing a visual readout of the sound. At the thought of Bunsen burners on stage, the Podewil house manager put his foot down: German regulations prohibited flame on stage. I spent a week in daily discussions to resolve the problem. He suggested performing the piece outside in the courtyard; I mentioned the threat of rain or wind. I offered the option of a fire extinguisher on stage; he countered that it would have to be accompanied by a fireman. I asked whether house managers in Germany, like those elsewhere, were designated as fire marshals for the building; he acknowledged that this was true, but that he would have to be on stage no further than five meters from the flame. Deal! He placed fire extinguishers at either end of Lucier's table and sat in the wing during the performance. The flames did nothing more dangerous than whistle on cue.

Given the breadth of these events, I proposed we complement the usual program brochure with a book, modeled on the look and format of the famously authoritative eleventh edition of the *Encyclopedia Britannica*. Assisted by Volker Straebel, then a student of Dr. Helga de la Motte, doyenne of Berlin contemporary musicology, we wrote and solicited dozens of alphabetically sorted entries linked by the thread of whistling.

Figure 17.1 Border collie in sheep herding trial in the Podewil courtyard during the "Pfeifen im Walde" festival, Berlin, October 1994. Photo by Nicolas Collins.

Swiss artist Valerian Maly, whom I had invited with his partner Klara Schilliger to present one of their durational performances (eight hours of whistling in the Podewil atrium), ran an art book press in Cologne and published the beautifully designed hardback, *Pfeifen im Walde—Ein unvollständiges Handbuch zur Phänomenologe de Pfeifens* (*Whistling in the Woods—An Incomplete Handbook of the Phenomenology of Whistling*).[2] It included a bookmark ribbon of audio tape containing one second of a Maly/Schilliger performance, and a cut-out cardboard model of a subsonic whistle by Cologne artist Gunter Demnig.

The festival was gratifyingly popular, attracting a diverse audience of listeners and whistlers from across Europe, as well as a flurry of media coverage. An enthusiastic Valerian then brokered a meeting with the management of the annual Luzern Festwochen to propose an expanded version of the *Pfeiffen* festival. With a budget almost ten times what we had at Podewil, we produced a two-week festival-within-the-festival in August and September, 1997. Resembling the Berlin project on steroids, it included additional sound installations, a symposium, whistling workshops, a guided daybreak tour of songbirds in the Swiss countryside, and opening festivities that included whistling fireworks and a recital by the grand dame of German cinematic whistlers, Ilse Werner (1921–2005).[i] The sheepdog trial took place on the great lawn of Richard Wagner's Tribschen estate. The whistling competition, which now drew a broadly international roster, was staged in the main train station. The concert series included performances by whistlers of the Banda Linda and Aka tribes of the Central African Republic and Wayana musicians from the Amazon. (A flurry of last-minute international phone calls succeeded in securing shoes for the Wayana performers so they would be allowed to board the plane.) Our friends from the Canary Islands returned and Silbo echoed across Lake Lucerne.

Pfeifen im Walde distilled everything that attracted me to curating and production. As with the open-form scores that bridge improvisation and compositional structure, a good festival is an exercise in balancing centralized artistic decisions with distributed responsibility. I might select the acts and advise them on their material, but the unfolding of any individual event—a sonata by Biber or a sheepdog trial—is beyond my direct control. In an interview with a Lucerne newspaper, I compared festival rubrics to the scaffolds within which a boatyard builds a sloop: ultimately, the framework is taken away and the boat has to float on its own. Seeking out and interacting with experts on medieval musicology, whistled languages, dog training, or ornithology felt unexpectedly akin to my approach to improvisation: throw something interesting out there, then listen and adapt to what comes back.

In the fall of 1996, we sublet our Palestrinastraat apartment and moved to Berlin, where I had been awarded a one-year residency as a guest of the DAAD's Berliner Künstlerprogramm. By the mid-1990s, unified Berlin was no longer an isolated island within a hostile power I remember from my earlier visits, but it was not yet

---

[i] Werner had appeared in some late-Nazi era musicals, which hampered her post-war career.

the international art capital it has now become, and the Künstlerprogramm—well connected and well supported in the political order of things—continued to thrive, Wall or no Wall.

The DAAD managed a famously luxuriant array of prewar *Altbau* apartments scattered through the bourgeois heart of West Berlin, acquired on long leases when the city was still considered a hardship post by most West Germans. Ours, on a quiet street in the leafy neighborhood of Friedenau, was at least three times the size of our Amsterdam flat. Our Dutchified children commuted from room to room on bicycle and tricycle, zooming over the parquet floors and around the baby grand piano that sat in the dining room, a natural amenity for those apartments reserved for composers. (I never played it, but our son did.)

The whole experience of that year could be characterized as "large": the apartment, the stipend, the helpful staff, and the DAAD connections throughout Berlin's cultural institutions were far more generous than anything I had known before.

In contrast to the immigration snafu that greeted us when we arrived in Amsterdam, the preparations for our stay in Berlin were meticulous, reducing our interaction with the *Ausländerbehörde* (the German *Vreemdelingenpolitie*) to a mere ripple. They opened doors, made introductions, greased wheels, minimized bureaucracy. The DAAD produced my "Welcome to Berlin" concert in the middle of a Joseph Beuys exhibition in the enormous former railway hall of the *Hamburger Bahnhof* museum.[ii] To record an album, two years after my residency officially ended, I was installed in a studio at the Sender Freies Berlin (SFB) radio station, which possessed so many priceless vintage Neumann microphones that some were used as door stops.

We settled into the rhythm of Berlin life. In Amsterdam, we had gone everywhere by bike, with children and groceries strapped front and back. Berlin was much bigger, however, and the Berlin British School was in the former British sector by the Olympic Stadium, an impractical commute by public transit. For the first time in our adult lives, we needed a car. Matthias accompanied us to a used-car lot in the blue-collar neighborhood of Neukölln, where he kicked a few tires and walked us through the paperwork provided by a shady Russian salesman. Off we drove in a careworn red Audi.

If you had an American driving license you did not need to take a road test or a written exam to get a German *Führerschein*, but the process required a notarized German translation of your American license, a vision test, and a seven-hour first-aid class that included giving artificial respiration to an inflated sex doll. Going through the process two weeks after me, Susan found that the first-aid class had mysteriously been dropped. On the other hand, when submitting her documents, she had to deal with a surly woman who spoke in difficult-to-understand local *Kiezdeutsch* and whose nameplate revealed her to be "Frau Unglaub"—"Mrs. Unbelievable."

[ii] Small world: the recording engineer for the evening was Gerhard Behles, then a student at the Technische Universität Berlin, who went on to start Ableton, whose software was inspired by STEIM's "Lick Machine."

There were parts of the Berlin cultural landscape I knew well by this time— Matthias, his Freunde Guter Musik organization, Podewil—but the DAAD introduced me to a wide range of new organizations, performers, and resources, including the instrumental ensembles zeitkratzer and Kammerensemble Neue Musik Berlin (KNM).

Ironically, my years at STEIM—that most electronic of music foundations— coincided with my rising interest in acoustic instruments. Perhaps this was a question of saturation—spending every day surrounded by loudspeakers—or of parenthood. (When I told Peter Cusack that I found acoustic sound more visceral and three-dimensional than what emerged from loudspeakers, he observed: "It's been a while since you've been in a club with a good PA, hasn't it?")

Mostly, however, I think it came down to my experience with improvisers and adventurous conservatory-trained musicians like the Soldier String Quartet, Leslie Olsen, and the Barton Workshop—my approach to notation reflects the dual education I received from both types of musicians. Even when I write a score, it generally does not dictate specific phrases—instead, it makes tactical suggestions as to how players should *act*, and I depend heavily on their individual instincts to fill in the details and complete the work.

The Berlin ensemble zeitkratzer included both improvisers and players familiar with scores, and they were open to a wide range of notational alternatives. They had transcribed and arranged Lou Reed's *Metal Machine Music* (1975), a studio recording of layers of feedback and other electronic noise, which the ensemble meticulously notated to be mimicked by amplified acoustic instruments. They invited composers who worked directly with electronic sound to submit audio tapes instead of a written score (Merzbow did so); each member of the group would study the tape and figure out how to use their instrument to imitate some line running through the recording. The individual transcriptions and comments would be compiled into a master score, and players would often monitor the original tape as a cue-track during performance.[iii] Seldom was there the sort of commissioning fee one might expect from more established European ensembles, but Reinhold Friedl, zeitkratzer's director, made a point of approaching composers for whom the mere fact of a performance by a large group was incentive enough, if supplemented with a modest fee and travel expenses for attending the premiere. They adapted quickly to the open form of my skipping CD pieces, improvising over the modal harmonies of early music recordings, and prompted a new work, *Broken Choir*, which was premiered in 1997.[3]

Thomas Bruns, the director of Kammerensemble Neue Musik Berlin, had reached out to me before I arrived in Berlin to ask if I would be interested in being a composer-in-residence in the ensemble while a guest of the Künstlerprogramm. I wrote some new pieces and adapted some older ones. Claiming that even the minimal technology of *Still Lives* was too complicated for their touring program, they asked if I could develop an all-instrumental variant of *Still Lives* without the hacked CD player. The result, *Still (After) Lives* (1997), directs the ensemble to imitate acoustically the electronic artifacts

---

[iii] This was the same mechanism that Alvin had proposed for the instrumental evocation of environmental sounds in his 1970 composition, *(Hartford) Memory Space*.

of the earlier piece, from looping to glitching, much as *It Was a Dark and Stormy Night* had distilled the electronic innovations of *Tobabo Fonio* into a score for a largely instrumental ensemble.[4]

My work with the Kammerensemble encouraged me to merge my computer music practice with their familiarity with historical repertoire, resulting in a third, expanded version of *Truth in Clouds*. I photocopied dozens of pages from scores written before 1850 (works that could have been familiar to the nineteenth-century protagonist) and programmed small electronic displays that told the musicians when to turn to particular pages and how to perform variations on the notation using techniques drawn from sampling: loop measure 2; play it backward; add a beat; drop a beat; speed up; slow down; and so on. Sometimes everyone would be brought together on the same page, other times they'd be distributed across the centuries, but the collective outcome always sounded more or less like music. We premiered the work at Podewil in an event that was part concert, part installation.

DAAD connections opened the door to the Deutsche Oper's props department, which supplied period chairs, tables, vases, and decorative objects. ("Please be careful with that skeleton," I remember being told. "We need it for our upcoming *Wozzeck*.") In the former residential palace of Podewil, the audience strolled through our make-believe parlor, where an inverted wine glass stood on a table, and spirit writing beamed down from a video projector above—the longer you sat and moved the glass, the further the narrative unfolded into a proper Gothic ghost story. Solenoids hidden under and inside the furniture tapped out Morse code in imitation of spirit rappings. The musicians set up as for an evening of amateur *Hausmusik*, drifting in and out at various times each evening, flipping through their scores in response to directions generated by the moving glass (Figure 17.2). (Audience participation at the table was somewhat disappointing since, as I learned on the opening night, the wineglass-as-séance-accessory was unknown in Germany; several visitors turned the glass right-side up as if expecting wine to pour down from the projector that was beaming sentences onto the table.)

Berlin of the 1990s, shortly after reunification, still held onto some of its unique historic character. The city remained the first stop for artists coming West from the East, and a refuge for westerners exhausted by economic marginalization. The televised image of the fall of the Wall depicted East Berliners swarming West. The ensuing years saw a reverse flow of westerners gentrifying East Berlin (or colonizing, depending on your point of view): large prewar apartments, often in rough shape, were cheaper there than their counterparts in West Berlin neighborhoods like Charlottenburg. In the fall of 1990, a week after the formal start of German reunification, I helped a friend clean up an abandoned store in Prenzlauer Berg in which he hoped to start a gallery. We crowbarred open a door in the back to reveal a rubble-strewn room that had been sealed since the end of the war, a miniature of the landscape one sees in those black-and-white photos of the city in the spring of 1945.

By 1990, the former East Bloc no longer existed and everyone—whether thrilled or trepidatious—had to make adjustments. Traveling between Vienna and Berlin that fall, I changed from a bus to a train in Bratislava, with an hour's gap for a stroll. I went to

Figure 17.2 Installation views of the interactive séance table, part of *Truth In Clouds* at Podewil, Berlin, February 1999. Photos by Ingrid Lommatzsch-Sedgley. Used by permission of Thomas Bruns, KNMB.

drop off my gear-filled suitcase at the train station's left-luggage office. A stern-faced, middle-aged woman handed me a complicated form in Slovak. A to and fro in broken bits of several languages suggested that I was expected to list the precise contents of my suitcase. This I did, laboriously, only to be told that most of the items were not permitted. I had just started to plead my case when a smartly dressed woman in her twenties appeared from the back of the office.

"May I help you, sir?" she asked in only slightly accented English.

I explained the situation. She turned and lit into her colleague in rapid-fire Slovak. The older agent slunk back through the curtain, and the younger one turned to me with a broad smile.

"Please, sir, this will be no problem. Enjoy our beautiful city."

Which I did, having glimpsed the cusp of profound change. In the not-too-distant future, young people with freshly minted degrees in "hospitality" would replace the grim enforcers who had previously defined the experience of travel in the East. Everything would get easier for us visitors, and new generations in these new nations would have new careers. But older workers, trained for a world that no longer existed, would be swept out.

This had repercussions in music as well. I returned to Bratislava in 1997 for a residency with the Vapori del Cuore ensemble, whose members were mostly in their twenties and included several composers. None were using any electronics, though by this time synthesizers and effect pedals had infiltrated most of the groups I'd worked with in the Netherlands and Germany. Their work had a vaguely Frank Zappa quality, mashing up pop music, Slovak folk tunes, and classical repertoire. One member explained that electronic sounds were associated with "official" party-line composers of the old regime, who had been the only ones allowed to work in the state-run studios. In those early transitional years, the younger generation had no interest in those politically tainted sounds. Fifteen years later, however, I returned to Slovakia for a workshop in hardware hacking, which was embraced by a wide swathe of young artists—though what they made might well not have been recognized as music by the studios of the former Czechoslovakia.

When I moved to Berlin in 1996, John Corbett (a writer and concert organizer in Chicago) and guitarist Jim O'Rourke told me to look up Markus Popp, whose group Oval was ascendant on the Ambient music scene. (The term had been coined by Brian Eno in his post-Gavin Bryars phase and represented the popularization of the kind of looping and droning tonalities explored earlier by LaMonte Young, Pauline Oliveros, and John Hassell. With the rise of electronic dance music like House and Techno in the late 1980s and early 1990s, Ambient entered clubland as the soundtrack for "chill rooms" where exhausted ravers could retreat to recoup.) Ambient interested me because it seemed to violate the basic precepts of pop music—it had no beat and no lyrics—and yet it was popular and made money. Markus Popp was using hiccupping loops from damaged CDs—"things you did ten years ago," as Corbett told me—smoothed over by nice pop textures, drum machines, and rather beautiful, wobbly temporal shifts.

Markus insisted on hearing examples of my music before agreeing to meet at the Café Adler, an artist and spy hangout right by Checkpoint Charlie (a curiously formal request compared to the relaxed fraternization of artists of widely differing fame that had been my expectation since Alvin introduced me to the likes of John Cage, and John McLaughlin agreed to sleep on my dorm room floor). To break the ice, I inquired about his musical interests.

"I'm not interested in any music," he replied. "For me music is just an entry point to the media."

I soldiered on, despite the unpromising start to what was already looking like the blind date from hell. Noting his flawless English, I asked if he had perhaps grown up in the UK.

"No, I have a lot of English friends, but I grew up in Germany. A small town. You wouldn't know it."

"Try me."

"Darmstadt."

Since Darmstadt was the single most famous center in the development of post-war German music, I realized he must have been serious about not being interested in music.[5] The lunch dragged on, but just before the check arrived, he asked, "You actually knew John Cage?"

I acknowledged I did.

"Would you like to remix our next album?"

This was my first foray into pop music since producing Robert Poss's projects in the 1980s, and I quite enjoyed it. I shared remix duties on *Microstoria's Reprovisors* (Microstoria was another studio-centric "band" of Popp's) with ten other artists, most from the pop world, each of whom was assigned one track.[6] Given its relatively abstract character, the original material could be bent pretty far and retain the feel of Microstoria—my contribution did not stick out as the work of the one weirdo.

As East and West Berlin re-assembled themselves, unusual sites for performances and installations blossomed. Some had been hidden or forgotten (like the backroom in Prenzlauer Berg), some forbidden (countless bunkers and abandoned tunnels), some had simply become redundant (two sets of radio stations, two opera houses, lots of museums). Many of these had first been opened to the larger musical public through *Sonambiente*, a massive festival of site-specific sound installations and performances all over the city organized by Matthias and the Akademie der Künst in the summer of 1996. I was offered a two-lane bowling alley (*Kegelbahn*) in the basement of the Sophiensaele, a nineteenth-century workers' meeting hall and recreation center in former East Berlin. In the 1980s, I had returned to the Pythagorean underpinnings of my first sound installation, *Under the Sun*, and replaced the austere, almost invisible mechanism of a sliding Teflon loop isolating harmonics of a plucked wire, with a more overt, possibly goofier, one: the long wire now ran above a model train track, and its harmonics were elicited by the pantograph of an engine shuttling back and forth from one end to the other—like a guitarist dragging a pick up and down a string. The train image arose in the wake of the drumming panda bears I had used in *Killed in a*

Bar When He Was Only Three, as I sought to position experimentation in the context of familiar objects. The first version was executed in affordable HO scale. But the *Sonambiente* commission came with a European-level budget, so for *When John Henry Was a Little Baby* (1996), we laid twenty meters of larger G scale track down each bowling lane. An expensive historically accurate tram ran along each, its pantograph scraping the steel piano wire overhead. The resulting harmonics were picked up by contact mics plugged into a pair of massive Marshall guitar amps at the dark far ends of the lanes. Visitors adjusted the speed of the trains with controls at the start of the track. A glorious din ensued (Figure 17.3).[7]

Reunification also set off a building boom. In empty tracts where the Wall once cut through the city center, real estate developers and corporations competed to construct a business center for the once and future capital. Architectural leading lights were brought in to design headquarters—Renzo Piano for Daimler-Benz, Arata Isozaki for Berliner Volksbank, Helmut Jahn for Sony—and Europe's biggest construction site arose from the lifeless plain where the remains of bustling prewar Potsdamer Platz had been razed to create a no-man's-land between the inner and outer Wall. In the long run, this proved a miscalculation—Potsdamer Platz remains a weirdly desolate spot despite all the adventurous glass and steel. In the short run, it produced a surfeit of unused office space that could be commandeered by artists for short-term projects.

A still-vacant office building designed by Philip Johnson near Checkpoint Charlie inspired a concert that, like the 1987 networked Hub concert in New York, made use of multiple performers in multiple spaces playing some form of "together." In "Büromusik: Musik in Unvermieteten Neubauten" ("Office Music: Music in Unrented New Buildings," a play on the name of the German industrial band, Einstürzende Neubauten), Jim O'Rourke and I played guitar and trombone-propelled electronics respectively from the concrete shell of a floor not yet built out with hallways or rooms; Markus Popp sat in the building's model office behind a large street-level window. Markus had protested that he didn't do performances but agreed to participate when Matthias and I explained that he could just sit at a desk and continue work on his next album as if he were in his own studio, while the resulting sound connected to speaker hung outside. Bypassing anything as sophisticated as modems, the three of us were linked by many meters of audio cable, while the audience wandered in, out, and around.

Berlin had been a major center of improvisation since the introduction of the annual "Free Jazz" Total Music Meeting in the 1960s. Three decades later, improvised music was threaded throughout the Berlin music world, from the most prominent city-supported festivals down to door-gigs in twenty-seat kinos and clubs that exhibited the same cooperative spirit I'd left behind in Downtown New York.

I moved throughout these various Berlin scenes—working with KNMB one night, playing in a squat the next. I wielded the new STEIM-built trombone-propelled electronics in a computer music festival, following on the heels of my Sonambiente installation. This free-for-all was refreshing after years of Dutch *zuilen*. But even friends who knew my work well were sometimes baffled. After the premiere of two pieces from the *Sound Without Picture* series at the Berlin *Musik-Biennale* festival in 1997, Matthias commented, "You really shouldn't be programmed on electronic music

Figure 17.3 Installation view of *When John Henry Was a Little Baby* in "Arts Le Havre" (Le Havre Biennale), Musée Malraux, Le Havre, France, June 2008. Photo by Nicolas Collins.

concerts. Your music uses electronics and computers, it's true, but it's never *about* them. And it doesn't sound like electronic music." Which struck me as strange, having rooted so many of my decisions in the affordances of circuits—how could my music not sound like *electronic* music, even when played by acoustic instruments? But I had to admit that it didn't sound like much of what passed for electronic music as a genre. I couldn't say what my music was, but by now, thirty-five years after feedback first jumped out of my Tandberg, I was getting a clearer idea of what it wasn't. Feeling myself at a musical crossroads, wondering whether I should focus on ensemble compositions or technologically centered pieces, I pressed Matthias, "Which way should I go?" "Make music that is a pleasure to play. I love Bach, but I love to *play* Chopin, the way it feels under my fingers."

We had no plans for what to do after the DAAD year, but I promised myself six months of living in the present before starting to panic about survival. When March rolled around, I discovered that staying in Berlin for the foreseeable future was a workable non-decision. We ceded the Friedenau apartment and moved into a freshly renovated *Dachgeschoss*—a previously unfinished attic space under the peaked roof of a prewar apartment building. It had two proper bedrooms, windows that looked out on the Olympic Stadium, and, up a narrow stair of Dutch verticality, a workspace under the eaves.

Strange Heaven

After four years at STEIM and one on the DAAD's dime, I was once again a freelancer, but somehow every time things started to get tight, a paying project would come my way (Figure 18.1). One of the first was a commission from Radio Bremen's *Pro Musica Nova* festival. The premiere was set for May 1998, and I had cleared the two months leading up to it for uninterrupted work on the piece—the last in the *Sound Without Picture* cycle about the senses. This one grew out of conversations with a blind friend from my childhood, Denyse Eddy, about her experience of touch. I planned to use the trombone-propelled electronics to process the voice. Every morning I'd climb up to my garret and program away, and every week or so I'd decide what I had was crap, throw it away, and start over. The text itself was good, the tonalities it evoked through the trombone-propelled-electronics system were lovely and mellifluous. But it all felt wishy-washy. There was no snap, no disruption, no edge.

A week before my deadline for submitting the finished score, I still had nothing, but I had to break for a quick trip to Austria to discuss an installation project at the Offenes Kulturhaus in Linz. On the night train back, just before I fell asleep, a simple—possibly stupid—idea popped into my head. (My little brother often chided me, "It's a fine line between simple and stupid, Nicky, and sometimes I don't know which side you're on.") Since the post-STEIM trombone worked with MIDI, I could hook it up to any MIDI device, including the drum machine I had been carting around since *Dark and Stormy Night*. My night train inspiration was to use the movement of the slide to scratch through a drum kit, bouncing my virtual sticks across a changing array of skins, cymbals, woodblocks, and cowbells. My composer's block crumbled, and forty-eight hours later I had finished *Strange Heaven*.[1]

Did the piece take two days or two months? It came together in those last forty-eight hours, but even though every time I threw out my work and began again I thought I was starting from scratch, each restart took place under conditions affected by all the activity of the previous weeks. The process reminded me of one of the many Zen-ish stories David Tudor told:

An emperor visits a man reputed to be the greatest artist in the land. "Paint me a picture of a cat." "OK, but it will take a year, and I'll need a fine house with servants while I work." The emperor complies and returns twelve months later. "Sorry, it's not finished, I need another year." The emperor comes back, the painting's still not

Figure 18.1 Chalkboard announcement outside The Spitz, London, December 1997. Photo by Nicolas Collins.

finished. "OK, you can have one more year, but if it's not ready I'll have you killed." Another year passes, the emperor returns, still no painting. "OK, that's it. Guard, cut off his head!" "Wait," says the artist. He grabs a paper, a brush, a bottle of ink, and five seconds later hands over a drawing. The emperor stares at it. "This is the best picture of a cat that I have ever seen! But it only took you five seconds!" "No, it took me three years, you only saw the last five seconds of work."

The Offenes Kulturhaus exhibition, "Archiv X," included a dozen artists from Europe and the Americas—Guillaume Bijl, Clegg & Guttmann, and Christian Marclay among them. Susan and I drove down with the kids for the opening, stopping at castle after castle along the way. My installation, *Burn Daylight,* used parabolic focused loudspeakers suspended from the ceiling in a dark room; visitors used their ears to follow a narrow path that took them through a sequence of disembodied voices narrating a story of sorts—text fragments drawn from Patrick Leigh Fermor's account of walking through central Europe sixty years earlier as he made his way on foot from the Hook of Holland to Istanbul.

The room I had been given looked out on a historic plaza, and I realized it was a perfect setting to create a camera obscura—an inverted projection of the present to accompany the aural representations of the past. I knew nothing about optics, but the term "pinhole camera" lodged in my brain, so I blacked out the windows with poster board, cut a circle the size of a quarter in one panel, and covered it with aluminum foil through which I poked a pin. The opposite wall remained black. I enlarged the hole to pencil diameter. Still nothing. Frustrated, I tore off the foil. As I turned to leave the room, there was the plaza in front of me, upside-down, luminously splayed across the wall. Coin-hole camera, not pinhole.

For his piece, Christian had borrowed a hundred empty cases from a nearby museum of brass instruments and laid them out open, on low plinths that filled a large gallery in parallel rows. The velvet linings of the interiors showed the wear of their long-nestled, now absent instruments (the piece was dedicated to cellist Tom Cora, who had passed away a few weeks earlier). For me, the most poignant aspect of the experience was the cloying scent of verdigris, spit and mold that enveloped me when I entered the gallery as Christian was finishing installing. By the morning after the opening, *Empty Cases* was as visually evocative as before, but that special smell had been replaced by the fug of cigarettes and spilled beer.

As a freelancer in New York, I had learned never to say no to an invitation to work, no matter how unqualified I felt, which is how I began writing. I never learned to touch-type and had somehow made it through high school and college on my execrable handwriting, hunt-and-peck keyboard pounding, and the occasional paid typist for my theses at Wesleyan. In the 1980s, the advent of word processors (hello WordPerfect!) enabled me to bang out grant applications with moderate success. Then in the spring of 1990, composer Larry Polansky asked me to submit an essay about the trombone-propelled electronics for the premiere issue of the *Leonardo Music Journal,* a spinoff from the *Leonardo Journal* that had been covering technological art since 1968. The writing experience, concurrent with the last months of anxious waiting for the birth of our son, was excruciating but in the end cathartic, forcing me to think through processes and responses in revelatory ways. I took on more writing projects, including a catalog for a festival marking STEIM's twenty-fifth anniversary and various entries in the *Pfeifen im Walde* faux-encyclopedia.[2] The more I wrote, the more self-reflection gave way to larger analyses of the interaction of musical aesthetics with technological and economic developments (by the end of the 1990s this style of self-centric methodology would acquire the lofty label of "Practice-Based Research").

During our first year in Berlin, British trumpet player and composer Jonathan Impett came to visit and told me that *Leonardo Music Journal* was looking for a new editor-in-chief, and he thought I should apply. Still on the DAAD residency, I was mindful of guarding my time for my own music but recognized that the journal served a vital function. Popular music was documented in periodicals and fanzines; classical music had academic journals that addressed both historic subjects and current developments, but experimental music was pretty much absent from the library. This was partly because extant musicology had no analytical tools suited to compositions based on echolocation, computer networks, CD error correction, doppler shift, or speech patterns, rather than melody and harmony; but also because experimentalism had chosen to champion the ephemeral and casual, usually outside of an academic framework. In real time, that approach felt exciting and poetic, but now we were left with a body of music conveyed largely through remnants—oral traditions, unlabeled circuits, obsolete synthesizers, and forgotten computers; a music whose aesthetic had (by the 1990s) never been adequately articulated or archived. By emphasizing writings by composers and audio artists, *Leonardo Music Journal* documented ideas and works that might otherwise float away on a cultural River Lethe. (This was several years before critical theory sank its teeth into experimental music and sound art.) *LMJ* had given me my first serious prompt to analyze my own work, and I liked the idea of offering others a boost onto the same soapbox. I saw the three-year editorial post as an opportunity to produce, at someone else's expense, beautiful books with stories, pictures, and sounds by artists I admired.

My first issue, *Ghosts and Monsters*, took its title from a diatribe that appeared in Cornelius Cardew's post-political-awakening rant against avant-garde music, "Stockhausen Serves Imperialism." The tension between the Maoist bête-noires of techno-futurist aesthetics and traditional humanist values was addressed, if obliquely, in submissions by Alvin Lucier, Ron Kuivila, David Behrman, Richard Barrett, Pauline Oliveros, David Gamper, Ricardo Arias, Robert Poss, and Scott Gresham-Lancaster. I was off to a start.

The editorial office was in San Francisco. I was living in Berlin. We gave the internet an early remote-work stress test, but once a year I would be flown into town for a few days to meet with the board and lay out the issue. My older brother and his wife lived in Sausalito and, while my cat allergies prevented me from bunking up in their townhouse, they owned a sleep-aboard sailboat moored just down the hill. Its cozy cabin had a magical ability to erase whatever jet lag accrued from the nine-hour time difference between Berlin and the Bay Area; not even the croaking ruckus of amorous toadfish could disrupt my slumber.[3] In the morning, under a nozzle in the Sausalito

Yacht Club's communal showers, I'd listen to guys complain about the partner who'd kicked them out of the house and onto the boat. After breakfast at Café Trieste at the base of the dock, I'd walk a hundred feet, board the ferry to the city, then stroll up Market Street to the *Leonardo* offices—a commute to rival the bike ride home from STEIM through twinkling lights.

Though I originally assumed the job would be rotated every few years, at the end of my first term my contract was renewed, and then again, and again, and again. For twenty years I assembled an annual issue, each organized around a rubric—there was *Southern Cones: Music Out of Africa and South America*; *Not Necessarily 'English Music': Britain's Second Golden Age*; *Groove, Pit and Wave: Recording, Transmission and Music*; *My Favorite Things: The Joy of the Gizmo*; and more. I pursued sound practitioners underrepresented in print, often convincing them to publish for the first time. The result was twenty little festivals that sit quietly on your shelf long after the music has stopped.[4]

Back in Berlin, meanwhile, sitting in the makeshift bleachers of the Berlin Little League baseball diamond (one of our few regular forays into the American sector), I got chatting with a fellow British School parent. Andrew Woodmansey had parlayed an interest in music and a background in Chinese studies at Cambridge into a successful business career and was now Chief Financial Officer for Sony Europe. (Expat communities can be great levelers and, counterintuitively perhaps, broaden one's social horizons. At nursery school pickups, sports events, and birthday parties, artists mingle with bankers, musicians with embassy fleet mechanics, academics with CEOs.)

Among Andrew's responsibilities, he explained, was overseeing the construction of Sony's new headquarters on the Potsdamer Platz. (Which is how our son ended up pulling the lever on a concrete mixer to help pour the foundation for that landmark building—a highly satisfying experience for a nine-year-old.) A review of the blueprints after work had begun revealed an oddly shaped slice of unallocated space, leftover from divvying up the retail area on the ground floor. Andrew proposed a hands-on "music experience," like the interactive exhibits in a science museum, but with a music focus that reflected Sony's brand. Sony accepted the idea but saddled him with a location-based entertainment company they had acquired when they purchased the Columbia Records conglomerate. Andrew was erudite and fluent in multiple languages, both Asian and Indo-European, but his new colleagues were Texans who built amusement parks. Their cultural expectations sparked by the phrase "music experience" were very different from Andrew's.

I was brought in as a consultant, in part to translate American into European, and in part to help steer the project toward an outcome in keeping with Sony's sophisticated self-image—to bring some frisson of cutting-edge music and technology to something that would appeal to a broad public. I drew on the expertise and artist contacts developed at STEIM, on my experiences as a designer of my own esoteric musical devices, and on a familiarity with existing music-related museums and research facilities. I proposed a variety of exhibitions that would allow hands-on musical engagement by the general public, and developed guidelines for an artist-in-residence program to generate new exhibits. Finally, I helped broker a cooperation with the influential Karlsruhe music-technology museum ZKM (*Zentrum für Kunst und Media*) for a modest artist's commissioning program.[i]

The Sony Music Box took four years to build, and by the time it was completed, Andrew and I had both left Berlin. Many of the more adventurous pieces of the project gradually slipped away, and the main attraction came down to a Yellow Submarine amusement-park ride. For me, however, the entire experience was both fascinating and remunerative (my consulting fee supported the family for six months).

In the space of six years, I had gone from hourly wage day jobs in New York, to a salary with benefits in Amsterdam, to the cushiest grant of my life in Berlin, and back to freelance consulting and gigging. Our financial situation wasn't desperate, but neither was it secure. We had a large apartment in a nice part of town and two kids in fee-paying international schools. I was over forty. It was time to look for a proper job.

My father's dinnertime tales of woe from the trenches of Columbia University had left their mark: none of his sons chose to pursue academic careers. But just as the Sony project was wrapping up, pianist Peter Hill, who'd performed Messiaen in *Pfeifen im Walde*, contacted me to ask if I would be willing to apply for a faculty position at Sheffield University to teach composition and run the electronic music program. They had an inside candidate, but Peter said, "We have to go through the motions and I thought you might shake things up a bit." The insider got the job, but I found that chatting with the other candidates in the holding pen was so interesting, and the interview process itself so surprisingly enjoyable, I figured what the hell—maybe I *could* do this professor thing.

I applied for a similar post at Huddersfield University, made the first cut, and was flown over for an interview. I quite like the North of England. I had enjoyed my time in Newcastle, and Sheffield, which backs onto the Peak District, has great charm. Huddersfield, however, felt very different. The city was bleak and the interview process far less jolly. The candidates were reminded that this was a junior post with a prescribed teaching load. We were also informed that our travel expenses would not be reimbursed if we were offered the position but declined to accept. Three of the six invited candidates were thrown from the lifeboat at the end of the first day. I went on to the second round of interviews with a 33 percent chance of being chosen for a job that I now knew I did not want; nor could I eat the cost of an international plane ticket in that pricey era before Ryanair.

I did not know much about the department, but I was aware that the chair of the hiring committee had enjoyed a late-career bump writing music for local brass bands of unemployed miners (a legacy of Margaret Thatcher). When the committee asked what I might like to do in the way of research while at Huddersfield, I saw my opening.

"I've done some pieces based on Peruvian brass music," I said. "I believe there are a lot of colliery bands in the area and I'm really looking forward to working with them."

Stony silence, a line through my name, and the return ticket covered.

[i] Founded in Karlsruhe, Germany, in 1989, ZKM produces exhibitions and events focused on the interaction of art and technology.

Matthias, meanwhile, was working behind the scenes to secure me a position as music curator at Haus der Kulturen der Welt, a Berlin arts center with an emphasis on non-European cultures. He had more confidence in my qualifications than I did. As the review process ground slowly on, I got an email from my friend Mark Trayle, listing an opening in the Department of Sound at the School of the Art Institute of Chicago. He appended the comment, "You could play trombone with the AACM."[ii]

No one in the family had any desire to leave Europe, but a month later I was in Chicago on the short list once again, giving a lecture, critiquing student work, and sitting through more interviews. The dean proposed the rank of assistant professor. I countered that, given my experience (twenty years as a freelance composer, significant grants, and administrative work), I deserved associate status with tenure. She reminded me that the committee had no proof I could teach—a fair point. In any case, I explained, I was considering another job in Berlin so I'd appreciate a quick decision one way or another. The phone rang before I left for the airport the next morning. After a family conference twelve hours later in Berlin, we were in agreement: moving back to America was not ideal but, hey, it was a job for at least a year or two.

Our knowledge of Chicago was rudimentary. Susan had attended the Art Fair on Navy Pier a few times. I had visited my younger brother, who worked in finance there, and played a few concerts. We had both been on Frank Lloyd Wright architecture tours. That was pretty much it.

Because European schools run through mid-July and we had obligations on Cape Cod in August, we were left with about ten days to find a place to live that would provide a roof over our heads, a workable commute for me, and acceptable schools for the kids. Our blithe assumption that a city the size of Chicago would have an international school full of Third Culture Kids like ours was swiftly quashed. Then it turned out that Chicago public schools did their intake at age four, and the desirable ones had no spaces for older arrivals. The same was true of the handful of nonsectarian private schools. The fact that we weren't Catholic and our children did not speak French crossed the last options off the list. Thus began our experiment in a kind of living none of us had ever experienced: the suburbs.

As many ex-expats will tell you, no move is harder than the one back to the country you're supposed to think is home. It was rough on everyone. The payoffs came in the form of a rescued elkhound-shepherd mix of sublime sweetness and reassuring bulk, a house large enough to build two-story marble runs and indoor papier-mâché forests, and teaching.

[ii] The Association for the Advancement of Creative Musicians is an important Chicago-based collective of experimental composition and improvisation. Given the virtuosity of its members, Mark and I both knew there was no chance of me being treated seriously as an instrumentalist in any of their ensembles.

Art School

The School of the Art Institute of Chicago's Department of Sound was founded in 1972, and by the time I arrived, sound was treated seriously as an art material throughout the school. Even the foundation year curriculum had a module on working with it. The school as a whole is strategically interdisciplinary: undergraduates study across the curriculum, rather than majoring in a specific discipline; graduate students apply to particular departments, but once accepted, they too are free to forage anywhere.

SAIC has a long-standing commitment to digital technology, but balancing the ubiquity of the computer in 1999 was a shared belief that there was no such thing as "obsolete" technology: photography students had access to not only high-end digital cameras and printers but also darkrooms; the printshop interspersed computers with acid baths for etching; and the sound studios were equipped with programming languages and recording software alongside rare analog synthesizers and reel-to-reel recorders that dated back to the 1970s. Facility managers seldom threw anything out, so when some older gear came back into fashion a working example could usually be dragged out of a storage room. (This is in marked contrast to many music departments that have blithely cast off past generations of technology when upgrading to the next— exchanging idiosyncratic analog equipment for generic MIDI devices in the 1980s and 1990s, then becoming increasingly software-centric at the end of the 1990s.) A student at SAIC might shoot footage on a Super 8 camera, digitize the processed film, edit on a computer, and finally make a 16 mm optical print for screening.

Soon after arriving, I was handed a box of business cards emblazoned with the title "Assistant Professor of Sound." This inspired a lot of quips from old friends along the line of "are there also professors of Light? Weight?" but I found the institutional word choice helpful: As with many composers working outside the mainstream, I had occasionally been told that what I did was "not music," but nobody ever accused me of not making *sound*. My colleagues stressed that we were a department of *sound*—not specifically "sound art"—and that sound should be taught as a material to be shared freely between the domains of music (in multiple styles, high and low) and various genres of ostensibly visual art.

I'd never identified with the term "sound art," instead regarding almost any artistic practice with a strong sonic component as being subsumed under my generous definition of "music." I'd often (snidely) commented that sound artists were merely composers embarrassed to admit they're composers. (Luke DuBois—a polymath whose purviews include music, computer science, and, yes, sound art—once commented, "sound artists are composers who are afraid of their own shadow.") But as sound art became more established in museums and galleries, and as I spent hours working with my students, my opinion shifted, and I came to see sound art as a distinct, if poorly defined, genre. The sensibility behind its use of sound was different than in what is commonly accepted as music, reflecting instincts and skills often rooted in visual art practices rather than making at least a tacit reference to the long sweep of European art music or even the fundamental acoustic building blocks of harmony shared by musics across the globe.

Our faculty often had to adapt musical concepts, techniques, and aesthetics for students who hadn't studied music in any formal way. The challenge felt familiar, given my own experience of coming to music as an adolescent after a childhood immersed in visual art, and also from the time I had spent with Stuart Marshall's students at Newcastle Polytechnic. In conceptual and aesthetic terms, there was a fair amount of crossover between the canonic experimental music of the 1960s and 1970s and visual art movements such as minimalism, Fluxus, and performance art, and the practice of appropriation spread across both music and visual art in the 1980s and 1990s. The techniques and structures, however, were quite different between domains, and reconciling them often required inventive pedagogy. Conventional musical notation, for example, is off-putting to those who can't read it, but asking an art student to view a Bach score as a graphic representation of things going up and down starts to demystify it. Bob Snyder, the senior member of the Sound Department faculty, employed methodology from cognitive psychology—the roles of memory and perception—as an alternative method of explaining fundamental aspects of music composition.[1]

Digital technology and the ubiquitous cut-and-paste syntax of *command-x/command-v* made it possible for anyone to rearrange words, photos, drawings, video, code, or sound (I often describe those paired key commands as the world's most powerful pencil and eraser). Artists no longer needed to master discipline-specific techniques like tape splicing or darkroom practice just to get started. This ease of cut-and-paste was reflected in the ongoing aesthetics of appropriation that could be heard in most of the music my students consumed. Art schools had been birthing bands from the Beatles onward, but nobody at SAIC at the turn of the millennium seemed to be picking up a guitar and forming a group. The musics they loved—mostly variants of House, Garage, or Techno (styles rooted in Chicago and Detroit)—were made alone on computers in bedrooms.

And there lay a conundrum: recording and editing software like Garage Band or Fruity Loops or ProTools led to an emphasis on visual tools for structuring sound. This approach was natural for editing film and a boon for aligning a soundtrack with video, but the reliance on the eye over the ear led to the emergence of what I often heard as "visual music"—music made by looking rather than listening. The software relied on colored bars representing the duration of musical patterns on the screen—quicker to recognize, but decisions being made about an experience taking place in time, were now based on static visual proportion and balance. To sensitize them to this distinction, I would ask students to edit a track by ear alone: to mark the edit points by hitting a key when it *sounds* like the right place rather than gazing at a grid on their screen.

One semester, I had a student who produced a new dance track almost every week. The tempo of sampled drums, minimal bass lines, and wiggly synth riffs never varied. When I pressed him to experiment, he sped it up by a barely perceptible three beats per minute. Exasperated, one day I presented a lecture on Christian Wolff's notion of "reducing the tempo to zero," replacing an underlying metronomic pulse with cues between musicians. I illustrated the idea with examples such as Feldman's *Piece for 4 Pianos* (in which each of four pianists makes their way independently through the same sequence of chords), Wolff's *For 1, 2 or 3 People*, Zorn's *Cobra*, and *alap* on a sitar (the languid introduction to a raga played before the tabla enters, often described by the musician as "water flowing down a stream"). As often happened when I designed a presentation around one individual, the student didn't show up until the last chord of the last piece was dying away.

"What did I miss?" he asked a classmate.

"Nic played examples of what happens when you reduce the tempo to zero."

A stunned silence followed. Then,

"That's not possible!" he insisted. "You *can't* reduce the tempo to zero . . . Maybe to 48 beats per minute, but not zero."

48 bpm must have been the minimum clock speed in his sequencer software and thus the horizon of his musical world.

The rise of video as an artist's medium undoubtedly helped integrate sound into visual thinking. Movie film cameras require separate audio recorders to capture sound, but after Sony's introduction of the Portapak in 1967, most video cameras have recorded audio in sync with the visual material. When you review or edit the video footage, the soundtrack plays back as well, whether it's wanted or not. So while film is silent by default, video is always shadowed by audio unless you reach for the mute button. This constant exposure to sound as a byproduct of editing visuals imposes an unconscious immersive learning—like children in the Netherlands unwittingly acquiring English from watching American cartoons whose soundtracks aren't dubbed into Dutch.

My undergraduates generally fell into three categories: students working in film, video, or some other discipline who wanted to incorporate sound into their primary medium; creators in various styles of pop music who wanted to access the cool gear in our studios (and get course credit for what they would be doing anyway); and a smaller subset interested in genre-fluid sonic experiments. This last group worked with the same hardware and software you could find in any music department, and the *sounds* that emerged from their computers were not so very different, even if the decisions on how to put them together were informed by different skills and desires (as I had noticed with Stuart Marshall's students in 1976).

When I arrived at SAIC, students in our core Introduction to Sound course worked with current versions of the tape recorders, mixers, and other standard studio gear that I had learned on in my youth. Only in more advanced classes were they introduced to the digital equivalents of those machines—computers on which they used a mouse to move the virtual slider of the virtual mixer in imitation of the physical slider on the physical mixer in the studio next door. Within a few years, however, incoming freshmen usually arrived with prior experience of those digital tools (think Garage Band) but none with their physical antecedents.

New tools are commonly modeled on their predecessors—automobiles on carriages, computer keyboards on typewriters—and the decision to design the first-generation audio-editing software with visuals that looked familiar to established engineers made sense. Eventually, however, that kind of heritage can become an impediment (imagine if we were dialing our fingers in circles on our mobile phone screens). Teaching young people how to use the heritage equipment (mixers, patch-bays, and reel-to-reel tape recorders) became more difficult every year. The hardware-software-hardware transition reminded me of the "severe tire damage" barriers in rental-car lots: it's more difficult to go backward than forward. Why? Robert Poss suggests that audio software used analog elements (faders, meters, transport buttons, etc.) as metaphors, but when a generation grows up knowing only the software version, the images on the screen no longer reference anything in particular and lose the helpfulness of their metaphoric value.[2]

In my introductory classes, I asked the students to share studio time in pairs—two wrongs sometimes *do* make a right, and often one bumbler can see the solution to a fellow bumbler's problem. Instead of confronting beginning students with a fully equipped facility, I would ask them to construct a studio in an empty room, adding one piece of gear every week as they mastered it (echoing my experience of having to rewire the Electronic Studio at Wesleyan every time I entered). This tactic gave them a greater sense of control over their working environment than walking into a complete studio.

SAIC studio classes ran from 9 a.m. to 4 p.m. once a week. This schedule is well suited to a life-drawing class, where students sketch and the teacher wanders the room, peering over shoulders and making the occasional suggestion, but six continuous hours of explaining audio mixing or computer programming was brutal. One unexpected benefit was honing my performance skills: holding student attention all day kept me in shape between concert tours, since a similar focus is needed in performing complicated concert sets.

I arrived at SAIC at a moment of paradigm shift in the recording industry. The file-sharing site Napster had not yet been shut down, and I was impressed by the impact peer-to-peer file exchange had on the listening habits of my students. At their age, I had accumulated what I regarded as a pretty eclectic record collection, but records cost money, while shared files were free (hence the recording industry's panic and legal actions). Many of my students had far more adventurous libraries than anything I could have put together in 1974. The legal Achilles heel that would bring Napster down was also its greatest asset: users could see whose files they were downloading (each computer on the Napster network was identified with a unique username). Leaving class one afternoon, a student mentioned that the three best songs he'd downloaded recently had all come from the same source. "Whoever this guy is, he has great taste," he enthused. "Before I go to bed I'm connecting to their computer and grabbing everything on the drive while I sleep." This activity was conducted with slow dial-up modems, but if you had a phone plan that charged per call rather than per minute, eight hours connected to a local number cost no more than three minutes. Years before social media influencers, Napster provided a forum for accidental tastemakers—a virtual version of making a friend in your freshman dorm on the strength of the music heard through a shared wall.

There was an important difference, however. Whether paid for or downloaded for free, digital music arrived with no jacket, no label. There were no liner notes of the sort I had scrutinized as a teenager for information about the artists, their instruments, and their network of connections to the rest of the musical world. Now there was only *sound*. This was liberating on the one hand—music free of all that baggage and accreditation, to be enjoyed purely on sonic merit—but limiting on the other, since each song was framed only by the tracks that preceded and followed it in a playlist. As Alex Petridis observed later in *The Guardian*:

> Streaming encourages a kind of decontextualised discovery. It's a world where albums are less important than single tracks, where you're encouraged to focus not on the artist, but the song; where music is served up with any accompanying visuals relegated to a tiny corner of the screen; where historical context, image, subcultural capital—all the other stuff that was once part of the package—no longer really matters.[3]

The material facts of how music is recorded, distributed, and consumed have knock-on effects for how subsequent music is conceived and produced. As my colleague John Corbett pointed out, "When we were students, if somebody played a record we liked by Iannis Xenakis we'd ask, 'Who is this Xenakis guy? What else has he done?' But now the kid will say, 'Cool, I can use that.'"

My students' ways of making, sharing, and playing music had roots in DJ culture, but that culture had changed in the twenty years since Grandmaster Flash. Gone, along with thrashing guitars at CBGB, was the physicality of DJ performance, of Flash spinning around in front of his mother's sink, of scratching and rhythmic crossfades, of the virtuosic hand. One student routinely brought in recordings of the DJ sets he produced in his apartment studio for upload to some distribution website. He had composed none of the tracks; he did not cut or scratch between them creatively. He simply picked songs and played them, complete and unaltered but for crossfades, in a certain order. The sequence was so seamless that I asked him to hold up his hand to mark the duration of each fade he had made, and over the course of twenty minutes, his hand was in the air for under thirty seconds. His contribution was like a cassette mix-tape smoothed out with beat matching. The line between playing back someone else's music and claiming ownership of it was getting even murkier than when early hip-hop artists sampled Clyde Stubblefield's iconic break from James Brown's "Funky Drummer."

Using standard sound editing software, aspiring pop musicians could now assemble competent if not compelling rhythm tracks. When, however, it came to writing a hook—even the most minimal three-note riff—my students struggled. I brought in numerous examples of compact melodic writing from multiple genres of music—from Miles Davis to Blondie to Prokofiev—to no avail. I had never thought of melody as being more challenging than rhythm—if anything, I assumed the opposite to be true (I find it easier to whistle than drum). But the cut-and-paste paradigm disproportionately benefits rhythm and structure over melodic design.

Their response to my harangues was to ask if the department could run a class on how to write a hook. I invited Julia Miller—a composer with a recent PhD from Northwestern University—to design a course in songwriting for non-musicians. The students learned basic melodic writing, harmony, counterpoint, and how to use software to notate their creations. They had to compose works to be performed, on instruments, by their classmates. Emails flew home requesting clarinets and flutes not played since middle school band, and the class formed a de facto local chapter of the Portsmouth Sinfonia. Unlike the facile workings of software, this was difficult and messy, but the hooks gradually improved.

A lot of incoming SAIC students had been the Weird Art Kid in their high schools, but this was often more a statement of alienated identity than an engagement with art itself (much like I had assumed the mantle of "composer" thirty years earlier). If I asked first-year students which artists they admired or responded to, the reply was often a look of puzzlement, sometimes followed by a tentative "Picasso . . .?" (seriously). For some, finding a community of like minded individuals was a boon, but for others, landing on a campus where *everyone* is the odd kid could be traumatic, one factor behind the high drop-out rate after the bootcamp-like first-year program in art schools.

I was often asked to accompany the school's admissions personnel on global recruiting tours, probably because I could speak Parent as well as a smattering of foreign languages. Not without reason, many mothers and fathers questioned the prospect of spending vast sums of tuition dollars on an art school. The harsh reality is that very few art school graduates become self-supporting painters or sculptors or sound artists. Some will go into teaching; some will find success as graphic designers, animators, or web developers; many will make a more radical sidestep to marketing or law or whatever. That reality does not discount the importance of what can happen in art school; it confirms it.

A good art school nurtures an instinct for invention and a competence in research. Every artist begins a project by inventing a problem and then inventing solutions to that problem. Good artists also give serious thought to what constitutes a successful resolution to their problem. These are skills whose applications extend far beyond the confines of the studio, but usually remain unacknowledged as such. At one of the "branding" sessions the administration periodically inflicted on the faculty, I suggested we promote ourselves as a "school for invention." Sadly, the idea went nowhere, perhaps because it muddied the distinction between Art and Liberal Arts, a habit that has defined my whole career.

Our decision to return to America from Europe had not been easy, but for me, the deal was sweetened by the dean's declaration that they wanted someone with an international reputation and were willing to provide me with a travel budget and scheduling flexibility to maintain this reputation. So, in and around teaching and administrative obligations (I served as department chair for many years), I was able to participate in concerts and festivals, workshops, and symposia around the globe.

Another enticement was that the job came with an invitation to design the first MFA program in Sound at an American art school. Shortly before I arrived, I read an interview with John Baldessari, who was famous both for his own work as a visual artist and for his mentoring of a remarkable number of young influential artists at CalArts and UCLA. "The way to get a good art school," he told *The New York Times'* Deborah Solomon, "is to hire interesting faculty. Then they attract good students and the students teach themselves."[4] Ours was a small department with reasonably talented faculty, but it included nobody of the stature of Baldessari. There was no budget for new tenure-track positions, so I ramped up our Visiting Artist series to bolster the new MFA track.

Our grad students arrived from art schools, music departments, and liberal arts colleges. They reflected the aesthetic soup out of which sound art was emerging: music, yes, but also sculpture, video, film, writing, community organization, and even one mathematician. Our faculty, in turn, ended up advising students from diverse backgrounds and had to become adept at critiquing everything from video and performance, to ceramics and fiber arts.

The biggest problems for grad students were the knots they would tie themselves into constructing conceptual frameworks in advance of making any sound. Like me, many of the faculty across the school had been educated in the era of conceptual art, but what was usefully provocative in 1967 (when LeWitt wrote his "machine that makes the art" statement) had aged into less-than-useful dogma. By the time I got to SAIC, I could be described as a "reformed Conceptualist": I understood the appeal of Conceptualism and loved much of the art that emerged from under its umbrella, but I'd also experienced its drawbacks as a methodology for sound work (as exemplified by my moment of doubt before a Parisian audience in 1977). I resisted its pull like an alcoholic passing a pub. LeWitt, for his part, spent his later life designing wall works that follow a programmatic logic while also luxuriating in chromatic nuance, surface texture, and the fall of light. LaMonte Young formed the Forever Bad Blues Band, of which Neil Strauss wrote, "even if you know nothing about mathematics and music theory, you can dance to it."[5] Art has never not been about beauty.

In the 1990s critical theory set its sights on sound as a subject of analysis (Douglas Kahn's *Noise, Water, Meat: A History of Sound in the Arts* was an influential early example), and SAIC was all in for Team Adorno.[6] Whatever his merits for examining the social conditions of art reception, I find that despite, or because of, being a trained pianist firmly rooted in the Second Viennese School, Adorno had little to say of relevance to the process of writing music after Schoenberg.

Sound is a physical thing. You hobble it by not reveling in that element, like the guy who glued himself to the sub-woofer during Marianne Amacher's concert at The

Kitchen, or the psychoacoustic phantoms in your ear when listening to Alvin Lucier's _Bird and Person Dyning_, or the strange pressure of _Pea Soup_'s feedback as it filled an underground ice cellar in Brussels (described by one listener as "church of sound"). Words are wonderful, but what they do is very different from what sound does. Stuart Marshall, who read deeply in Freud, Lacan, and semiotics in general, once observed that "critical theory is a wonderful instrument for analyzing art. As a tool for making art though it's rubbish."[7]

The painter David Salle—one of those artists who studied with Baldessari—has described the problem as it plays out in visual art:

> Ever since Duchamp decoupled art from retinal experience early in the last century, there has been a misapprehension about the relationship between means and ends. Critical writing in the last forty or so years has been concerned primarily with the artist's intention, and how that illuminates the cultural concerns of the moment. Art is treated as a position paper, with the artist cast as a kind of philosopher manqué. While that honorific might in some instances be well earned, the focus on intention has led to a good deal of confusion and wishful thinking. A visit to any of today's leading art schools would reveal one thing in common: The artist's intent is given far greater importance than is his or her realization, than the work itself. Theory abounds, but concrete visual perception is at a low ebb. In my view, intentionality is not just overrated; it puts the cart so far out in front that the horse, sensing futility, gives up and lies down in the street. "Intent" is very elastic in any case; it can stand for a variety of aims or ambitions. What has a greater impact on style is how an artist stands in relationship to his or her intention. This may sound complicated, but it's not. How someone holds the brush will determine a lot. Intention does matter, but the impulse guiding the hand often differs, is even of a different type, from that described in the wall text. Call it pragmatism.[8]

Interlude

How Things Work

1

Composer and trumpet virtuoso Jonathan Impett once told me that because of the cost of paper in the early eighteenth century, Bach drafted his compositions on a wax tablet. As a result, there are relatively few surviving sketches of his works in progress. By Beethoven's time, a century later, paper had become less precious and he went through reams, leaving behind hundreds of pages of working notes. As with the transition from pens to typewriters to word processors was for writers, this must have affected the way composers conceived, drafted, and edited their ideas. This might be a factor in why Baroque music makes such heavy use of double dots and strict measure repeats rather than writing out subtle variations: less paper for more time. I also hear the double dots in *Einstein on the Beach* (1975), whose hours of music Philip Glass wrote freehand in the days before software tools for music notation—here more to ward off tendonitis than to save paper.

2

The Phase-Locked Loop (PLL) is a control method commonly used in electronics to track the frequency of a signal. It appeared in the form of an integrated circuit in the 1970s as one of the building blocks of Touch-Tone phone systems, where it was used to identify the pitches a phone generated for each button pressed. The charm of the PLL lies not so much in what it produces—a square wave matching the frequency of the incoming signal—but in how it gets there. Instead of measuring frequency in absolute value by counting the number of times a waveform crosses its midpoint each second, the input is compared to an internal voltage-controlled oscillator (VCO) whose frequency is also unknown. The chip generates an "error signal" in the form of a voltage that represents the *difference* between the two mystery pitches. This voltage is connected to the internal VCO's control input, which forces it toward the frequency of the external source—a kind of informational feedback. As the internal oscillator gets closer to the pitch of the external signal, the error voltage gets smaller, reaching 0 when the two signals match. We can follow this process by listening to the VCO output: depending on how quickly it responds to the error signal (set with a few components the user attaches to pins on the chip), the VCO glides slowly into tune like a guitar string being tightened, or snaps to the pitch, or weaves drunkenly up and down before settling.

What I find so charming about this behavior is its relativism, the extraction of information without appealing to a fixed reference. It's as though two people agree to meet somewhere not by sharing the address but by texting "warmer/colder" as they stumble across town—an electronic version of Hunt the Thimble.

3

I have observed a musical manifestation of Moore's Law (the number of transistors in an integrated circuit will double every two years) in concerts over the years. When digital delays emerged in the early 1980s, composers grabbed them as cheaper, more portable alternatives to paired reel-to-reel tape recorders. But whereas the maximum delay time using two tape machines was constrained only by the width of the stage separating the machines (which, at a tape speed of 7.5" per second, could easily exceed half a minute), in the digital devices, the delay was limited by the capacity of their memory chips, which periodically increased by doubling, as per Moore's Law.

At every *New Music America* (an annual festival held in different cities between 1979 and 1990), at least one artist would perform a work for a solo instrument and a digital delay. One year I heard several pieces with the exact same tempo: a whole note = 240 BPM, which was a function of playing in time with the maximum delay time (256 ms) at decent bandwidth given the capacity of then-current RAM. Two years later tempos halved to 120 BPM (512 ms) as the size of memory doubled. At the following festival, we had various subdivisions of measures with a duration of about one second (60 BPM). By the end of the decade, memory was big enough and cheap enough that Moore-Collins' Law (loop length doubles every twenty-four months) no longer exerted a structural stranglehold on performance, as delays increased beyond the threshold of what would be perceived as an echo or repeat to what could be regarded as a distinct, separate event. By the 2000s, the ubiquity of affordable, quasi-unlimited capacity looping pedals led to a widespread revival of modal improvisation that harked back to Terry Riley's two, pre-digital Revoxes, spread across a virtual stage.

4

Effect pedals became problematic for me when they started to affect *time* (mostly through looping and delays) rather than just *tone* (distortion, wah-wah). All loops sound like loops, whereas tone comes in a thousand colors. As more improvisers adopted pedals, I've been struck by the contrast between the inventiveness and individuality of the playing and the generic quality of the processing: I hear the same effects from the feet of multiple musicians. Pedals are like quotes of another sound; it's hard to make them as personal as the minds and fingers of individual players.

5

One summer night I was walking down Water Street in Woods Hole when my attention was drawn to the astonishing din of a cicada perched on a car roof. The sheet metal acted like the hubcap-shaped metal resonator on a Dobro guitar, making him easily the loudest bug in town. I'm not sure what the Darwinian factors in the cicada's song might be, but I assume loudness plays a major role in asserting suitability as a mate. Similarly, in recent years we have been regularly visited by a woodpecker, who settles on the chimney in the early morning. Hammering away on the metal cap, which resonates through two stories of metal flue, the bird has devised a hearty and effective PA system to those outside, and an alarm clock to those inside.

This is animal busking. For me, proper busking is incompatible with electronic amplification; it demands site specificity: you set up in an underpass or atop a hot tin roof to harness the feature's natural resonance and projection. Wherever you play, you accept your subservience to traffic and other ambient sounds. The skill lies in cutting through background interference by means of guile—choice of instrument, pitching of voice, placement—rather than sheer loudness. Electronic amplification, on the other hand, lifts you above your surroundings, and electronic effects craft an artificial space that overwrites the real one. The cicada and the woodpecker were both making use of human innovation, but in a natural context.

Hardware Hacking

As in the old adage "when you have a hammer everything looks like a nail," these days it's easy to assume that any problem, whether aesthetic or technical, can be solved with a computer, especially if you're a "digital native." I was not—I had learned computers as a second language, after the technical motherese of circuitry—and I could see that sometimes the computer was preselecting a limited, less-than-optimal set of options where a simpler and more direct tool would open things up.

My students were not unaware of this. Among the most popular offerings of the Sound Department at SAIC were classes in musical instrument building and audio installations. Artists like to make *things*. But if few of them had any grounding in traditional instrumental music, even fewer knew anything about circuitry. As with hook-writing, they knew there was something missing. More than one asked if the department might offer a class in making electronic music *without* computers, so in 2002 I designed "Hardware Hacking."

I saw the course as bridging the gap between the sound world of our thoroughly electronic culture and the timeless tactile habits of the human hand. Reaching back to my earliest forays into electronics, I tried to remember what it was like to be completely incompetent. What kind of advice or information had helped me out of my jams? There was no reason to waste students' time replicating processes and effects now more easily produced on a computer, but there were sounds and forms they were unlikely to reach through software.

We begin with *listening*: using speakers, microphones, making contact mics, and experimenting with inductive pickups for eavesdropping on electromagnetic signals emitted by all the electrical devices in our world (as well as natural phenomena like lightning and meteor showers). We pull tape heads out of broken cassette players, solder them directly to audio cables, and swipe them across the magnetic strips on credit cards, playing back their digital data as sound. These non-standard microphones extract unexpected sounds from familiar objects and places and are cheap enough that you can do things with them you wouldn't attempt with a Neumann. I show examples of what other artists have done with a particular device, then leave it to them to experiment: record a firecracker in a bottle, or a banana in a blender, or a penny being flattened on a railroad track.

Then we *play* electronic sound, as directly as possible: we lick our fingers and lay them gently on a transistor radio circuit board. Small currents flowing through the skin create feedback paths that push the circuit into oscillation and transform the radio into a touch-sensitive synthesizer, a cheap imitation of the STEIM Cracklebox.

In the mid-1990s, instrument-builder Reed Ghazala began publishing articles in the journal *Experimental Musical Instruments* on what he dubbed "Circuit Bending": modifying inexpensive sound-making toys to create performable instruments.[1] Repurposing consumer devices had been common practice among experimental musicians since the 1960s, but circuit bending took advantage of the plethora of recent toys containing remarkably advanced sound circuitry, while pointedly abjuring the study of the electronic principles behind them. (David Tudor, by contrast, extended the paltry range of available circuits with a hard-won understanding of what was going on inside each one.) Ghazala advocated what he called "anti-theory": make new random connections between points on the circuit board, take a photo when you get a cool sound, upload it to the web for others to copy, and don't worry if you don't understand it. This dismissal of expertise had obvious appeal among art students who had bypassed science in high school, so I include a session or two of circuit bending. We listen to video signals from cameras and games—low-pitch drones whose overtones shift balance as the image changes—and hack LCD toys to create tiny pixel animations and crude video projectors.

We progress to building circuits from scratch: oscillators, fuzztones, gates, and panners. We cover "glue" circuits: simple mixers and amplifiers that have multiple uses. We wrap up with a ten-step sequencer that has been used for the bass lines in a thousand techno tracks—a gift to those students obsessed with dance music.

The designs I prepared for the class were easy to understand and build, virtually impossible to blow up, and could be assembled like Lego bricks to create complex networks. This process is facilitated by bypassing traditional analog approaches in favor of circuits based on digital CMOS chips, which can run on a 9-volt battery for months and use fewer parts than their analog equivalents (the chance of making a mistake in assembling a circuit is directly proportional to how many pieces you have to stick together.)[i] Performability is stressed throughout: the projects make extensive use of photoresistors (devices that change resistance with light level), direct skin contact, pressure pads, and other intuitive interfaces for playing the circuits through physical gestures.

I was guided by five basic goals:

- Keep the students alive. To avoid the experience of the young Michel Waiswisz, we use batteries rather than the potentially lethal voltages running through the walls.

---

[i] CMOS (complementary metal-oxide-semiconductor) refers to a fabrication process for integrated circuits that came into prominence in the 1970s in the design of digital chips. This technology was used not only in early microprocessors like that in the KIM-1 computer but also in smaller integrated circuits that performed discrete logical operations (AND, OR, NOT, etc.), such as those I describe in earlier chapters. They were popular among my circuit-building peers in the 1970s because they were cheap, consumed very little power, and could be tricked into performing functions normally associated with more complicated analog designs.

The early stages of unsupervised electronic play activity are thus kept safer and less daunting.

- Keep things simple. We get cool sounds quickly by starting with a small number of axiomatic circuits that can later be combined with permutational richness.
- Keep things cheap. Students don't need a full electronics lab, just a soldering iron, a few hand tools, and a modest number of parts easily obtained online.
- Keep it stupid. They learn to design by *ear*, not by gazing at test instruments or engineering texts. The little bits of theory that are introduced arrive only after direct experience.
- Forgive and forget. There is no right way to hack. The circuits we build are robust, tolerant of wiring errors, and accept a wide range of component substitutions. The designs are starting points from which one could go on to create many variations with minimal help or risk.

Some of our projects escaped the classroom and spread through the school like the flu. At the cusp of the 1980s, composer Richard Lerman had discovered that the piezo disc, which had been in use as an inexpensive and energy-efficient speaker for beeping alarm clocks and truck backup warnings, made a wonderful, cheap, loud contact mic. When my class started making piezo disc contact mics, my department's facilities manager, Robb Drinkwater, coated one in Plasti-Dip, a rubber paint normally used to create soft grips on tool handles. Plasti-Dip protects the delicate soldered connections, improves the sound quality by deadening the resonant peak at the beep frequency, and also waterproofs the mic, effectively creating a one-dollar hydrophone. (I brought home a can of the stuff, and our five-year-old asked if she could dip her toothbrush. I didn't realize she meant the bristles, but the result was a surrealist object worthy of Méret Oppenheim.) Suddenly, every department seemed to find a need for contact mics—filmmakers used them to record Foley sound effects; performance artists amplified floors; sculptors converted mute objects into sound installations.

Part of the ethos of the hacking class is making maximum use of the minimum of materials, for reasons both economic and ecological, and much of what we do is repurposing found technology. (My early adoption of the KIM and VIM aside, I often approach most technology not at its cutting edge, but at its trailing hilt, adapting it for new use after it has become culturally familiar.) One semester an overstock of "Big Mouth Billy Bass" was being unloaded at the local Walgreens for five dollars each (marked down from forty). Billy was a rubber-skinned mechatronic fish mounted on a fake wood plaque like a trophy. When someone passed by, a motion sensor triggered playback of a few bars of Bobby McFerrin singing "Don't Worry, Be Happy" or Al Green's "Take Me to the River," while the fish flopped its tail and opened and shut its mouth in time to the lyrics. For one season this was deemed hilarious, and it sold like crazy at a premium price. Five years later, five students chipped in a dollar each to buy shares in a remaindered fish. One took the circuit that played the music and hacked the clock to slow down the chipper song to a spooky growl. The second student used the motion sensor to turn on a different bent toy whenever someone came near. The third mounted an oscillator inside the rubber skin, instead of the usual plastic or metal box

(Altoid tins were the default housing for many of my students), with a photoresistor embedded in the eye. The fourth built a small keyboard into the woodgrain plaque. The fifth glued an aluminum lampshade to the plastic skeleton and positioned it over a speaker: when the motor flapped the tail, the lampshade moved up and down, filtering the sound like a toilet-plunger wah-wah mute on a trumpet.

Italian musicologist Veniero Rizzardi refers to my hacking workshops as *quinto quarto* or "fifth fourth." There's a traditional Roman recipe with that name, he told me, that uses the entrails (tripe, brains, tongue, etc.) leftover after an animal carcass has been divided into the quarters that provide the best meat. "Your classes remind me of that dish."[2]

Every project is accompanied by examples of what other artists and musicians have created with similar devices. Many of the designs were adapted from the work of my musical colleagues, and are best understood in the context of the music they made with them. So just as students of painting might take a gander at van Gogh if they're experimenting with impasto, hacking gives insight into music and aesthetics about which most students know nothing. The class perpetuates the craft of handmade electronic instruments while contributing to the ongoing archive of music made with them. By the end, students acquire both technical skills and an appreciation of their aesthetic implications.

There is a beautiful moment, usually around the time a student discovers the ticklish spot that causes a radio circuit to swoop and warble, where euphoric self-confidence sets in. Most leave the class happy and fearless, if a threat to the electronic possessions of their roommates. The syllabus is designed as a roadmap to this euphoria and to suggest that it could have a higher utility in music and art. The students might still go home and assemble sounds on their computers at will, but now they could choose between ultra-processed downloads and chewy whole-grain electronics. Every class seems to have an aspiring techno producer who starts off merely wanting to add something new to her sound palette, only to leave making stranger things and tracking down obscure recordings by someone we had discussed. Although most of the artists whose work I demonstrate are, like myself, from the experimental fringe of the musical spectrum, I try to make the class as tolerant of aesthetic diversity as possible: that techno producer would feel no shame had she limited her semester's takeaway to new tools for her primary obsession.

The class has been remarkably popular—not just because it was, as Susan put it, "Gameboy for Credit," but because it offers a hair-of-the-dog remedy for the contemporary world's digital hangover. A lot of people, it seemed, had woken up in the new millennium with a headache from software overindulgence and a desire for something physical. Hardware hacking was their prairie oyster (Figure 20.1).

The hacking class handouts eventually grew into a crude PDF handbook that escaped the walls of the school. Emails arrived inviting me to give workshops elsewhere in the United States and around the world. Whereas my SAIC class met once per week, 9 a.m. to 4 p.m., for a full semester, my outside workshops ranged in duration from forty-five-minute sessions I presented for schoolchildren in branches of the Chicago Public

Figure 20.1 Hardware Hacking. Workshops in Crest, France, September 2023 (above) and in the Sound Studies program, Universität der Künste, Berlin, Germany, May 2022 (below). Photos by Nicolas Collins.

Library in the summer of 2011, to residencies of two to five days at maker spaces and academic institutions on multiple continents. Then in 2005, Richard Carlin, the music editor at Routledge, contacted me about doing a proper book. Routledge is an academic publisher, and while I was happy to see the project get better distribution than hand-to-hand PDFs, I had no interest in rewriting everything in proper academic prose.

"We have no problem with your writing style," Carlin assured me. "But your drawings are terrible." This is objectively true. He asked if I could find a student to make them more legible, and also suggested adding sidebars to provide more information about the artists and composers mentioned.

Carlin further recommended including a CD of what the finished projects sounded like. (This was 2005, when books with CDs were still a happening thing.) I worried that including audio samples might kill the delight of hearing your own circuit for the first time, so I countered with the offer to gather examples of actual musical works that employed elements similar to those in the text. The sidebars would be no problem, and I hired as an illustrator one of my ex-students, Simon Lonergan, who had worked for a T-shirt company converting photos of hot-rods into high contrast silkscreen stencils— roughly equivalent to translating schematics and photos of rat-nest wiring into legible figures. (I can only assume that when peers familiar with my original PDF expressed dismay at my drawings' replacement in the published book there was some sarcasm involved.) He was also a good commercial photographer and could document objects and instruments. The result was *Handmade Electronic Music—The Art of Hardware Hacking*, published in 2006.[3]

Much of the book was written at 35,000 feet above oceans between workshops and concerts. For all the discomfort of long-haul flying in economy class, I found the disconnect from daily life inspirational. I considered crediting United Airlines in my acknowledgments until I totted up the money I'd paid for tickets as an unofficial Writer-in-Residence, which amounted to thanks sufficient.

The book was published amid yet another round of hysteria over "the death of the printed book." But as someone who had struggled to distribute independent records (selling out of my suitcase on tour, giving away promo copies, a tiny number of store and mail-order sales), I was amazed by the reach of a book from a reputable publisher. It was available internationally through web retailers (mostly Amazon) who never handled my records, and modest royalties arrived steadily. For many years, it was Routledge's top-selling title outside the United States, perhaps as a result of its simple prose and profuse illustrations—a graphic novel among the dense thickets of critical theory that populate Routledge's roster. While marketed as a textbook, it was equally (if not more) popular as a how-to guide for the distinctly non-academic hacker.

I had thought that with the book now widely available, invitations to conduct workshops would decrease, but the reverse happened. People could now study and build the projects on their own, but they preferred doing it in groups, and my presence was a convenient catalyst for people to come together in a particular place at a particular time. The term DIY (Do It Yourself) had long been applied to the "maker" movement, but the workshops were DIT (Do It Together), and this represented a significant shift in the way they were valued: not just as a way to learn a skill, but as a way to build or strengthen community.[ii]

As time went by and I ran hacking workshops in a wider range of venues, the depth and contours of the rift between the worlds of software and hardware became increasingly apparent. In 2004, I presented one at the brand-new Sonic Arts Research Center (SARC) at Queen's University in Belfast, Northern Ireland. The participants included faculty and staff, along with doctoral students in electronic and acoustical engineering, composition, and computer science. Midway through the second day, I noticed that one guy seemed completely clueless. Anything that could be done wrong, he did wrong: his chips were installed backward, his battery polarity was reversed, and so on.

"Are you by any chance a composer?" I probed gently, since I'd found that composers often have poorer manual skills than visual artists.

"Oh no," he answered cheerfully, "I'm an electronic engineer."

I was dumbstruck.

He went on: "I got my BSEE last spring and I designed a Digital Signal Processor chip for my senior project. But we did everything in CAD [computer-aided design] software. This is the first time I've actually touched a component or a soldering iron."

SARC was planned as a very high-tech facility, the UK's answer to IRCAM. I was presenting material from the opposite, feral end of the technological spectrum, which had a mysterious appeal. One student raised his head from circuit rapture and turned to the center's director to ask, "So what the fook did we buy all those computers for?"

In every workshop I am called upon to debug recalcitrant circuits by novice hackers. I circulate around the room like the grandmaster in old photographs playing a dozen kids at a chess club, walking from one table to the next, inspecting the boards, making moves, holding all those games in his head. Toward the end of a workshop in Vienna in 2010, a student called my attention to a circuit and explained, "It only works when I breathe on it." She blew gently, and indeed an oscillator sprang to burbling life but then, over the course of ten seconds, sputtered and went silent. Turning the board over, I discovered a tiny crack between a blob of solder, the leg of a chip, and the copper trace on the circuit board. The moisture of breath was sufficient to bridge the gap, but as the flow of current heated the water, it would evaporate, breaking the connection again. The problem could be eliminated with a fresh drop of solder, but appreciating the peculiar breath-of-life quality of her circuit, she opted to keep it in its poetic state and built a second, "normal" version in the day's remaining hours.

Workshops begat other workshops. People who participated in one went on to organize others elsewhere. Alejandra Perez Nuñez, a Chilean artist studying in Rotterdam, attended a workshop in Brussels in 2004. After returning home to Valparaíso, she

---

[ii] When the third edition of *Handmade Electronic Music* was published in 2020, I expanded it to include new chapters by thirty younger authors. Several of these contributions cover aesthetic and historical aspects of hacking culture rather than technical instruction, and two of them focus specifically on the development of DIT movements worldwide.

loaned her early PDF version of the hacking book to Fernando Godoy, a local musician and concert producer, who set up a modest business buying parts in quantity for the projects and distributing them to local hackers by bicycle (no mean feat in so hilly a city). In 2011, Fernando—unaware that my mother had grown up a few miles away in Viña del Mar—invited me to present a workshop and concert in the *Tsonami* festival.

The book spread like a virus. Against all reasonable expectations, *Handmade Electronic Music* has had a profound impact on how electronic music is made and thought about. I have given more than 200 workshops and classes in hardware hacking to some 3,000 participants. They have taken place on every continent except Antarctica (though the *Cielo de Infinitos* festival in Punta Arenas, Chile, "The southernmost arts festival in the world," did get me within 900 miles). And while I am still invited to give workshops in person, the book has traveled even further without me. People I've never met are reading the it and conducting their own workshops, from Trondheim to Jakarta.

Everywhere I go, I now encounter what I call "elemental electronic music," with similar background stories: boy/girl buys a guitar/bass/keyboard and forms a band with friends. They can't play very well, so they buy a pedal that makes things sound better. They buy another pedal to sound even better. And another. Soon they are spending more time experimenting with pedals than playing their instruments. They build a contact mic and discover that the pedals sound just as interesting with a contact mic instead of the guitar/bass/keyboard. Then they come to a fork in the road: they either get brave enough to open up the pedals and play the circuit boards with their fingers, or they abandon their pedals and play just the contact mic. The greatest exuberance in the workshops often accompanies the most fundamental projects: making an oscillator out of nothing more than a speaker and a battery; recreating the light saber sound effect from *Star Wars* with a freshly soldered contact mic and a Slinky; passing a coil pickup over a cell phone to reveal the inner voices of the circuitry.

But the workshops do something still more powerful, something that stretches beyond the fun of boops and beeps. Again and again, I hear from participants that the great takeaway was not any specific circuit, but a sense of empowerment, of exerting control over technology that is widely used, but seldom understood in its material specificity. After a couple of days with an eviscerated toy and a soldering iron, the ubiquitous label "no user serviceable parts inside" ceases to be a prohibition and instead becomes a challenge. It is often difficult in an art school to gauge the long-term benefits of classroom teaching, but the impact of the hacking curriculum has been profound.

That said, my children's attitude toward my profession has fluctuated over the years. The eldest, surveying a glitchy circuit of mine with the gimlet eye of a middle-schooler, pronounced: "In this world there are Makers and there are Breakers. Steve Jobs is a Maker. Dad, you are a Breaker." A few years later, however, when we were depositing this same child in his dorm, a curious fellow student picked up a recently unpacked object on the dresser.

"What's this?"

"It's a Scratchmaster. My dad made it. It lets you hear the sounds of the magnetic stripes on credit cards and IDs." The kid ran his school ID through, eliciting a sound similar to scratching a record. They were still scratching away when we left. To break the ice, it can help to know a Breaker.

The intergenerational benefits have been reciprocated. In elementary and middle school, our youngest would periodically spend an afternoon with friends making a movie. They would write a script, design costumes, shoot, edit, and upload to YouTube by dinner time. The results were rarely longer than a minute and always contained a dizzying number of cuts. I had sat on grants panels where we reviewed artists' videos, and I commented that one minute into those tapes we would still be looking at color bars, waiting for the action to begin. "No video needs to be longer than a minute," came her stern response.

When I was called upon to assemble a DVD for the second edition of *Handmade Electronic Music* (replacing the first edition's CD), I heeded this advice and circulated a call for video contributions with a one-minute cap. The DVD also included thirteen largely improvised tutorials, a cross between my typical workshop banter and the late-night televised "open universities" that bring education to insomniacs around the world. Reviewing the book in *The Wire*, a UK music magazine, Chris Sharp described the DVD as "surprisingly watchable."[4] You can't buy press like that.

Salvage

In workshops I regularly found myself immersed in the din of twenty fledging hackers working independently on contact mics, oscillators, or bent toys. It was glorious. Here was the raw sound of primal electronics, stripped of the niceties of reverb, echo, and equalization. It had the scruffy quality of the experimental analog electronic music of the 1970s, in contrast to the polished, synthesizer voices of MIDI or pre-produced samples on digital audio workstations.

The sounds themselves were unexpected, as was their distribution over time: the semi-controlled instability of parallel but unsynchronized exploration with less-than-cooperative circuits. Lacking the collective intentionality of most music, it verged on chaos, while still suggesting some ineffable, ineluctable law of physics and social governance—glitches, whoops, spoings, intermittent bursts of extreme loudness and feedback. At any moment most of the sounds arose from similar circuit designs (usually the most recently introduced topic), and initial exposure usually prompted users to experiment in similar ways: scrape the contact mike along different surfaces, waggle one's hand over the photocell, and so on. The result had something of the complex, autonomous structure of sounds in nature—the quality Cage had hoped to emulate with indeterminacy. Indeed, composer and musicologist You Nakai has argued that Cage's sprawling collaborative multimedia event *Variations V* (1965) employed crowd-sourced decision-making as a kind of a parallel to indeterminacy. In the words of Leta Miller:

> By superimposing the inputs of an increasingly large number of imaginative personalities, Cage and his colleagues created a work with so many collaborators and such intricate linkages that each participant could influence the sound, but none could control it. The greater the number of participants, the more unpredictable the result. Thus Cage increasingly buried his own intentions under the weight of those of his artistic partners.[1]

Cage's interdisciplinary extravaganza used large numbers and elusive connectivity to subvert any perception of organized intentionality. Something of this effect happened in the hacking classes where there were no structural links—just individuals tinkering on their own unstable instruments. They were investigating, not performing, and in some mysterious way, that difference in motivation was audible. I began to think about how to replicate this quality in a composed work: something with multiple hands, a shared task whose parameters were learned on the spot by listening, and that lurched between comprehensibility and chaos.

I constructed an instrument that would extract sound from any dead circuit board—a cell phone, an old VHS player, a computer motherboard—otherwise destined for the rubbish heap or, more likely, China. (Despite the "quinto quarto" ethos of hacking, there was always e-waste left at the end of class, and awareness of the environmental impact of this waste on the communities where it was sent for recycling was growing.)[2] In *Salvage—Guiyu Blues* (2008) six performers use probes to investigate sonically a circuit board while a seventh directs the action. A camera above the circuit projects the action onto a screen, revealing hand movements otherwise blocked by the clustered performers, a modern update on Rembrandt's anatomically explicit painting of *The Anatomy Lesson of Dr. Nicolaes Tulp*.

I built a circuit with six simple oscillators on a single chip often used in my hacking workshops. Each voice was constrained to a certain frequency range—from subsonic through audible notes to ultrasonic whistling. In the design we follow in the workshop, the precise pitch within that range would normally be set by a feedback resistor (such as a potentiometer or a photoresistor) that connects the oscillator's output to its input, but in my implementation each output and input is connected to a handheld test probe, like that on a multimeter.

On older circuit boards the electronic components (transistors, chips, resistors, etc.) are distributed on one side, with their legs and leads sticking through holes to the other side, where copper traces make connections from one point to another. The salvaged board is placed on a plinth with the trace side up. When a pair of probes from my circuit is pressed against the traces, the oscillator's frequency is determined by whatever components happen to lie in the path between them—an unknowable array of resistors, capacitors, diodes, transistors, and integrated circuits, now hidden from view on the other side—rather than a simple resistor. Sometimes the path between the probes yields a clear pitch, but more often the array of components generates an unsettled response. As a result, moving the probes across the board elicits an unpredictable and unstable series of pitches and noises. When multiple probes from multiple oscillators touch the board at the same time, short circuits and feedback among them further complicate the texture.

The performance begins with a single player moving their two probes across the trace side of the dead circuit board, hunting for different sounds. Every minute or so, an additional player is cued to join the group. The complexity of the sound increases with each new pair of hands, and the effect of probe movement becomes more obscure to players and audience alike. Once all six players are active, the conductor occasionally shuts off a light illuminating the board from above, and everyone freezes (like tabletop "Red Light, Green Light"), shifting the texture from energetic glitches to semi-stable suspended pitches. After three such freezes the conductor mutes the audio from the circuit, leaving only the unamplified sound of the probes scratching

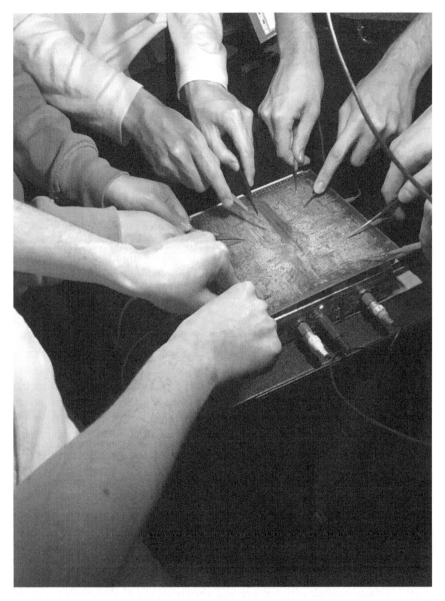

Figure 21.1 Student performance of *Salvage*, Arnold Schönbergzaal, Koninklijk Conservatorium, The Hague, March 2019. Photo by Nicolas Collins.

across the board, which reaches the audience's ears like distant cutlery in a quiet restaurant (Figure 21.1).[3]

Each musician is a rational actor: a few minutes of solo playing with the probes is enough to learn cause (movement) and effect (sound), even if the exact sound at any moment is unpredictable. This causality is apparent to the listener as well. But with each additional pair of hands, causality becomes harder to identify, including the effect of one's own actions, evoking what I love about those hacking workshop moments. I cannot perform *Salvage* by myself: even if I could tape twelve probes to my fingers and wiggle them across the board, I could not get the same effect. The piece requires six brains connected to twelve hands.

That said, as much as I appreciate the chaotic totalism of *Salvage*, there is a certain brinksmanship to rounding up performers and scheduling rehearsal time in my typically too-short sound checks (the intended mayhem exists, after all, within an *a priori* structure). After a few years with *Salvage* in repertoire, I searched for a way of adapting its essence to a practical solo format, as I had earlier distilled elements of the ensemble piece *It Was a Dark and Stormy Night* into the more portable solo, *Sound for Picture*. Carrying over the sound palette and disjunctive transitions of circuit recycling was not difficult, but I puzzled over an interface that could imbue my two hands with something like the character of the dozen employed in *Salvage*. I tried metal fingerpicks, wire brushes, and rivets punched through beer coasters, before finally settling on spherical fishing weights connected by thin wires to my oscillator circuit: a dozen small lead shots could be rolled and nudged under ten fingers; their precarious resting state mimicked the instability of *Salvage*'s probes held in nervous hands, and the small differences in motor control between my ten fingers imbued each shot with its own personality—not exactly a brain, but close enough.

Salvage invariably degenerates into frenetic fluttering of hands. The fishing weights of *The Royal Touch* (2014), however, impose on hand movement the tranquillity of a trout stream, zooming in on and freezing the broad chaos of its predecessor (the pressure of the little spheres against my fingertips encourages gentle, massage-like movement rather than the more aggressive scratching brought out by the probes). To make these motions visible to the audience, I fold the lid of my laptop half down to focus its built-in camera on the circuit resting on the table in front of the trackpad and project the live feed, as I had used an overhead camera in *Salvage*.[4]

As the 2000s progressed the flow of ideas from my workshops into my own compositions and installations increased. In the suitcase I brought to workshops, I carried an Altoid tin containing a circuit with four oscillators, each controlled by a photoresistor, along with a box of birthday candles. I'd demonstrate the versatility of light as a performance medium by lighting a candle stuck onto the circuit board. As the flame wiggles the oscillators, tuned roughly in unison, would swoop around, beating against each other and sounding a little like bent guitar notes through heavy distortion. The guttering flame is a classic example of turbulence, and when sonified with this simple circuit the flickering flame becomes a turbulent four-dimensional controller. I'd tell my students it's not enough to build a light-sensitive circuit and then wave your hands over it: if light is the controlling element, then light is your instrument, and you need to learn how to play it.

In June 2008 as I was wrapping up a workshop in Rovereto, Italy, and preparing for a concert that evening I learned that Michel Waisvisz had passed away the night before. I'd known Michel for twenty-five years. He introduced me to STEIM, opened the door to my European touring and ultimate residence, fostered ideas and a scene of great value to me, and was an important friend. He'd been ill for a few years, so the news was not unexpected, but the timing was. *In Memoriam Michel Waisvisz* (2008) came into being in the brief time between hearing the news and going on stage with a birthday candle, my oscillator circuit, and a small battery-powered fan. Holding the fan, I walked slowly toward the burning candle. The closer I got, the more the flame flickered and the more violent the sound became until the wind got too strong and the candle sputtered out, leaving the audience in darkness and a silence punctuated by slow polyrhythmic ticking. The fan became a bow for the flame's string, so to speak, and the performance grew out of pushing the limits of the flame's motion before snuffing it out, like bending a string to the breaking point. The sound was reminiscent of the progressive-rock guitar parts for which Michel harbored a secret fondness, and the candle's demise after a good struggle spoke for itself.[5]

In classes and workshops I demonstrate the versatility of contact mics by amplifying all kinds of objects—tongue depressors, soda straws, slinkies, cymbals. One day I brought in sparklers left over from Fourth of July celebrations with my kids. I clamped a wire stem to the piezo disc, turned off the lights, and lit the tip. The dazzling sparks elicited the predictable oohs and aahs (do we ever outgrow the delight of fireworks?) as well as a filtered resonant whoosh that slowly rose in pitch as the magnesium burned down the wire, like the spoing of a wooden ruler snapped and drawn against the edge of a desk. Darkness, brief silence, and then an unexpected denouement of pings and pops and gong-like tones as the wire stem attempted to reconcile the insanely high temperature of its burnt end with the room-temperature end clamped to the mic.[i]

At the invitation of the Diapason Gallery in Brooklyn (the first gallery devoted to sound art, run by composer Michael Schumacher) I exploited this phenomenon for my first video installation, *Tall Poppies* (2009). Three different takes of sparklers burning down were projected on three walls of the gallery, each with its own speaker. The vagaries in the burn-times and the cool-downs produced a beguiling percussive polyphony of surprising strength for such small pieces of wire. The two-minute cycle looped all day for the duration of the exhibition.[6]

If the great professional boon of Amsterdam had been the genius bar of STEIM, and that of Berlin was its breadth of instrumental talent, the upside of the Chicago burbs was a fully equipped home basement workshop right out of *Popular Mechanics*. My father would have been thrilled at his granddaughter's creative mastery of the drill press, and I had room to anatomize all manner of consumer audio equipment.

The once-quixotic musical effects that had so delighted me with the skipping CD pieces had become well ensconced in the musical mainstream, and my original hack

---

[i] In 2004 I flew to England for the first of my foreign hacking workshops. Along with other supplies, I included in my checked bag a can of Plasti-Dip and a handful of sparklers to demonstrate the contact mic. To keep the wire stems from bending, I rubber-banded the sparklers to the side of the paint can. When I opened the suitcase in Bristol, the Plasti-Dip and sparklers had been replaced by a note from the TSA informing me that prohibited materials had been removed. On an X-ray machine, sparklers attached to a can must have looked almost as malevolent as the alarm clock, coiled wire, and sticks of TNT I remember from cartoons.

had been made redundant by various technological advances, but now I returned to the ambition that drove me to crack open my first CD player: approximating a DJ's tactile vinyl interventions, such as scratching. I opened up an old Discman, flipped over the drive mechanism so the sled that held the laser was now on top of the disc, and removed the motor that moved the sled back and forth. I could then slide the exposed sled across the disc with a flick of my finger, producing an amazing racket as the machine furiously piled on error corrections in a futile attempt to get the music back on track (literally).

Having now eviscerated the machine, I poked around the exposed circuit board with an audio cable in search of other sounds. The data on a CD passes through a labyrinth of transformations along its path from reflective divots in the disc to the audio output, and a signal can be picked up anywhere along the way. The circuits that control the motors and coils that spin the disc and guide the laser produce remarkable noises as well, completely unrelated to the content of the audio tracks. I picked four of my favorite sounds and wired them through switches to mix with the disc's audio output. I added another switch that shuts off the spindle motor and collapses the audio into silence with a sound reminiscent of black hole effects in sci-fi movies. Slapped between two scraps of acrylic plastic, with the disc protruding like the blade of a circular saw, the resulting *Sled Dog* (2003) is a paean to glitch and a noisily satisfying capstone to my extended engagement with the unloved CD.

I wasn't sure exactly how to use this new instrument when I first took it on stage. Every concert was an occasion for experimenting, after which I would tweak both the circuit and my performance. By the fourth outing everything clicked: the device and the music merged into a coherent package. The result represented a welcome break from the lilting swing of the prior CD pieces, reflective of my emerging interest in chaos. All I needed was one more switch.

Back in my basement after that fourth concert I figured there was just enough space on the plastic to mount the switch. It would have been the work of but a moment to remove the screws holding the acrylic in place and drill it safely in a vise, but I assumed I was nimble enough with the Makita to skip the first step. Of course, I slipped and the drill passed through the plastic, the circuit board, and a ribbon connector, emerging on the other side disturbingly close to my palm. Gazing morosely at the carcass, I pondered where on earth I might find a duplicate ten-year-old Discman, and then remembered this new thing I'd read about called eBay. I set up an account, typed in the model number, and found three for sale. Now the painful question arose: how much was it worth to reopen this enticing door to my musical future? I entered a maximum bid of $12 (reflective of my low self-image?). A week later the player was mine for $11.38. I transplanted the circuit board from Sony's clamshell to my holey plastic, resoldered the wires, and was soon back on stage, chastised but glitching away.[7]

Circuits, hacks, and hands—the strange leaps and buzzes that erupt from electrons doing their thing—had powered my auditory imagination since I was a teenager. I loved what they did, how they looked, what they felt like. But I've long known that this love has its drawbacks: they were heavy to carry around, a lot of work to replicate, and they were mortal.

The cusp of the Millennium was marked by growing interest in early live electronic music among younger artists working with technology: Cage's *Cartridge Music* (1960), Kosugi's *Micro 1* (1964), Reich's *Pendulum Music* (1968), and Tudor's *Rainforest IV* (1973) were being performed again after years of hibernation. Some works were easier to revive than others. Phono cartridges could still be sourced with relative ease, but handmade circuits, artist-hacked boxes, or more obscure commercial devices presented problems.

In 1997, the Kammerensemble Neue Musik Berlin asked me to revive *Pea Soup* after some twenty years. However, the Countryman phase shifter it required had not been manufactured for decades. I was able to approximate the phase shifter circuit with the aid of a schematic provided by Carl Countryman himself (with the proviso that I never ask him for tech support) and performed it with KNM that year and at the wonderful Limbo festival in Plasy, Czech Republic, in 1999. But I was not entirely satisfied, since I had been unable to replicate one custom-made sub-module and certain behaviors of the original system remained out of reach.

By 2000 it was possible to use music programming software to emulate the behavior of analog devices. Software like Max/MSP specifically modeled their graphic interface after analog synthesizers: software equivalents of oscillators, filters, and lower-level signal processors could be arranged on the screen like the module faceplates on a Moog, with lines drawn to interconnect them like patchcords. I just had to get my head around the idea of replacing hardware with software.

Since my first exposure to the KIM-I I had divided my musical resources into three categories according to what I perceived as their intrinsic strengths. Hardware—handmade circuits, hacked digital reverbs, backwards electric guitars—was great for interesting sounds and instability. Software was best for making logical decisions, generating compositional structure, and interfacing controllers. People, meanwhile, made the most nuanced and often unpredictable, choices.[8] My musical tool chest resembled a cautious investment portfolio, sensibly balanced between these three sectors. In the early 2000s, however, the edges began to blur.

In 2001 I emulated *Pea Soup*'s original hardware in Max/MSP. It can be tempting to "improve" a circuit when modeling it in software: physical sliders and knobs have limits past which they will not move, while numbers in a program can always be made larger or smaller. To preserve the essential character of the original composition, however, it can be important to retain some limitations that in software seem "artificial." Other aspects of the original, meanwhile, might be the result of unwanted technological limitations or economic compromises whose correction can benefit the work without violating its spirit.

Preserving the core properties of the original analog *Pea Soup*, I added some new innovations made possible by the software: a half-a-dozen "feedback nulling filters," activated with a tap of the keyboard, that detect the current pitch of feedback and attenuate that frequency just enough to silence it and allow a new pitch to emerge and take its place. In the 1970s I had to determine the pitch of the feedback by ear and then use equalization on the mixer or tone controls on the amplifier to null it, but the software could accomplish the same thing faster and more accurately. The primary use of both the original and automated nulling techniques was to keep the feedback changing and avoid it sitting on a single frequency for too long. I now found that judicious use of the filters could steer *Pea Soup* through changes in tonality as pitches are dropped and others added as the performance unfolds, which creates a new sense of forward harmonic motion in what was previously a rather static modal piece— different from the original, but an intriguing extension.[9]

I also replaced the rather severe performance guidelines I had penned in 1976 with something more akin to "improvising with architecture". A few years later, when I designed my first website, I uploaded the program with instructions so it could be downloaded by anyone with a computer and performed anywhere, anytime, without custom circuitry or my presence, almost as easily as one might prop the score of a Beethoven sonata on a music stand. (In my formative years, I had understood the rise of the composer-performer as marking the end of scored music; the advent of software distribution has led me to see it as more of a temporary expediency until the technology arrived to facilitate performances in a more practical form.)

The sonic character of the new *Pea Soup* is no different from its parent. Feedback is still feedback, and the physics of acoustics are the same now as they were in 1974. In the hands of a sensitive musician with a good ear, the updated piece proved virtually foolproof and has been presented in more than a hundred performances and installations around the world. I do miss the quaint look of a table of esoteric homemade circuits replaced by familiar, stolid computers, but for ease of distribution, downloadable software cannot be faulted (and the rather minimal equipment needed for the original *Pea Soup* was never as visually seductive as the classic Tudor sprawl). Already site-specific in terms of its tonality, *Pea Soup*'s new portability often imbues the instrumentation with a corresponding regional twang: a Shō in Hong Kong, an alphorn in Bern, a musical saw in Miami.

In 2002, John Corbett, then a colleague at SAIC, invited me to revive *Devil's Music*. (His interest was piqued after finding a cassette dub of the *Devil's Music* LP under his car seat and listening to it on a long drive.) The required Electro-Harmonix digital delays were a thousand miles away in my Cape Cod attic, so I took another stab at using software to replicate circuitry. Like *Pea Soup*, the work gained a second life through online distribution of the program.[10] There was an important amendment to the performance options for the piece—while the original version could only be performed by one person, the update could be run on multiple computers simultaneously, or sequentially, like a DJ battle. It was premiered by a half-dozen "Radio Jockeys" at the Empty Bottle in Chicago in May 2002.

Group realizations have since become the norm for *Devil's Music*, with each player contributing personal musical preferences from the smorgasbord of local radio. By 2015 the Web had emerged as the dominant source of music and news, and radios were receding. The local variety and moment-to-moment site specificity that I loved about the piece was evaporating. I took the step of incorporating software that shuffled the computer's internal music library as an alternative sampling source when a radio was unavailable—the geographic site-specificity of local radio transmitters would then be replaced by the microsite of the performer's own taste.

In the transition from hardware to software, *Pea Soup* lost nothing but gained both easier distribution and the option of tonal movement. The replacement of radio with personal playlists in the latest *Devil's Music* iteration represents a more fundamental shift in the essential character of the piece. This was not a decision taken lightly, but it reflected a changing reality: not only were radios themselves becoming less common, but the very idea of *local* radio broadcast was disappearing under the global reach of the Web. However, the retriggering effect of the stuttering circuit, which was a defining trait of the original version, remained. It imposes such a strong rhythmic signature on the musical texture that whether there was one performer or six, sampling radio or internal playlists, every performance still *sounded* like *Devil's Music*, regardless of input. I think of the piece as my contribution to the world of the "standard": a tune that could be interpreted by artists as different as Miles Davis, Dean Martin, Cyndi Lauper, or Poly Styrene and still be recognized as "My Funny Valentine" (Figure 21.2).

The update of *Devil's Music* was well timed to the proliferation of laptop ensembles, which had become to the 2000s what Glenn Branca's and Rhys Chatham's massed

Figure 21.2 Ensemble performance of *Devil's Music* in its software iteration, Sonic Arts Lounge, MaerzMusik, Berlin, March 2003. From left to right: Christof Kurzmann, Jen Brand, Ed Osborn, Andrea Neumann. Photo by Gerlind Fichte, courtesy Berlin Festspiele.

guitars were to the 1980s. During my first sabbatical in 2007, I was a Visiting Fellow in the Music Department at Princeton University, where PLOrk (the Princeton Laptop Orchestra) invited me to compose a piece. Having attended several concerts by similar groups, I was surprised that, although their instruments were *lap*tops, they always sat on tables like *desk*top computers. So I wrote a program for a laptop marching band that reached back to my oldest analog trick, feedback. The over-amplified built-in microphones fed back, soaked in distortion, through the tinny built-in speakers. Every time the player hit the return key, a filter shifted the feedback into a different range, shifted the balance between feedback and sound files of scratchy lead-in grooves from antique records, and changed the color of the screen, which lit the player's face. With a dozen performers stumbling around in the dark, *Waggle Dance* bore more than a passing resemblance to a swarm of colorful buzzing bees.

I learned things from doing these conversions and extensions of hardware into software. Listening to *Pea Soup*'s fresh tonal modulations after the introduction of the nulling filters was the spark for a new work that pushed this minor utility into a central role. *Roomtone Variations* (2013) opens with ninety seconds of controlled feedback through which twenty-four nulling filters map the resonant frequencies of the room. Those frequencies are then displayed in conventional staff notation by a video projector—strongest resonances on the left, weakest on the far right. Once the staves are filled, the electronics go silent and acoustic musicians improvise variations on the notes as they are highlighted on the screen above the stage, gradually stepping through a site-specific architectural tone row. After a premiere by the TarabúsT ensemble at the Museo de Arte Contemporáneo in Santiago, Chile, in 2013, the piece has been performed by soloists and ensembles of various sizes, in spaces including the notorious Berghain club in Berlin, the Concergebouw Brugge in Belgium, and—by an orchestra of 144 mostly amateur musicians—in the St Pauli Elbtunnel crossing under the Elbe in Hamburg. Since only minimal sight-reading skills are required, *Roomtone* is accessible to musicians from a wide range of backgrounds with minimal rehearsal—a boon to organizing performances with local improvisers or amateurs.

One last story about the hardware-software relationship: In 2001 I applied to the ICMC (International Computer Music Conference) in Cuba to present a duo with Peter Cusack. I received an acceptance for a cello suite that I had never written. I asked for clarification and was told they had made a mistake and our invitation was rescinded. A few months later a colleague at SAIC asked me about a symposium in Sheffield where I was to give a paper. Except I wasn't. The paper looked like something I might have produced, but I hadn't.

Some Google-sleuthing led me to a British composer twenty-one years my junior whose webpage bio consisted of a single sentence: "Nick Collins is not the Editor-in-Chief of *Leonardo Music Journal*." The "k" was the giveaway. Nick, it turned out, was a composer with an interest in the kind of computer-assisted DJ-style crosscutting I had pursued in the early 1980s, but working exclusively with programming (he proudly claimed never to have held a soldering iron). To further foster our identity confusion, I invited him to write an article for LMJ, and he obliged, under his full name of Nicholas (with an "h") Collins. We became friends.

The *Handmade Electronic Music* book had cemented my reputation as a "hardware guy," while Nick was an early proponent of "live coding," in which software is written live on stage and projected for the audience to follow. In 2007 Nick asked me to pair up for a presentation at the upcoming NIME (New Interfaces for Musical Expression) conference in New York. The performance would be both duet and duel—hardware versus software, physical gesture versus the keytaps of coding. No swords or pistols, but there would be a trophy—an elegantly rugged small vase created and donated by the Devon-based wood-fire-kiln potter Nic Collins. A brass plate on the wooden presentation box announced the official "Nic(k) Collins Cup."

We took the stage at Galapagos in Williamsburg at 3 a.m. on June 10. Ballots were distributed to the audience. Nick warned me that he "fought dirty" and was planning to embed video clips by yet another Nic Collins, a star of gay porn. I fought back, using a hammer to extract a tape head from an old boombox, and closed my performance with a piezo disc amplifying the sound of a sparkler. Porn is no competition for fireworks. I won the audience vote and carried home the Cup to display on my mantel.

Like the America's Cup, ours demanded rematches. In the years that followed, we battled it out in London, Mexico City, and New York again. Though vindicating my instinct that watching people code is less entertaining than watching people play with fire, the results did nothing to sway Nick's aversion to solder. Now a professor at Durham University, Nick went on to publish important books on computer and electronic music, and never did become editor of *Leonardo Music Journal.*

22

The Missing Switch

In 1999, soon after I accepted the job in Chicago, I had a chinwag with British improviser Fred Frith who had just taken a position at Mills College. Like me, he'd been a freelancer all his life and had his doubts about long-term jobs in general and teaching in particular. We agreed we'd last three to five years and then return to freelance life in Europe.

In 2013, I was visiting Mills as the fondly named "David Tudor Composer-in-Residence," and Fred's ensemble of graduate students was performing *Roomtone*. He was still in Oakland, and I was still in Chicago. Our planned trajectories had been scotched by tenure's rare allure of job security and health insurance.

SAIC had hired me in part for my international profile and recognized that maintaining that profile would require frequent travel. For twenty years—from the time I arrived in Chicago until the curtain-fall of the Covid pandemic—I crossed oceans and continents often enough that some United cabin personnel knew me by name. A few years ago, I receiving a tacky Lucite paperweight honoring the dubious distinction of having flown 1 million miles. The vast majority of those miles took place on long-haul flights in economy class seats, though Alvin had given me a useful piece of advice: "Wear a tie when you fly—you might get upgraded." Having gone to a school where jackets and ties were mandatory, I was all but allergic to them, but I acquired a couple of nice ties and Alvin's trick yielded a high success rate. I was grateful every time it did. A Chilean colleague called it my "*corbata mágica*." (Being white and male no doubt helped. Friends who weren't had less luck, regardless of income level or sartorial statements.)

Tenure kept us in Chicago, but it never came to feel like home, despite being one of the most important cities for the development of multiple threads of American music. Maybe I hit it too late in life after too many other scenes. Summers and sabbaticals were spent on the East Coast and in Europe. The children evolved hard-to-place accents that amended their early British school immersion with a thin topcoat of American. Both would depart for the East Coast at the first opportunity and return to Europe for graduate education and beyond.

The one moment we really felt that Chicago was the place to be was November 4, 2008. Standing in Grant Park with our youngest and her best friend, we were immersed in the joyous roar of the crowd when Barack Obama's election became official. I recorded both the roar and the ensuing applause—a testament to just how deliriously long three minutes can be.[1] Eight years later, a sociopath entered the White House and we started looking for an overseas foothold.

Berlin was fiscally manageable, culturally lively, and we still had friends and professional contacts there. Our youngest was planning to move there after university. The music scene sported a dynamic mix of improvisation and electronics in concerts at dozens of small venues across the sprawling city. A friend of a friend of Susan's rented us a lovely small apartment in Charlottenburg—quiet, convenient to public transport, and evocative of the Berlin I remembered from my first visit forty years earlier. I was also now a visiting Research Fellow at the Orpheus Institute in Ghent, Belgium—a foundation devoted largely to historical musicology but, as Research Director, my old friend Jonathan Impett solicited me as a test case for more contemporary topics.

New Year's Day 2020 found our extended family celebrating in Lisbon. In the following forty-five days, I crossed the Atlantic five times—woodshedding in Berlin, teaching in Chicago, meetings in Ghent, workshops and concerts in Canterbury and Ithaca, visiting the kids in Edinburgh and London. On March 11, I landed in Chicago holding a return ticket to Berlin for the following week. Two days later, Susan was in the air between a conference in London and a show to review in New York when the world shut down. Unable to get back to Germany, she grabbed a flight to Chicago so we could sit out the next few days together. Those days of lockdown turned into weeks and then to months.

The challenge of teaching online was particularly acute in art schools, where studio courses are hands-on, in facilities with equipment or supplies people don't have at home. The terrible audio quality of Zoom, irritating enough in routine meetings, made any reasonable evaluation of sound-based art impossible. Everyone improvised alternatives.

In May, the semester finally ended. Susan and I rented a car and drove to Cape Cod. George Floyd had just been murdered, and every city we passed through, from Chicago to Cleveland to Buffalo to Boston, was in the throes of protests. People were dying everywhere from Covid.

A year previous we had inherited my parents' West Falmouth cottage, in which I had summered every year since childhood—a building high on charm but low on recent maintenance. Our youngest arrived from New York to find that the walls of the upstairs shower had failed, leading to a catastrophic droop of the ceiling below. We had mildew problems and a dynasty of empowered mice. But it was a welcome port in the storm. By August both our children and their partners had arrived, with friends occasionally visiting as local and international regulations allowed. We worked remotely in five different time zones, in six corners of the house. We upgraded the WiFi and the cocktail cabinet, and shared croquet mallets at sunset.

Supply chains were in shambles and plumbers, electricians, and carpenters seriously overstretched. We tore things down, nailed things up, ran electrical lines, painted, and ferried dozens of anxious small mammals to remote woodlots. We sold our own house down the road to finance repairs, and nobody seemed to mind group dinners beneath a duct-tape-and-cardboard ceiling. We were aware of being extraordinarily lucky.

I had spent the previous eighteen months compiling a third edition of *Handmade Electronic Music*. The previous iteration was a decade old and in need of updating. The Do-It-Together ethos had taken on a global life in ways that had to be acknowledged, so I invited twenty-five young hackers and writers from around the world to contribute new material, hoping to expand the book's scope beyond the white, male, Eurocentric base out of which I had operated. I figured half of those invited might submit usable material by the deadline. Instead, I ended up with a surplus of contributors, as invited authors brought in their own enthusiastic collaborators. The new chapters were divided between the printed book and a substantial supporting website with streaming audio and video (replacing the now-outmoded DVD of the previous edition).[2]

The original publication date came and went in the stasis of the pandemic, and the scheduled release events in New York, Chicago, London, Berlin, and Buenos Aires were cancelled. The publisher struggled to get the book out in time for the academic fall book orders, but their website production had stalled, so I took a week off from home-repair triage to kluge together an interim site (the official one would not be completed until six months after publication).[3] The new edition garnered a lovely spread in *The Wire* along with enthusiastic support from what the family calls my "cult."

In September, I began a year-long sabbatical. The plan had been to spend it in Berlin, with junkets hither and thither, composing, performing, attending concerts and conferences, collaborating with musicians, and immersing myself in the kind of conversations about art, music, and technology that, for some reason, never took place in Chicago. But summer crisped into New England fall with lockdown measures still in place. The laziness of August still clung to the house and hammock, immobilizing the art part of my brain. The house decay was stabilized, and time began to trickle back into my hands but it brought no new ideas along. My music had always felt out of place in the country. Since childhood, the point of the West Falmouth had been its distance from real life: from school, from concerts, from selling audio gear, from hacking. As I told our friends, "I leave my music on the other side of the Cape Cod Canal."

Susan often remarked that I needed a community to function, and by November 2020 I had not attended a concert for seven months. The election arrived, yet its anxiety continued. With no live input, and no prospect of a stage for my output, I was rendered incapable of creative thought. I did my best to stimulate myself remotely, scheduling regular Zoom calls with colleagues like Ben Neill, John Bischoff, David Behrman, Stuart Jones, and James Fei. But this was not enough to unstick me. In the hopes of righting my own ship, as an alternative to crafting anything new, I forced myself to dig deeper into my existing repertoire.

I had for years bounced back and forth between soldering and programming. There remained an irrationality and instability in some circuitry that I had never found in software, epitomized in the pieces inspired by my hacking workshops. (The circuits I had successfully emulated in software—those for *Pea Soup* and *Devil's Music*—happened to be comparatively stolid in their behavior.) By 2017, however, I was curious about whether it would, after all, be possible to write a program that would emulate not only the sounds of unstable circuits but their behavior as well—could I persuade my most rational resource to act irrationally? This led to the first improvising instrument I had built since retiring the trombone-propelled electronics a decade earlier.

With a forty-dollar trumpet acquired on eBay as a core, I created a mashup of trombone-propelled electronics and my recent hacking-inspired experiments, with a speaker mounted inside the bell, and sensors to measure breath pressure and read the position of each valve. I embedded seven switches and an infrared transmitter in a toilet-plunger mute. An Arduino microcomputer on the trumpet gathered data from the sensors and sent it to a Max/MSP program on my laptop.

The program incorporated a collection of voices that emulated the kind of glitchy, unstable output of *Salvage* and *The Royal Touch*, as well as some of the weird sounds I had heard emerging from the bells of (proper) trumpet-playing friends. I shunned the sampling vocabulary that had characterized my trombone, and replaced it by digital synthesis. The sounds are sent to the speaker in the trumpet, where they can be acoustically filtered by valving, the movement of the mute and, when more oomph is desired, to the PA.

The resulting system occupies a sweet spot between controllability and unpredictability such that I have to improvise with the instrument itself as well as with other musicians. Players often long for the freshness and accidental discoveries that accompany first acquaintance with an instrument, qualities difficult to recreate once one becomes competent. (According to Joe Zawinul, in the recording sessions for *In a Silent Way* John McLaughlin had some difficulty playing in the manner Miles Davis wished of him. Davis told him to "play as if you don't know how to play the guitar. As a result John's playing was among the best of his career.")[4] To frustrate any incipient virtuosity, I wrote software that changes the trumpet's behavior every time it's turned on. The valves (like the slide in my trombone) act like faders on a mixer, but instead of controlling some sound parameter linearly—gradually increasing volume as you press it down, for example—the program scrambles the relationship between a valve's position and the control value sent to a sound generator, as if every time you sat down at a piano its keys were rearranged to strike different strings. Each valve slides through its own unique scramble, so that each of my fingers in turn effectively emulates one performer in *Salvage*, moving across the same uncertain terrain as the others but following a different path.

In a nod to Tudor's first electronic composition, *Bandoneon!*, I dubbed the new instrument "!trumpet." Where Tudor's exclamation point referenced the factorial symbol borrowed from mathematics (alluding to the complex interaction between the keys on his hacked bandoneon and the resulting sounds), mine was the negating symbol from logic: this is *not* a trumpet (see Figure 22.1).[5]

For three years leading up to the pandemic, I had used the !trumpet regularly in improvised collaborations with musicians in the United States, Europe, and South America, tweaking the code from time to time and occasionally adding new voices (often in imitation of my partners). But what was I to do with this instrument in isolation? Musicians talk about the differences between performing live and in the studio—some work best in isolation, others need a crowd to push them. The Grateful Dead, long one of the most successful touring bands in the world, was incapable of

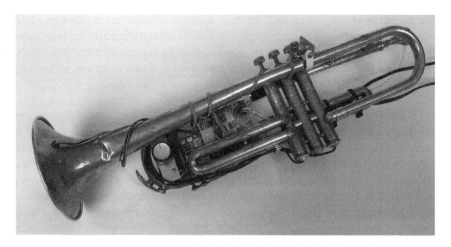

Figure 22.1 The !trumpet, 2020, showing embedded Arduino microcontroller with wires leading to sensors in valves and speaker in bell, and vinyl tube from air-pressure sensor to mouthpiece. Photo by Nicolas Collins.

producing a studio recording that could rival its live shows. Going the other direction, both the Beatles and Glenn Gould eventually chose the studio over the stage. I had always fallen into the Dead camp: I had never embraced the notion of "playing to the mic" for a recording session in an empty studio. I needed an audience, but after nine months of Zoom I thought it was just possible that a video camera might convince me someone else was watching and listening.

Another thing I dislike about recording, however, is that it inevitably exudes a false sense of completeness and commitment. The record is presumed to be the final, most authoritative, most perfect instance. Choosing the "best" of three takes can feel like an existential crisis, but also a misrepresentation—there likely remain others of equivalent quality if different character.

When my parents renovated and winterized the Cape house in 1976, they asked the children for design suggestions. My younger brother, then in his surly teens, requested a spiral staircase. As it happened, Columbia was renovating the art history library and removing the old cast-iron spiral stairs that led to the upper stacks. My father and I rented a U-Haul truck whose bay had a long enough hypotenuse for the central pole, paid off a construction worker to load in the parts, and drove up to our gutted cottage. The architects added a curved tower to the plan to accommodate it—now one of the house's distinguishing features. Like Marian the Librarian in *The Music Man,* I thought that this spiral stair might provide an enlivening backdrop for my private performances.

Beginning the morning after the election and continuing every day through the failed insurrection and eventual inauguration, I would set up and record a few solo improvisations on the !trumpet. To assemble *Lucky Dip* (2020) I returned to the principle of an earlier web project, *Pea Soup to Go* (2014), which shuffles and crossfades between dozens of audio files of *Pea Soup* performances around the world, producing an endless, random sequence of slow key modulations and changes in instrumental accompaniment as it drifts from Amsterdam to Hong Kong to Zurich.[6] In *Lucky Dip*, a JavaScript app randomizes a collection of fifty short video clips for an online album that delivers the material in a new order every time you visit the site.[7]

On January 1, 2016, I made a New Year's resolution to write a story a day. The content was not prescribed—one day it might be an anecdote from childhood, the next a statement about my creative habits, another day an observation about a concert I had seen. The critical thing was just to write. The project got a little out of hand: by the politically distressing end of that year, I had accumulated over 1000 stories. And now I had a habit. The stories continued to pile up through the following years, but I showed them to no one until Susan unexpectedly requested the collection as a Christmas present.

Undaunted by the word count, she worked her way through a thumb drive, commenting on individual stories as she went ("tidy summary" or "potentially libelous?"). By the end she thought it had the makings of a book that connected my own eccentric path to the often undocumented musical and artistic scenes of the past several decades. But many tales had to go, and the remainder needed to be given context. A string of anecdotes, she pointed out, is fun at first but then it begins to feel like a dinner party dominated by one guy who can tell a good story but never shuts up. So I set to work on editing.

We finally returned to Berlin after more than a year away, landing at the appalling new Brandenburg Airport in May 2021. The city was enjoying a double spring: parks and gardens were in bloom, and communal life was finally starting to thaw. We met friends in small numbers (fully vaccinated people were allowed to visit other fully vaccinated people at home). I went to the opening of a sound installation in the cavernous Parochialkirche near Alexanderplatz, the perfect venue for the still-mandated social-distancing. (Signs posted around town gave animal-referenced equivalencies for that 150 cm separation: one Shetland pony, three corgies.) Then on June 6, sixteen months after I had last heard a live performance, I attended an open-air concert outside the Theaterhaus Mitte (Figure 22.2).

The audience sat in meticulously spaced chairs, gazing up at an outdoor stage flanked by a good PA. The crowd buzzed with the simple euphoria of "wow, a concert!" The performance started. It wasn't bad or brilliant, but it *was*. My mind drifted, as it often does in concerts. And then suddenly, out of nowhere, there appeared an *idea*. It was not a great idea, not the start of a new piece, just an add-on to some material I'd been experimenting with prior to the quarantine. But still—*I had had an idea*! Something threw a hidden switch inside my head.

As clubs and concert halls gradually re-opened, I went out as often as possible. At every event something new popped into my head. And the switch didn't reset when I left the venue—I now had ideas even when sitting in our apartment. Baby steps, perhaps, but at least I was vertical.

Figure 22.2 View from the author's seat at Theaterhaus Mitte, Berlin, June 6, 2021, during a performance by Rudi Fisherlehner (left) and Olaf Rupp (right). The first in-person concert attended after the sixteen-month pandemic hiatus. Photo by Nicolas Collins.

That first Theaterhaus inspiration was one of those last-one-percent details that help material finally cohere into a composition. In the hacking workshops, we construct inductive pickups for "sniffing" electromagnetic fields. In 2001, I connected a pickup I was using to detect signals from a CD player to the driver coil under the strings of a backwards electric guitar; when I passed the pickup over the driver by accident, the pair began to feedback like a mike and speaker would, resonating the strings with an eerie siren-like swoop. Discovering a new order of feedback decades after my first inspiring encounter with the phenomenon was the kind of serendipity that periodically reinvigorates my musical thinking.

I built a glove with a pickup on each fingertip, feeding back with driver coils strewn across the table (leaving the guitar behind), but by the time of the pandemic, I had not advanced beyond exploratory improvisation. At the Theaterhaus concert, I envisioned a method for organizing the swoops and chirps that the five channels of feedback produced: the performer would control the sound by mimicking the gestures of hands in old-master drawings; a video camera would superimpose my hand on a drawing, and I would try to align the two by watching a projection above me. This turned out to be just as overwrought and clumsy as it reads in print, but it got me thinking of imposing strategies and structures rather than improvising freely. Within a few months, a less affected approach snuck into place, and *Roll, Pitch & Yaw* made it to the concert stage (Figure 22.3).[8]

A few weeks after the Theaterhaus event, I went to a concert of local improvisers and foreign guests in bassist Alexander Frangenheim's studio just outside the S-Bahn ring that defines the perimeter of central Berlin. The playing was workmanlike, the acoustics good, the ambience friendly. Heading home on the S-Bahn, I mused about the notion of *quality*: great composition and great improvisation are both rare, but where poor composition seems labored, even lackluster improvisation displays occasional spontaneity. It came down, I thought, to the difference between dependence on editing or invention, between the results of methodical work or unexpected inspiration.

A week later at another club, Sowieso, I heard a quartet of voice, trumpet, trombone, and guitar. There was a beautiful moment halfway through the first set, and another one a little while later. But getting from one of these moments to the next struck me that night as haphazard. The effect, common in improvised concerts, was one of navigating in the dark: making careful, tentative steps to avoid banging a shin on a coffee table while seeking the door or the light switch. This raised a caveat to my observation of the relative virtues of invention and editing: invention often entails a lot of failure, or at least unwanted outcomes; editing potentially eliminates them before the final result

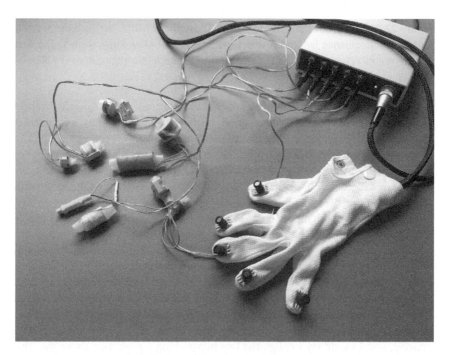

Figure 22.3 Driver coils and glove with inductive pickups for *Roll, Pitch & Yaw*, 2021. Photo by Nicolas Collins.

is presented. This is why I'm at my happiest when my musical life balances between improvisation and composition, both as a listener and as a creator, with access to the benefits and risks of both options. In the words of dieticians everywhere, a colorful diet is a healthy diet.

My first performance after sixteen months loomed at the end of June. It had been on my calendar for over a year, the only scheduled event that hadn't subsequently been cancelled. By now I wasn't sure I still remembered how to play a full concert. I had never been one of those people who enjoyed practicing. (My downstairs neighbor in graduate school taught flute; when he spoke of his delight in a weekend "with nothing to do but practice," I was astonished—I assumed it was always a chore but that some people were just more self-disciplined.) I usually prepared for concerts by blocking the critical moments in a piece and the transitions between compositions, but running through the full piece repeatedly from beginning to end would have been counterproductive, since I preferred to preserve that sense of the unpredictable.

Now, however, I felt too out of shape to take this cavalier approach. For three weeks, I rehearsed my entire set in full every morning. I invited the Hamburg-based trumpet player Birgit Ulher to perform in a couple of the works and contribute a solo of her own. Even if I flamed out, I reckoned she could rescue the night. But I didn't fall off the bike I'd learned to ride so many years ago (and had been stashed in the garage for a year).

By the end of June, Susan and I were back in West Falmouth, the ocean beckoning as it had every year since I was four. The idea-switch clicked off again like the lights in a European stairwell that you punch on at the bottom and that always time-out when you're halfway up. But that's okay. I made it to the third floor. I was in the dark again, but now at least I knew where the ON switch was.

Interlude

Things I'd Like to Own

1

While working for Studio Consultants, I was given a tour of NBC's sound effects department (a client). Down the hall from the luxuriously equipped modern studio, replete with the latest digital technology, lay a storeroom full of devices that dated back to radio plays of the 1930s, including a plethora of mechanical devices for sound effects: slapsticks, doorbells, wood blocks, bullwhips, and so on. My favorite was a black cube, about one foot on each side, of ebonized wood. On each of three sides was a large wooden knob below an engraved legend in block capitals, filled with white paint. One read "CREAKING RIGGING," another "CART WHEEL," and the third "CRUSHING BONES." Like Marcel Duchamp's *A Bruit Secret* (*With Hidden Noise*, 1916), the mechanism inside remained a sealed mystery, but turning any knob produced a stunning likeness of the designated effect.

2

Solid State Logic (SSL) is a British company that makes very expensive recording consoles. At an industry trade show in the 1980s, one of the sales reps told me about a huge crate that had recently been delivered from Brazil to their headquarters in Oxford. Inside was a 1:1 replica of their latest mixing desk, carved out of wood and realistically painted. The recipients were understandably baffled. The next day, an envelope arrived from a major recording studio in São Paulo containing a check for the full cost of a new mixer, along with a letter asking SSL to "repair the returned console and bring it up to current specifications."

The backstory was that the Brazilian government had recently imposed hefty tariffs on the import of products for which the government believed there was a domestically manufactured equivalent. The recording studio, however, needed an internationally recognized, state-of-the-art console to attract high-level clients, so they employed the loophole of "repairing" an older asset, and sent the replica to reinforce the ruse with a shipping trail. Had we space sufficient in our loft, I would have bought the wooden one in a New York minute.

3

Benthos, a small company on Cape Cod, builds instruments for oceanographic research. In 1972, they applied their skills to an unusual commercial product. In the wake of a series of botulism scares, the food industry was looking for a way of testing cans for the presence of botulinum without opening them. Drawing on their experience with sonar, Benthos designed a machine that tapped each can with a solenoid (an electrically activated plunger) as it came off the assembly line; the sound was analyzed and compared to the sonic "fingerprints" of a healthy can and that of a can in which botulinum was present. Bacterial growth produces a gas that increases pressure inside the can, raising the pitch of the ping like a timpani player tightening his drum.

4

In the mid-1980s, I read a story in *Studio Sound* about a retired LA session musician who, driving by the site of one of the legendary 1960s recording studios, noticed that the building was slated for demolition. The studio had moved out years earlier, the building itself was less than nondescript, and the location made it a valuable site for commercial development. But the musician remembered how the stairwell had produced a massive reverberation when tracks were played back through a speaker at the bottom of the stairs and re-recorded with a microphone a few stories up, which became a signature effect in the records of Phil Spector, The Beach Boys, and others. He called some of his old colleagues and gathered signatures on a petition to the landmarks commission for Los Angeles, requesting that the building be preserved for the acoustical properties of the stairwell. Sadly, the appeal fell on deaf ears. Call for Rachel Whiteread!

5

On a trip back to New York not long after 9/11, I called on David Behrman. We met at his loft on Beach Street, then walked around the corner to Walker's restaurant. Life felt gray and grim. Behrman said that the ratcheted-up surveillance and security reminded him of McCarthy days. During a lull in our despondent conversation, a Teac 4-Track reel-to-reel tape recorder rose slowly out of a dumpster outside our window like the conning tower of a surfacing submarine. It was the same model we had had in the Wesleyan studios when I was a student. It was followed by four arms, then two heads, as a couple of skinny guys in their late twenties wrestled the machine out and onto the curb. They jumped back in and hauled out a few more pieces of old audio gear as we watched in silence.

By 2001, most recording studios had shifted from tape recorders to computers, and once-coveted technology was being tossed. The world had recently changed so radically and so quickly that I couldn't help viewing our morning metaphorically. David and I would have liked to be the ones to discover that Teac, bring it home, and recreate yesterday's studio. We finished our coffee. At the door, David said he needed to buy a pair of shoelaces. I walked with him to a cobbler down the street. As we left, he commented, "This is the sort of thing my father would have done, bought shoelaces."

Surprise Me

Just before the pandemic, I attended a concert of tape music by the American composer Tod Dockstader at the Akademie der Künste in Berlin. I was struck by how similar his work from the 1960s and 1970s sounded to my own juvenile experiments from that same time. He had "performed with tape" as much as I had, and listening to his pieces, I heard the familiar sonic elements that arise naturally from the gap between the record and play heads: metronomic rhythms, crude reverb simulation, cascading feedback that morphs from tape hiss through resonant noise to become pitch and cascading distortion, and oscillator swoops with head-delayed offsets.

Dockstader's work was more sophisticated, his textures more complex, than anything I could have managed with my one tape recorder and oscillator in my bedroom. Not only did he have more equipment at his disposal, he also made use of a large library of sound material from which to build work of a musique concrète nature. And he was obviously musically more accomplished than a self-taught seventeen-year-old. But our shared repurposing of a neutral piece of technology had nonetheless created similar results.

I used to say there were two kinds of concerts that I enjoyed: performances of great music that gave me something to strive for, and evenings of music worse than mine, which gave me an ego boost. Now I have added a third category: music that reminded me where I came from, and how I might fit into the larger picture.

When I first flipped the switch hidden inside my Tandberg tape recorder in 1971, what came out of the speakers could only have been described as "electronic." Likewise, the oscillator circuit I built a few months later. The cover of the spiral-bound notebook in which I transcribed Alvin's lectures my first semester at Wesleyan bears the scrawled course title "Introduction to Electronic Music."[1] But within a few weeks of immersion in the music and writing of Cage and his followers, I adopted the expression "experimental music" to describe what I heard in class and what I wanted to compose in response. Cage had introduced the term and Alvin applied it freely. Many artists shun labels, but I was comfortable with the word "experimental."

"Electronic music" was pinned to a technology in use across various genres, many of which I snobbishly shunned—everything from Switched on Bach to Stockhausen to Kraftwerk. "Experimental music," on the other hand, denoted an aesthetic philosophy: "an experimental action," wrote Cage, "is one the outcome of which is not foreseen."[2] On that basis, I freely attached that tag to compositions such as Alvin's

I am sitting in a room, Terry Riley's *In C*, or Takehisa Kosugi's *MICRO 1*. Those three compositions, along with many others, were discussed by Michael Nyman in his 1974 book, *Experimental Music—Cage and Beyond*, which bears some responsibility for promulgating the label.[3]

For me, "experimental" doesn't describe what something sounds like, but rather the methods from which it arose. Consider one decade of Alvin's output: we have *Music for Solo Performer* (1965), in which percussion was played by subsonic brainwaves; *Vespers* (1969), with its sparse clicks and blindfolded players; in *Still and Moving Lines of Silence in Families of Hyperbolas* (1973–4) sine waves beat against conventional instruments; while *Bird and Person Dyning* (1975) feedback prompts in-ear psychoacoustic phantoms. These pieces differ so radically from one another in sonic character, form, and performance technique that it would be difficult in a blind listening test to link them to the same composer. Alvin's compositional process itself was unforeseeable from one work to the next.

Once, when I was his student, Alvin told me that after hearing *I am sitting in a room* Steve Reich had commented, "If I had come up with that idea I would have spent the next three years just making variations on it." Alvin, proud of his heterogeneity, recounted this with a certain smugness, and yet even Alvin eventually began to narrow his focus. It was not *I am sitting in a room* but *Still and Moving Lines* that prompted him to concentrate on a single phenomenon—the acoustical beating of close pitches—in piece after piece.

Many other composers who struck eighteen-year-old me as paragons of the experimental music method eventually settled into more stable, recognizable styles: Robert Ashley, Pauline Oliveros, Terry Riley, Steve Reich, Annea Lockwood, and Gavin Bryars. Over the centuries, most composers—radical or conservative—explored multiple materials and methods in their youth before settling on a "mature style" for the balance of their careers.

So, is there such a thing as "Experimental Music"? Or, in the words of parents everywhere, is it just a phase they're going through? In her 2016 book *Experimental Music Since 1970*, Jennie Gottschalk embraced Nyman's stylistic premise, extended its timeline to the present day, and made much-needed steps toward diversifying the gender and racial balance of artists represented.[4] Nonetheless, a colleague of mine commented in response, "I can't believe anyone still believes in the idea of the 'experimental.'" And even in its heyday the term attracted derision. Robert Ashley, for one, explicitly disowned it:

> When you have thought about other kinds of musical ideas, and worked with, say, electronic music for most of your composing life, the composition is anything but experimental. It is the epitome of expertise. It may be aleatoric or purposefully unpredictable in its specific sounds, or purposefully exploratory of a sound, but experimental is the wrong word, and its use has more or less divided composers among themselves . . . Scientists do experiments. Composers

make music. The making of music is an act of absolute confidence. It could not be otherwise.[5]

Bob makes valid points. When Alvin began messing about with brainwaves, he may have been drawing on scientific discoveries, but he was not conducting a scientific experiment. He had no *a priori* hypothesis or clearly identified variables; he was not collecting data. He had an idea for a musical mechanism and was curious to hear what it would sound like. And in music, he had expertise.

What Bob's argument misses is that we use the verb "experiment" in different ways. At one end of the spectrum, you have scientific experiments. At the other, you have the infant who tries eating Duplo bricks. The accumulation of data and the diminution of Duplo-chewing both produce learning, which in turn reduces the locations where surprise is likely to erupt. All art exists somewhere on that spectrum: strict species counterpoint at one end, the first day of hardware hacking at the other, and most other musical activities somewhere in between.

As we develop skills—whether as scientists, infants, or composers—we have greater choice about that balance between expertise and surprise, between certainty and discovery. We pick and choose which learned skills to employ according to external factors (mission of the lab, impact on digestion) or personal preference. Perhaps what *I* mean by "experimental" is simply this: the desire for a structure or instrument that can surprise me.

I have never had Bob's "absolute confidence," but I have enough confidence to enjoy certain kinds of risk. Some musicians prefer making recordings where everything can be fixed in the mix (thumb on the certainty side of the scale); others prefer performing live (thumb on the side of surprise). Even in my recorded work I've tried to facilitate uncertainty: encouraging the use of the shuffle mode on my first CD, my JavaScript apps of *Pea Soup to Go* and *Lucky Dip*.

George Lewis has said that he prefers "the provisional—the idea that something is *not* complete, that I can return to it."[6] Although George doesn't say this, his observation points to a commonly accepted distinction between traditional *composition*, which tends toward completeness, and *improvisation*, which doesn't. I side with George and with Robert Rauschenberg's reflection, "I want to put off the final fixing of a work as long as possible."[7]

Often, I will bring a composition to the stage when all I have is the beginning and the end. The middle gets filled in as I go, like building a bridge from either bank, adding new details with each performance. The audience observes me figuring things out—which is what I like to feel I'm witnessing at a concert by someone else. The piece is finished when the final board drops into place, but at that point, the challenge is gone and I typically stop performing the work. Weeks, sometimes years later, I might become aware of some divergent path suggested by one of those earlier, "finished" pieces—some still unanswered response to "what would happen if . . .?"

As I mentioned earlier, soon after acquiring my first microcomputer, the atavistic VIM, I read a 1947 paper describing a form of computer memory that relied on a pulse of sound in a column of mercury. This prompted the thought of using sound in architectural space as a kind of lossy, reverberant memory. I spent a year programming *The Time It Takes* (1980), figuring out how to encode linguistic data as sound and then reverse the process as the sound died away and the data reverted to entropic nonsense. The piece was performed twice and justifiably panned.

My father had taught me that good workers never blame their tools, so I chalked up the failure to my modest programming skills. The truth is, though, that a computer designed for controlling a microwave oven wasn't the right tool for the task I had set. Its constraints, as well as my own shortcomings, had limited the scope of my imagination before I even started working.

The piece was not good, but the idea of memory occupying acoustic space had value and would periodically jump back into my mind. Thirty years later, digital resources had reached a level of sophistication unimaginable in the days of VIM. Encoding and decoding data were no longer the problem—bytes could be taken from statistics, medical imaging, or hydrothermal measurements, and output as sound, text, images, or money. The question of imagination, however, remained. If the problem in 1979 had been a surfeit of limitations, now it was a surfeit of options.

Among those options competing for my attention now were visual ones. After teaching in an art school for over a decade, and having started using video as a frequent, if usually utilitarian, element in performances, I was increasingly comfortable with my visual instincts.

Ideally (for me), a piece using space as memory would capture the magic of *Pea Soup*, where sound is reshaped by its experience and situation. *Pea Soup* was both nice to think about and rewarding to listen to. It's never the same—changing not just with the architecture, but with air currents, the movements of visitors, and other competing sounds in the space. The point of memory is preservation. The poignancy of memory is fragility. The tension between the two was what I wanted to explore.

Imagine a photo of a boy playing with a dog under a big maple tree. If you take the data file for the image and output it through a speaker in a large room, you'll hear a sharp burst of sound—something like a handclap that then dies away in a series of short echoes and a tapering smear of reverberation. Which frequencies trail away soonest and which hang on to the last audible moment depend on the acoustics of the space in which the sound was played back. If you record that shifting sonic data and translate it back into visual data, you see something like a sequence of images projected on moving clouds, with a wisp of an arm or a wagging tail or a tree emerging with a clear resolution for a moment before dissolving.

In our digital age, we tend to think of memory as absolute: either we can retrieve a document on our computer or we cannot, but the information doesn't fade away like an old thermal fax. Much has been written about the frozen distance of photography: the boy in the photo may now be in college, the dog buried in the garden, the tree lost to a hurricane, but the picture itself remains inviolate. Our own neurological memory, on the other hand, deteriorates in erratic ways: one parent may remember clearly the shirt the boy wore that day but recall the tree as a cherry; the other has no recollection of the shirt but remembers the excitement of the dog as she chased the ball; the boy—star of the show—may not remember the incident at all.

Figure 23.1 Three screen images from a performance of *Speak, Memory* (2016), showing the same NYC street corner from 2014 (top), 1968 (bottom), and the confusion of the sound-encoded photo data as it is "forgotten" in the reverberation of a concert hall (middle).

The combination of acoustic memory and images could easily produce something that wallows in nostalgia or offers a sappy evocation of the evanescent. It would also be possible to slip into a more convoluted retake of *I am sitting in a room*—recycling those few seconds of data decay into a long elegy. But the lesson of *Pea Soup* had been that in the interaction of sound and space, forgetting and creating are inextricably intertwined.

The spring of 2014 found me back on the Columbia University campus. Prompted by filmmaker Paul Cronin, who had contacted my mother seeking material for his documentary on Columbia '68 *A Time to Stir* (2018/2020), I had dug out the old negatives I'd shot when I was fourteen.[8] Our younger child was now a student on that same campus and a fine photographer, and together we spent a day identifying the locations of my earlier photos. I would hold up a print from 1968 and she would line up the same vista on a digital SLR. The university gates were the same, but where once a paddy wagon had stood, there was now a Halal food truck doing brisk business; the statue of Alma Mater still presided over the steps of Low Library, but in place of barefoot hippies strumming acoustic guitars, scattered rose petals marked the site of a proposal. Students still gathered around the sundial, now minus the bullhorn.

In *Speak, Memory* (2016) those competing visions share both visual and auditory space. A clap of sound bursts from a loudspeaker and swiftly dies away, but its few seconds of reverberation and decay have been recorded and analyzed. After a brief lull, they reappear, tail-end first and greatly slowed down in a series of some thirty suspended wispy chords. The swift "forgetting" becomes an elongated remembering— sound re-emerges from silence, and the haze of reverberation gradually coalesces into the original clap.

In that first moment of silence, the screen lights up with a chromatic blur—shapes as yet unspecified, colors unforthcoming. Then, in sync with the audio as it reconstitutes itself, bits and pieces of an image come into focus with each chord—the brown granite corner of Seely Mudd Hall, a gray-scale balloon against a gray-scale sky; a bit of blue sky. The irregularities of the sound's decay control how the image flickers between then and now (Figure 23.1).

This is not a linear process. We hear and see that neither the sound nor the image simply fades up from black. Certain frequencies decay, others sustain; in the image, certain regions or colors wane or bloom into vibrant presence; distortions and superimpositions disrupt the arc of decay; ghost images appear out of nowhere. The color image of a young man carrying folding lawn chairs comes into clarity for a moment, followed by a different young man in black-and-white wrangling a flotilla of balloons with scribbled logos—"WE LIVE HERE."

The present shakes hands with the past.

Notes

Chapter 1

1 See John Ochsendorf and Michael Freeman, *Guastavino Vaulting: The Art of Structural Tile* (Princeton Architectural Press, 2010).
2 The fruits of Davis's experiments can be heard on Davis's 1972 release, *On The Corner*, a record much maligned at the time but now considered a harbinger of subsequent developments in funk, hip-hop, and electronica. Miles Davis, *On The Corner* (Columbia Records, 1972).
3 *The New York Times* ran this photo with her obituary: https://www.nytimes.com/2018 /05/08/obituaries/christiane-collins-scholar-who-fought-a-columbia-gym-dies-at-92 .html?searchResultPosition=1 (retrieved July 12, 2023).
4 Paul Cronin, editor, *A Time to Stir: Columbia 68* (Columbia University Press, 2018).
5 *Rolling Stone*, No. 51, February 7, 1970, p. 44.
6 Nicolas Collins, *Tone Gen* (1972)—the only extant recording from this period of my work—can be heard here: http://www.nicolascollins.com/music/tonegen.mp3.

Chapter 2

1 Lucier tells a version of this encounter in his book Alvin Lucier, *Music 109: Notes on Experimental Music* (Wesleyan University Press, 2014), p. 5.
2 John Cage, *Cartridge Music* (Editions Peters score, 1963).
3 David Behrman in liner notes for David Behrman, *Wave Train (Music from 1959 to 1968)* (Alga Marghen CD, 1998).
4 See https://daily.redbullmusicacademy.com/2014/02/when-philip-glass-met-ravi -shankar (retrieved May 10, 2021).
5 Distilling the principles of species counterpoint that had been followed since the early sixteenth century, Fux's chapters lead the composer through an orderly series of rules, like steps in a mathematical proof, ensuring "correct" music. Johann Joseph Fux (author), Alfred Mann, translator, *Gradus ad Parnassum* (W. W. Norton & Company, 1965).
6 Philip Glass, *Music in Similar Motion & Music in Fifths* (Chatham Square Productions, 1973).
7 Alvin Lucier, score of *Vespers* (1969). In Alvin Lucier and Douglas Simon, *Chambers* (Wesleyan University Press, 1980), pp. 16–17.
8 See David Grubbs *Records Ruin the Landscape* (Duke University Press, 2014).
9 Much of the material from *Source* magazine was anthologized in Larry Austin, Douglas Kahn, and Nilendra Gurusinghe, editors, *Source: Music of the Avant-garde, 1966–1973* (University of California Press, 2011).

10 The only regular coverage of such work in mainstream media was Tom Johnson's column in the *Village Voice*, which I read religiously. These columns were collected in Tom Johnson's *The Voice of New Music: New York City, 1972*. Het Apollohuis. 1989. Michael Nyman's groundbreaking *Experimental Music—Cage and Beyond* was not published until 1974. (Michael Nyman, *Experimental Music—Cage and Beyond*. Originally published by Schirmer Books in 1974 [2nd edition by Cambridge University Press, 1999]).

11 Sol LeWitt, "Paragraphs on Conceptual Art" (*Art Forum*, June 1967).

12 John Cage, "Experimental Music: Doctrine" (1955) and "Experimental Music" (1957). In John Cage, *Silence* (Wesleyan University Press, 1961), Pp. 13–17, 7–12.

13 Mel Bochner, "Excerpts from Speculation (1967–1970)," in Ursula Meyer, *Conceptual Art* (E. P. Dutton, 1972), P. 57.

14 Felix Kubin, 2004 interview with Alvin Lucier, unpublished.

15 John Lanchester, *Reality and Other Stories* (W. W. Norton & Company, 2021).

Chapter 3

1 Wallace Clement Sabine, "Melody and the Origin of the Musical Scale" (1907), In Wallace Clement Sabine, *Collected Papers on Acoustics* (Harvard University Press, 1922), pp. 107–16. Sabine, writing in 1907, used language that equates "race" with culture in ways now difficult to read, but the essential observation about acoustics remains of interest.

Chapter 4

1 See David Bernstein, *The San Francisco Tape Music Center—1960s Counterculture and the Avant-Garde* (University of California Press, 2008).

2 John Cage, *Empty Words: Writings '73–'78* (Wesleyan University Press, 1979), p. 185.

3 John Cage, *M: Writings '67–'72* (Wesleyan University Press, 1973).

4 Harold Adamson (lyrics), Jimmy McHugh (music), *Comin' in on a Wing and a Prayer* (Robins Music Corp, 1943).

Chapter 5

1 Lucier's comment on circuitry (which irritated Ron Kuivila) was made during an interview with Robert Ashley for the video project *Music with Roots in the Aether* (Lovely Music video, 1976), but it was consigned to an outtake and does not appear in either the final video or the published book of transcripts.

2 Lecture in Music 184, "Introduction to Experimental Music," *c.* March 15, 1973.

3 David Tudor workshop at Mobius Art Center, Boston, MA, September 29, 1985. Quoted in You Nakai, *Reminded by the Instruments* (Oxford University Press, 2021), footnote p. 53.

4   Conversation with Paul DeMarinis, Paris, October 1976.
5   Ray Wilding-White, "David Tudor: 10 Selected Realizations of Graphic Scores and Related Performances (1974)," Box 19, Folder 2, David Tudor Papers, GRI. Quoted in You Nakai, *Reminded by the Instrument*, p. 112.
6   George Lewis, "Living With Creative Machines—An Improvisor Reflects," In Anna Everett and Amber J. Wallace, *AfroGEEKS—Beyond the Digital Divide* (Center for Black Studies Research, University of California Santa Barbara, 2007), pp. 85–6.
7   Nicolas Collins, Zoom interview with Stuart Jones, July 19, 2021.
8   See Cage's interviews with Michael Zwerin and Richard Kostelanetz. Michael Zwerin, "A lethal measurement" (1991). In Richard Kostelanetz, *John Cage: An Anthology* (New York: Praeger, 1970), pp. 161–8.
9   See George Lewis, "Improvised Music after 1950: Afrological and Eurological Perspectives," *Black Music Research Journal*, Vol. 16, No. 1 (Spring, 1996): pp. 91–122.
10 Conversation with Susan Tallman, West Falmouth, July 2021.
11 Phone call between Nicolas Collins and David Behrman, August 16, 2021.
12 George Lewis, "From Network Bands to Ubiquitous Computing—Rich Gold and the Social Aesthetics of Interactivity," In Georgina Born, Eric Lewis, and Will Straew, *Improvisation and Social Aesthetics* (Duke University Press, 2017), p. 91.
13 Collins/Jones 2021.
14 Christian Wolff at Orpheus Symposium, Ghent, fall 2015.
15 Cornelis W. H. Fuhler, *Disperse and Display: Structural Strategies for Modular Approaches in Composition and Instrumental Practice*. A thesis submitted in partial fulfillment of requirements for the degree of Doctor of Philosophy (Sydney Conservatorium of Music, University of Sydney, 2015), p. 64.
16 Gallery talk on Joseph Cornell by George Lewis at the Art Institute of Chicago, September 22, 2017.

Chapter 6

1   See You Nakai, *Reminded by the Instruments* (Oxford University Press, 2021).
2   Robert Ashley, *Wolfman* (Alga Marghen CD, 2003).
3   David Behrman, *Wave Train (music from 1959 to 1968)* (Alga Marghen CD, 1998).
4   These experiments were collected into a score that was included in my undergraduate thesis: Nicolas Collins, *Nodalings* (1973). See http://www.nicolascollins.com/texts/nodalingsscore.pdf.
5   Nicolas Collins, *Feetback* (1975). See http://www.nicolascollins.com/texts/feetbackscore.pdf.
6   Nicolas Collins, *Pea Soup* (1974). See http://www.nicolascollins.com/texts/peasoupscore76.pdf.
7   Adam Putz Melbye touches upon this latter point in his paper: Adam Putz Melbye, "Second-order Double Feedback—A Sonic Reconsideration of Ashby's Model of Double Feedback" (January 2020). https://www.researchgate.net/publication/344596144_Second-order_double_feedback_-A_sonic_reconsideration_of_Ashby's_model_of_Double_Feedback (accessed October 11, 2020).
8   The Center for Contemporary Music at Mills College began in 1966 with the move of the San Francisco Tape Music Center to the Mills campus under Pauline

Oliveros' directorship. With Terry Riley on faculty, under Ashley's leadership (later shared with Behrman), CCM became a center of experimental musical Zeitgeist in the 1970s. For a capsule history of CCM, see David W. Bernstein, "Thirty Years of Non-Stop Flight: A Brief History of the Center for Contemporary Music." https://performingarts.mills.edu/center-for-comtemporary-music/archives-history.php (retrieved July 20, 2022).

Chapter 7

1   Darryl Pinckney, *Black Deutschland: A Novel* (Picador 2017), pp. 27–8.
2   Georgina Born, *Rationalizing Culture: IRCAM, Boulez, and the Institutionalization of the Musical Avant-Garde* (University of California Press, 1995).

Chapter 8

1   Alvin Lucier, *Bird and Person Dyning* (Cramps LP, 1976). Stuart Marshall and I performed in the composition, "The Duke of York" (1970). This was my first credit in a published recording. Score in Alvin Lucier and Douglas Simon, *Chambers* (Wesleyan University Press, 1980), pp. 80–1.
2   See Stuart Marshall, "Zones," *Source,* Vol. 5, No. 2 (1971). Portions reprinted in Larry Austin, Douglas Kahn, and Nilendra Gurusinghe, editors, *Source—Music of the Avant-Garde, 1966–1973* (University of California Press, 2011), pp. 314–16.
3   Gavin Bryars, "1, 2, 1-2-3-4." On Christopher Hobbs, John Adams, and Gavin Bryars, *Ensemble Pieces* (Obscure LP No. 2, 1975).
4   Peter Todd, "Stuart Marshall's Ideophonics," *Leonardo Music Journal,* Vol. 26 (2016): pp. 97–9.

Chapter 9

1   On Gordon Mumma, *Live-Electronic Music* (Tzadik CD, 2002).
2   See Jeffrey Zygmont, *Microchip: An Idea, Its Genesis, and the Revolution It Created* (Perseus Publishing, Cambridge, MA, 2002).
3   Private conversation with Paul DeMarinis, Paris, November 1976.
4   See Rich Gold, *The Plenitude: Creativity, Innovation and Making Stuff* (MIT Press, 2007).
5   Email correspondence with Marina LaPalma, May 13, 2021. For more information on *Party Planner,* see A. K. Dewdney, "Computer Recreations: Diverse Personalities Search for Social Equilibrium at a Computer Party," *Scientific American,* Vol. 25, No. 3 (September 1987): pp. 112–15.
6   George E. Lewis, "Living with Creative Machines—An Improvisor Reflects." In Anne Everett and Amber J. Wallace, *AfroGEEKS—Beyond the Digital Divide* (The Center for Black Studies Research, University of California Santa Barbara, 2007), pp. 83–99.

7   See Brummer et al., *The Hub: Pioneers of Network Music* (Kehrer Verlag, 2022). Also, John Bischoff, Jim Horton, Tim Perkis, Paul DeMarinis, Rich Gold, and David Behrman, *The League of Automatic Music Composers 1978-1983* (New World Records CD, 2007). A good insider's history of the Bay Area computer music scene can be found at http://crossfade.walkerart.org/brownbischoff/. See also George E. Lewis, "From Network Bands to Ubiquitous Computing—Rich Gold and the Social Aesthetics of Interactivity." In Georgina Born, Eric Lewis and Will Straw, *Improvisation and Social Aesthetics* (Duke University Press, 2017), pp. 91–109.

8   Jared Diamond, *Guns, Germs and Steel* (W. W. Norton & Company, 1997), p. 243.

9   Conversation with Paul DeMarinis, Berkley, CA, July 1978.

10 See http://oldcomputermuseum.com/sym_1.html (accessed May 26, 2021). Synertek was soon forced to change the computer's name to "Sym" after being sued by MOS Technologies for trademark violation.

11 My only recording of this piece has deteriorated beyond playability. However, a text score and schematic of the circuitry can be found in my MA thesis: http://www.nicolascollins.com/texts/Collins_MA_thesis.pdf.

12 Nicolas Collins, *Little Spiders* (1981) on Nicolas Collins and Ron Kuivila, *Going Out With Slow Smoke* (Lovely Music LP, 1982).

13 Paul Doornbusch, *The Music of CSIRAC* (Common Ground Publishing, Melbourne, 2005).

14 T. Kite Sharpless, "Mercury Delay Lines As A Memory Unit," In *Proceedings of a Symposium on Large-Scale Calculating Machinery, 7-10 January, 1947*, pp. 103–9.

15 The SP-1 Speak & Spell Interface kit was made by Dave Kemp at East Coast Micro Products, one of the many small businesses started in the late 1970s to serve the growing market for microcomputer peripherals.

16 John Rockwell, "Avant-Garde: 2 Writers." *New York Times*, May 1, 1980.

17 Nicolas Collins, *Second State* (1981), on *Going Out with Slow Smoke* (Lovely Music Ltd. LP, 1982). http://www.nicolascollins.com/slowsmoketracks.htm.

Chapter 10

1   "Sound Corridor," PS1, April 4–May 30, 1982.

2   https://www.nytimes.com/2021/11/04/books/reading-around-new-york.html.

3   Tot Rocket and the Twins, *Security Risk* (Trace Elements Records EP, 1981).

4   "Guitar Trio," on Rhys Chatham, *Die Donnergötter* (Dossier LP and CD, 1987).

5   Nicolas Collins, *Handmade Electronic Music: The Art of Hardware Hacking* (Routledge, 2006, 3rd edition 2020).

6   For details on the technology of the backwards electric guitars, and their evolution over the next decades, see http://www.nicolascollins.com/texts/BackwardsElectricGuitar.pdf.

7   George Crumb, *Ancient Voices of Children* (Nonesuch CD, 2006).

8   Later published in edited form as Alvin Lucier and Douglas Simon, *Chambers* (Wesleyan University Press, Middletown, CT, 1980). Subsequently reissued in Alvin Lucier, *Reflections: Interviews, Scores, Writings (Reflexionen: Interviews, Notationen, Texte)* (MusikText, Cologne, 1995).

9   Nicolas Collins and Ron Kuivila, *Going Out With Slow Smoke* (Lovely Music Ltd. LP, 1982). http://www.nicolascollins.com/slowsmoketracks.htm.
10 *Computer Music Journal*, Vol. 8, No. 2 (Summer, 1984): pp. 62–3.
11 Nicolas Collins, *Let The State Make The Selection* (Lovely Music Ltd. LP, 1984). http://www.nicolascollins.com/letthestatetracks.htm.
12 See Mission of Burma, *Vs* (Ace of Hearts LP, 1982).
13 Western Eyes, *Western Eyes* (Trace Elements Records LP, 1984).
14 David Tudor, *Pulsers/Untitled* (Lovely Music Ltd. LP, 1984).
15 http://media.hyperreal.org/zines/est/intervs/branca.html.

Interlude

1   Joe Jackson, "Is She Really Going Out With Him?" (A&M Records, 1978).
2   Nick Hornby, *High Fidelity* (Victor Gollancz Ltd., 1995).
3   Conversation with Douglas Simon, New York, *c.* 1984.

Chapter 11

1   George Lewis. Gallery talk on Joseph Cornell at the Art Institute of Chicago. September 22, 2017.
2   Numerous clips of Flash's two-minute appearance in *Wildstyle* can be found on YouTube, for example, https://www.youtube.com/watch?v=JHIsNQ3eh2g (retrieved May 13, 2021). His memorable rotation occurs in the first half-minute of the scene.
3   Nicolas Collins, "Is She/He Really Going Out With Him/Her/Them" (1982), on Nicolas Collins and Ron Kuivila, *Going Out With Slow Smoke* (Lovely Music Ltd., 1982).
4   Conversation with Robert Poss, c. 1986.
5   Nicolas Collins, *Devil's Music* (Trace Elements Records LP, 1986). http://www.nicolascollins.com/devilsmusictracks.htm. Reissued by EM Records (Japan) LP and CD, 2009.
6   Nicolas Collins, *Real Landscape* (Banned cassette, 1988). http://www.nicolascollins.com/reallandscapetracks.htm. Included on the CD reissue of *Devil's Music* released by EM Records in 2009.
7   William Gibson tested by Emily Blick, "Invisible Jukebox," *The Wire*, No. 434 (April 2020): p. 25.

Chapter 12

1   Carin Drechsler-Marx, *Ich liebe New York* (Die Bibliophilen Taschenbücher, Munich, 1999). When, in 1991, the landlord finally installed a proper intercom, the old buzzer board was retrieved from the trash by our French babysitter as a souvenir of his time in New York.

2   Ann Barry, "A Nibbler's Guide to the Best in Free Hors D'Oeuvres," *New York Times*, January 29, 1982. Section C, p. 19.

3   See Jon Bellona, "Physical Intentions: Exploring Michel Waisvisz's The Hands (Movement 1)." Published online by Cambridge University Press, November 24, 2017. https://www.cambridge.org/core/journals/organised-sound/article/abs/physical-intentions-exploring-michel-waisviszs-the-hands-movement-1/3DA2B89E269A804 457D19329298073E2 (retrieved July 20, 2023).

Chapter 13

1   Banda Primavera de Tauca (Director Nemesio Olivos Z), *Cielo de Tauca*, (Decibel Records, no date).

2   Carl Stone, *Wave-Heat* (1983). See https://www.youtube.com/watch?v=Mw7gnDLuOtw (retrieved August 3, 2022).

3   See https://www.discogs.com/release/231483-Plunderphonic-Plunderphonic (retrieved August 3, 2022).

4   Conversation with Wolfgang Heiniger, Berlin, November 11, 2022.

5   Nicolas Collins, *Tobabo Fonio* (1986), on Nicolas Collins, *It Was a Dark and Stormy Night* (Trace Elements CD, 1992). http://www.nicolascollins.com/darkandstormytracks.htm.

6   Nicolas Collins, *Real Electronic Music*, on Various Artists, *Imaginary Landscapes* (Nonesuch CD, 1990).

7   Derek Bailey, *Improvisation—Its Nature and Practice in Music* (Da Capo Press reprint edition, 1993, New York), pp. xi–xii.

8   See Simon Rose, *The Lived Experience of Improvisation* (University of Chicago Press, 2017).

9   Carl Stalling, *The Carl Stalling Project: Music From Warner Brothers Cartoons 1936–1958* (Warner Records CD, 1990).

10 Including one featured in Derek Bailey's film *On The Edge: Improvisation in Music*. Channel 4 (UK), 1992.

11 Nicolas Collins, *100 Of The World's Most Beautiful Melodies* (Trace Elements Records CD, 1989).

Chapter 14

1   Yasunao Tone, *Solo for Wounded CD* (1985). On Yasunao Tone, *Solo for Wounded CD* (Tzadik CD, 1997).

2   Nicolas Collins, *Broken Light*, on Nicolas Collins, *It Was a Dark and Stormy Night* (Trace Elements CD, 1992).

3   Both compositions are available on Nicolas Collins, *It Was a Dark and Stormy Night* (Trace Elements CD, 1992).

4   Kyle Gann, "Nicolas Collins's 'It Was a Dark and Stormy Night'." *The Village Voice*, Vol. XXXV, No. 11 (March 13, 1990): p. 92.

5 The only other performance by the original group took place at the Open Space Gallery in Allentown, PA, in September 1990. Our studio recording was released on Collins, *It Was a Dark and Stormy Night*.
6 Various Artists, *Imaginary Landscapes* (Nonesuch Records CD/cassette, 1990).
7 Peter Watrous, "Music: Maryanne Amacher." *The New York Times*, February 28, 1988, p. 58.

Chapter 15

1 Nicolas Collins, *Sound Without Picture* (Periplum CD, 1999).

Chapter 16

1 https://nl.wikipedia.org/wiki/Adelbert_Nelissen
2 See https://opera.media.mit.edu/projects/hyperinstruments.html (retrieved April 12, 2024).
3 The only performance of the only composition I completed for the concertina took place at The Kitchen in 1993.
4 A video recording of a performance can be seen at https://www.youtube.com/watch?v =6UACmvCVDdg&t=320s (retrieved May 14, 2021).

Interlude

1 Nicolas Collins, editor, *A Call For Silence* (Sonic Arts UK, London, 2004). Audio files and a PDF of the book can be found at http://www.nicolascollins.com/acallforsilence tracks.htm. Subsequent to publication, *A Call for Silence* was included in several gallery exhibitions devoted to the increasingly popular subject of artists' silences.

Chapter 17

1 Fountains of Wayne, "Little Red Light," on *Welcome Interstate Managers* (S-Curve Records CD, Virgin America, 2003).
2 Straebel Collins, Maly Osterwold, and Moltrecht, editors, *Pfeifen Im Walde—Ein unvollständiges Handbuch zur Phänomenologie des Pfeifens* (Podewil/Editions Maly, Berlin and Köln, 1994).
3 Nicolas Collins, *Broken Choir*, on zeitkratzer, *SonX* (zeitkratzer records CD, 1999).
4 Nicolas Collins, *Still (After) Lives*, on Nicolas Collins, *Sound Without Picture* (Periplum CD, 1999). See score at http://www.nicolascollins.com/texts/stillafterl ivesscore.pdf.
5 See Amy C. Beal, *New Music, New Allies: American Experimental Music in West Germany from Zero Hour to Reunification* (University of California Press, 2006).

6 Nicolas Collins, "Microstoria.snd Remix," on *Microstoria: Reprovisers* (Mille Plateaux/ Thrill Jockey CD, 1997).
7 Akademie der Künste Berlin, *Sonambiente: Festival für Hören und Sehen* (Prestel, Munich, 1996). A video of a subsequent HO-scale installation for *Arts Le Havre (Le Havre Biennale)*, Musée Malraux, Le Havre, France, in 2008 can be seen here: https:// www.youtube.com/watch?v=F3AB4hWJyg0 (accessed June 9, 2021).

Chapter 18

1 Nicolas Collins, *Strange Heaven*, on *Sound Without Picture* (Periplum CD, 1999).
2 *De Zoetgevooisde Bliksem* (Balie Theatre, Amsterdam, Netherlands, 1993). Writing the texts for this catalog (main essay plus biographies for every artist) indoctrinated me in the production schedule of proper journalism. STEIM had contracted a well-respected author who submitted, shortly before the deadline, inadequate texts, leaving me forty-eight hours to write replacements.
3 https://coveringthecity.com/humming-toadfish-sausalito-california-mccosker-kgo -radio-sound/.
4 An inventory of the twenty annual issues of *LMJ* that I edited, along with links to the introductions I wrote, can be accessed here: http://www.nicolascollins.com/lmj.htm.

Chapter 19

1 Robert Snyder, *Music and Memory* (MIT Press, 2001).
2 Conversation with Robert Poss, November 2016.
3 Alexis Petridis, "Has Streaming Made it Harder to Discover New Music?" *The Guardian*. September 26, 2022.
4 Deborah Solomon, "How to Succeed in Art," *New York Times Magazine,* June 27, 1999, p. 39.
5 Neill Strauss, *New York Press*. Quoted here: https://www.melafoundation.org/fbbpress .htm.
6 Douglas Kahn, *Noise, Water, Meat: A History of Sound in the Arts* (MIT Press, 1999).
7 Conversation with Stuart Marshall, London, early 1980s.
8 David Salle, *How to See: Looking, Talking and Thinking About Art* (W. W. Norton & Company, 2016), pp. 2–3.

Chapter 20

1 https://barthopkin.com/experimental-musical-instruments-back-issues/ (accessed August 31, 2022). For more on Reed Ghazala, see http://www.anti-theory.com/bio/ (accessed August 31, 2022). Also Reed Ghazala, *Circuit-Bending: Build Your Own Alien Instruments* (Wiley, 2005).
2 Conversation with Veniero Rizzardi, 2008.

3 Nicolas Collins, *Handmade Electronic Music—The Art of Hardware Hacking* (Routledge, New York and London, 2006. Expanded 2nd edition (with DVD), 2009. Expanded 3rd edition (with website and thirty contributing authors), 2021). Translations have been published in Japanese (O'Reilly, 2013) and Korean (Hanbit Media, 2016). You can find the original PDF version I created for my students, in all its scribbly glory, here: http://www.nicolascollins.com/texts/originalhackingmanual .pdf.
4 Chris Sharp, "Handmade Electronic Music: The Art of Hardware Hacking," (review) *The Wire,* No. 207 (September 2009): p. 70.

Chapter 21

1 Leta E. Miller, "Cage, Cunningham, and Collaborators: The Odyssey of *Variations V,*" *Music Quarterly,* Vol. 85, No. 3 (2001): p. 553.
2 See https://edition.cnn.com/2013/05/30/world/asia/china-electronic-waste-e-waste/ index.html (accessed July 23, 2021).
3 Nicolas Collins, *Salvage (Guiyu Blues)* (2008). See https://www.youtube.com/watch?v =XV50-Cwy1RI&t=625s.
4 Nicolas Collins, *The Royal Touch* (2014). See https://www.youtube.com/watch?v =DtGcueEsuDE.
5 Nicolas Collins, *In Memoriam Michel Waisvisz* (2009). See https://www.youtube.com /watch?v=sBlIRdnPciw&t=6s.
6 Nicolas Collins, *Tall Poppies* (2009). A composite video documentation of the multi-channel original can be seen at https://www.youtube.com/watch?v=n_zNNYFyyqk&t =4s.
7 Nicolas Collins, "Sled Dog" (2001), on *AriaDA 2003* (AriaDA CD, 2003). Also available here: http://www.nicolascollins.com/music/ueasleddog.mp3.
8 For a more detailed overview of the distinctions between hardware and software resources, see Nicolas Collins, "What to Ware? A Guide to Today's Technological Wardrobe." In Jonathan Impett, editor, *Sound Work: Composition as Critical Technical Practice* (Leuven University Press, 2021). An earlier draft of this text can be found at http://www.newmusicbox.org/articles/what-to-ware-a-guide-to-todays-technological -wardrobe/ (accessed October 22, 2022).
9 The program for *Pea Soup* can be downloaded from http://www.nicolascollins.com/ software.htm.
10 The program for *Devil's Music* can be downloaded from http://www.nicolascollins .com/software.htm.

Chapter 22

1 "Grant Park, Chicago, November 4, 2008." http://www.nicolascollins.com/otherrecs .htm.
2 Nicolas Collins, *Handmade Electronic Music—The Art of Hardware Hacking* (expanded 3rd edition) (Routledge, New York, 2020).

3   The official site can be found at http://www.handmadeelectronicmusic.com. My stopgap version is still available at http://www.nicolascollins.com/HEM3/HEM3home .htm.

4   Paul Tingen, *Miles Beyond: The Electric Explorations of Miles Davis 1967–1991* (Billboard Books, 2001), p. 58.

5   For more on Tudor's *Bandoneon!* see https://www.soundohm.com/product/bandoneon -a-combine (retrieved August 6, 2023). !trumpet: Nicolas Collins, "The Development of the !trumpet," *Musica/Tecnologia (Music/Technology)*, Vol. 15 (2021): pp. 81–107.

6   Nicolas Collins, *Pea Soup to Go* (2014). http://www.nicolascollins.com/peasouptogo/

7   Nicolas Collins, *Lucky Dip* (2020). http://www.nicolascollins.com/LuckyDip.htm. Both *Pea Soup to Go* and *Lucky Dip* were developed with the programming assistance of Nick Briz, a former graduate student of mine from SAIC.

8   Nicolas Collins, "Roll, Pitch and Yaw—Toiling in Electromagnetic Fields," *Echo—The Journal of Music, Thought and Technology*, Volume 3: *Feedback,* January 2022.

Chapter 23

1   See http://www.nicolascollins.com/notebooks.htm.

2   John Cage, "Composition as Process" (1958), in John Cage, *Silence* (Wesleyan University Press, 1961), p. 39.

3   Michael Nyman, *Experimental Music: Cage and Beyond* (Schirmer Books, 1974).

4   Jennie Gottschalk, *Experimental Music Since 1970* (Bloomsbury, 2016).

5   Notes to Robert Ashley, *Superior Seven/Tract* (New World Records CD), 1995.

6   George Lewis, gallery talk on Joseph Cornell at the Art Institute of Chicago, September 22, 2017.

7   Calvin Tomkins, "The Sistine on Broadway," in Roni Feinstein, *Robert Rauschenberg: The Silkscreen Paintings, 1962–64* (Whitney Museum of American Art, New York, 1990), pp. 13–17. Originally published in Calvin Tomkins, *Off the Wall: Robert Rauschenberg and the Art World of Our Time* (Doubleday, Garden City, NY, 1980), pp. 192–200.

8   Paul Cronin, editor, *A Time to Stir: Columbia 68* (Columbia University Press, 2018).

Index